Mao's Children in the New China

In this inspiring collection of interviews with former Red Guards, members of the first generation to be born under Chairman Mao talk frankly about the dramatic changes that have occurred in China over the last two decades. In discussing the impact these changes have had on their own lives, the former revolutionaries give a direct insight into how they view both the past and the present, revealing an attitude perhaps more contradictory and critical than that of most western commentators.

These poignant memoirs tell the very personal stories of how people from all walks of life were affected by Mao's Cultural Revolution and Deng Xiaoping's economic reforms. They cover topics as diverse as politics, party leadership, nationalism, marriage and divorce, the privatization of industry, family relationships, education and the stock market. *Mao's Children in the New China* is essential reading for all those interested in learning more about modern China.

Yarong Jiang is Lecturer in Sociology at the University of Wyoming, USA. Her previous publications include *Sociology: An Introduction* with Shuqi Peng (Zhejiang People's Publishing House, 1990), as well as various articles for Chinese newspapers and journals. **David Ashley** is Professor of Sociology at the University of Wyoming. His previous publications include *Sociological Theory* with David M. Orenstein (Allyn and Bacon, 2000), *History Without a Subject: The Postmodern Condition* (Westview, 1997), and numerous articles on social theory and political sociology for scholarly journals in the UK, USA and Canada.

Routledge Studies in Asia's Transformations
Edited by Mark Selden
Binghamton and Cornell Universities

The books in this series explore the political, social, economic and cultural consequences of Asia's twentieth-century transformations. The series emphasizes the tumultuous interplay of local, national, regional and global forces as Asia bids to become the hub of the world economy. While focusing on the contemporary, it also looks back to analyse the antecedents of Asia's contested rise.

This series comprises two strands:

Routledge Studies in Asia's Transformations is a forum for innovative research intended for a high-level specialist readership, and the titles will be available in hardback only. Titles include:

1. The American Occupation of Japan and Okinawa
Literature and Memory
Michael Molasky

2. Koreans in Japan
Critical Voices from the Margin
Edited by Sonia Ryang

Asia's Transformations aims to address the needs of students and teachers, and the titles will be published in hardback and paperback. Titles include:

Debating Human Rights
Critical Essays from the United States and Asia
Edited by Peter Van Ness

Hong Kong's History
State and Society under Colonial Rule
Edited by Tak-Wing Ngo

Japan's Comfort Women
Yuki Tanaka

Opium, Empire and the Global Political Economy
Edited by Carl A. Trocki

Chinese Society
Change, Conflict and Resistance
Edited by Elizabeth J. Perry and Mark Selden

Mao's Children in the New China
Voices from the Red Guard Generation
Yarong Jiang and David Ashley

Mao's Children in the New China

Voices from the
Red Guard Generation

Yarong Jiang and David Ashley

London and New York

First published 2000
by Routledge
11 New Fetter Lane, London EC4P 4EE

Simultaneously published in the USA and Canada
by Routledge
29 West 35th Street, New York, NY 10001

Routledge is an imprint of the Taylor & Francis Group

© 2000 Yarong Jiang and David Ashley

Typeset in Sabon by Taylor & Francis Books Ltd
Printed and bound in Great Britain by Biddles Ltd, Guildford and
King's Lynn

British Library Cataloguing in Publication Data
A catalogue record for this book is available from the British Library

Library of Congress Cataloging in Publication Data
Mao's children in the new China: voices from the Red Guard
generation / Yarong Jiang and David Ashley
    p. cm.
    Includes index.
    1. China – Public opinion. 2. Public opinion – China – Shanghai.
    3. Hung wei ping – Interviews. I. Title. II. Voices from the Red
    Guard generation. II. Jiang, Yarong. III. Ashley, David.
DS706 .C5114 2000
951.05–dc21   99-049313

ISBN 0–415–22330–x (hbk)
ISBN 0–415–22331–8 (pbk)

For "Nini" and "Mei Mei."
May they learn from this book.

On youth

The world is yours, as well as ours, but in the last analysis it is yours. You young people, full of vigour and vitality, are in the bloom of life, like the sun at eight or nine in the morning. Our hope is placed on you ....

(Mao Zedong, Talk at a meeting with Chinese students and trainees in Moscow, November 17, 1957, in *Quotations from Chairman Mao Tse-Tung*, New York: Bantam, 1976, p. 165)

Contents

Foreword

Stanley Rosen

Oral histories, autobiographies and fictional accounts of the Red Guard generation have been appearing in China and the West since the 1970s. Far from abating, however, the outpouring of literature and film on this period seems to have gained momentum in the 1990s. Chinese participants in the Cultural Revolution (1966–1976) and its attendant "Up to the Mountains and Down to the Villages" movement (*shangshan xiaxiang yundong*) (which lasted until 1978) have fascinated western readers and audiences with harrowing tales of their experiences in those years.[1] Critical acclaim for Jung Chang's *Wild Swans: Three Daughters of China* – a compelling account of the life histories of her grandmother, her mother, and herself in the turmoil of twentieth century China that has achieved bestseller status in many parts of the world – has noted the volume's power to express "the tragic quality of life in China," "the survival of a Chinese family through a century of disaster" and the "shocking story."[2]

While Jung Chang was describing three generations of oppression, not just her own personal suffering during the Cultural Revolution, Anchee Min's *Red Azalea* – another bestselling personal memoir from the 1990s – is limited to her own experiences as a Red Guard and "sent-down youth." If anything, Min's account is even more harrowing, as well as titillating. As a Red Guard she denounces her beloved teacher as a reactionary, thus putting that woman's life in danger. Sent to the countryside she toils in near-starvation while fighting off leeches. Not allowed contact with the opposite sex she has a passionate lesbian affair with her squad leader, constantly aware that discovery could mean execution. More adventures – both political and sexual – follow, as Min becomes the star of Madam Mao's opera "Red Azalea." The *New York Times* chose *Red Azalea* as a Notable Book and observed that it told "the true story of what it was like growing up in Mao's China, where the soul was secondary to the state, beauty was mistrusted, and love could be punishable by death." The national advertisements used by the publisher – Pantheon – emphasized these same points, noting, again quoting the *New York Times*, how this remarkable story revealed both "the brutality of oppression and the incredible resilience of the human spirit."[3] Readers, to judge from comments on the Amazon.com website, had similar feelings. One noted how the book helped him "understand communism much better," while another found it "incredible to think these atrocities occurred in our lifetime … [It] makes you feel grateful to be residing in the United States."

More recently, Joan Chen's film *Xiu Xiu: The Sent-Down Girl*, based on Yan Geling's novella, *Tianyu* (Heavenly Bath), has received critical acclaim as a stark portrait of life in China, circa 1975, for a young girl sent to a remote area. As Roger Ebert noted:

> In a time of movies about sex and silly teenagers, here is a film that arrives with a jolt of hard reality, about a 15-year-old Chinese girl who was not lucky enough to be born into the consumer paradise of "American Pie". To those who find savage satire in "South Park: Bigger, Longer and Uncut" … here is a story about people who would weep with joy to have the problems "South Park" attacks.[4]

Joan Chen has defended her film from critics who object that this period has already been well covered in other Chinese films seen in the West, such as Zhang Yimou's *To Live*, Chen Kaige's *Farewell My Concubine*, and Tian Zhuangzhuang's *The Blue Kite*. As she puts it, "It's not just another Cultural Revolution movie. This was as important to my generation and my people as the Holocaust is important to the world. Why did Oliver Stone make three Vietnam pictures? Why do people still make World War II movies?"[5]

Joan Chen is correct to note the importance of this decade of upheaval for those who experienced it. Within China, former *zhiqing* youth – to use the term most commonly applied to those of school age sent to the countryside during the Cultural Revolution years – have produced an impressive collection of memoirs, reportage and historical fiction.[6] Chinese journals and magazines have also introduced feature stories on the Cultural Revolution experiences of the *zhiqing* and their current situation.[7] Up until now, however, with very few exceptions, the vast majority of westerners who have learned about this period have received their knowledge from a small number of widely circulated popular memoirs, novels or films. All the works cited above are extremely well done and provide important insights into various aspects of that period. But such polished accounts, written by expatriates and clearly prepared for a non-Chinese public, represent only one part of a much larger story. The twenty-seven interviews collected in *Mao's Children in the New China* certainly cannot compete with the dramatic, even lurid, details that emerge in books like *Red Azalea* or *Wild Swans*. On the other hand, as narratives related in conversations with Yarong Jiang, a native Shanghainese, these accounts are both more varied and, in a real sense, more "authentic" than even the best work published for western audiences. More importantly, unlike the accounts of Jung Chang and Anchee Min, both of whom end their story before the reforms, *Mao's Children* reveals the relationship between the Cultural Revolution years and the reforms that followed, bringing the individual stories that comprise the book up to the present.[8]

In most accounts of the Red Guard generation, including many written by participants, the Red Guards appear as thugs and the sent-down youth are portrayed as victims. In some cases, as in Ma Bo's *Blood Red Sunset* – another Cultural Revolution memoir that was very well received in the West – the protagonist is both a thug and a victim.[9] Unlike the works of Jung Chang and Anchee Min, Ma Bo's memoir was originally published in China, but it was quickly removed from circulation by the authorities. Indeed, given the restrictions that limit a thorough investigation of this complex and tumultuous era, the lack of understanding of the broader political context *within* mainland China, particularly among the younger generation, as illustrated by all the above-mentioned works, appears to rival that of the West. For example, in a recent book entitled *China Remembers*, that amassed a collection of thirty-four first-hand accounts of the crackdowns and campaigns that have shaped China since the founding of the People's Republic of China (PRC), An Wenjiang, a former Red Guard, explained why he wanted to tell his story:

> When I was teaching at middle school, one of my students wrote in an essay that the Red Guards were all thugs. She thought I was joking when I told her I was not only a Red Guard, but also the commander of a rebel group. It made me realize the importance of portraying a truthful picture of the Red Guards in history. ... Perhaps my story will help people understand us better.[10]

Generations in post-1949 China

Mao's Children in the New China tells the story of the Red Guard generation, also called the "Third Generation." While westerners frequently use generational terms as shorthand – the familiar Generation X, the baby boomers and so forth – it is perhaps even more common to use such categories in China. Thus, those who became leading directors after attending the Beijing Film Academy in the first entering class after the Cultural Revolution, such as Zhang Yimou and Chen Kaige, are widely known as "Fifth Generation Filmmakers." Perceived membership in a common generation – what Strauss and Howe writing about generations in the United States call "Awareness" – is also familiar in China.[11] For Strauss and Howe it makes a great deal of difference whether a person was born in 1942 or 1943. In China, there is a similar shared awareness among those who entered university immediately after the entrance examinations were restored in 1977 or 1978, when there were as many as 6 million applicants for a small number of places. Successful applicants are widely known as *qiqi ji* or *qiba ji* (class of 1977 or 1978). These students were considered – and considered themselves – to be the best and the brightest of their generation, since they emerged victorious in the first open competition after ten years without such examinations.

There is also a shared awareness among those who "graduated" from secondary school in 1966, 1967 and 1968 as being from the *lao san jie* (old three graduating classes). Most of the interviewees in *Mao's Children* fall into this category. One can find specialized restaurants in Beijing and other cities named for this generation (such as *lao san jie* restaurant) or for the bleak areas of the hinterland to which many were sent in the late 1960s and early 1970s (such as *hei tudi* restaurant, named for the wilderness area of Heilongjiang province). These are gathering places for former sent-down youth, providing very simple fare similar to what was served during their Cultural Revolution exile. At the same time, however, it is important to distinguish between those in the Cultural Revolution generation of educated youth who were eventually able to attend college or rise through political channels and those who ended up as farmers or factory workers with few opportunities to rise. Both are represented among these interviewees and, in a sense, provide a partial explanation as to why this generation can be called both the lost generation (*shiluo de yidai*) and the thinking generation (*sikao de yidai*).[12]

To understand the place the Red Guard, or Third, Generation occupies within Chinese society it is necessary to situate this group within its larger generational context. The discussion below is of necessity presented in general terms. It is useful, however, as a starting point because it is based on the analysis prevalent in China today and is drawn largely from a variety of works by Chinese authors. After this overview, we will return to the more complex picture of the Third Generation that emerges from this volume.

There have been five generations that have shaped the People's Republic of China.[13] The First Generation founded the Chinese Communist Party and, through various armed conflicts, established the PRC on October 1, 1949. The most well-known members of this generation were Mao Zedong, Zhou Enlai and Deng Xiaoping. Chinese writers sometimes refer to this generation as "the Rebel Heroes." This was a generation that found it necessary to break with old traditions in order to create something new. They often betrayed their families, their education and their social class. As one author put it, there was no authority they could not overthrow, no myth they would not question. They are also seen as a romantic generation since their struggle required unlimited imagination. They were convinced that human volition could be transformed into material power, and that virtually anything – for example the Long March of 1934–1935 – was possible. Despite some horrendous failures after achieving power – most notably the Great Leap Forward (1958–1961) and the Cultural Revolution – this generation has commanded and continues to command immense respect because of its revolutionary achievements.

If the First Generation were the Rebel Heroes, the Second Generation is often regarded as the Loyal Soldiers.[14] Although they also were born during hard times, they did not have the choices available to the First Generation. New authority structures were already in place by the time they reached adulthood. They came of age during the first seventeen years of "New China," before the Cultural Revolution. They accepted the leadership of the First Generation and many responded with both loyalty and enthusiasm to the call of Party and country. Because it was an era when the Chinese version of Marxism held sway, they had virtually no access to western or traditional thought alternatives. The only time this generation showed independent thought was during the Hundred Flowers Movement in 1956–1957, when some intellectuals raised criticisms of Party and state officials. After the anti-rightist movement of 1957, all such dissident voices were stilled. Politics, however, was very important in the lives of the Second Generation. Entering the Communist Youth League and then the Party was considered "glorious." As one commentator suggested, they were "collective animals," always putting state interests above individual interests. They were proud of their thriftiness and lack of material comforts. Their cultural lives were also circumscribed. They read Soviet literature and sang revolutionary songs. Even their family lives were politicized since political quality and social class background were priorities in choosing a spouse.

The Third Generation is often regarded as the generation that has experienced everything, having lived in three totally different eras. Indeed, it may be the only generation that Chinese writers have difficulty in characterizing. One author finds them "a combination of contradictions."[15] Yarong Jiang and David Ashley put it well in their introductory remarks to this book when they suggest that their subjects "develop themes that are contradictory, complementary and critical." It is a generation marked by paradoxes. Born in the late 1940s or early 1950s, it is often noted that the Third Generation experienced their happiest moments during their childhood, because they sensed the excitement of the 1950s. Some dissenting voices point out, however, that they were also confronted by the food shortages of the Great Leap Forward at an early age.[16] Still, most commentators suggest that elements of heroism and idealism have been deeply implanted within them and have affected them throughout their lives. As with the Second Generation, the Third Generation accepted mainstream state ideology unquestioningly. With the coming of the Cultural Revolution they transferred their complete devotion to Chairman Mao, competing to be the most loyal followers of the Chairman. Under these conditions they could commit the most violent crimes with the purest hearts. Objectively, therefore, these Red Guards should be seen as victims as well as criminals. They were compelled to forego their education and forcibly exiled to the countryside. When they were finally allowed to return to the cities, more than a decade later, there were often no jobs for them. Paradoxically, some of them are leading the market reform while others are unemployed. They are seen as realistic, flexible, highly adaptable and often nostalgic for an earlier era not tainted by corruption and material values. It is frequently suggested that it is the Third Generation that is managing China today, although some of the interviewees in this book take direct issue with that conclusion.

The Fourth Generation is made up of those who were born in the 1960s. While they may have some memories of the Cultural Revolution years, and some witnessed the persecution of family members during their impressionable childhood, they themselves were not direct participants. This spared them much of the pain experienced by the Third Generation. In school, however, their education was heavily influenced by Cultural Revolution standards, offering little beyond Mao quotations or stories of model heroes and performances of model operas. When China opened to the outside world they began to be exposed to a wide variety of western thought and culture. For some, this generation is at the same time the luckiest and the most confused.[17] Many have become pioneers in China's reform program.

One way of distinguishing the belief systems that characterized the Second, Third and Fourth Generations is to examine the works of leading intellectual theorists associated with these generations. Second Generation intellectual thinkers such as Su Shaozhi[18] and Liu Binyan[19] – both currently in exile in the United States following the events of 1989 – are still heavily influenced in their writings by socialist concepts. Despite – indeed, in some ways because of – developments in China, they appear to have retained a strong belief in socialism. The key theorists of the Red Guard generation, such as Yang Xiguang[20], the Li Yizhe group[21] and Yu Luoke[22], were different from intellectuals such as Su and Liu. Red Guard theorists might be characterized as very thoughtful individuals with limited knowledge, all trapped, to a greater or lesser extent, somewhere between Marxism-Leninism and its Maoist fundamentalist variant. Interviewee no. 8 in this book – the widely known and respected liberal Professor of History at Shanghai University, Zhu Xueqin – refers to his generation as "moral idealists" and, in a particularly apt expression, "amateur intellectuals."[23] Younger Fourth Generation theorists, such as Hu Ping[24] and Fang Zhiyuan[25], did not have the restrictions on information that had marked the Second and Third generations. A variety of translation series appeared in the 1980s, such as *Dangdai xifang wenku* (Collection of Contemporary Western Works) and *Zouxiang weilai congshu* (Toward the Future Book Series), exposing Fourth Generation theorists to more pluralistic ideas imported from the West.[26]

The Fifth Generation is made up of those born in the 1970s and growing up in the 1990s.[27] They are the generation most affected by "globalization." Thus, they are equally at home discussing the latest American films or the exploits of the superstars from the National

Basketball Association. Michael Jordan, until his recent retirement, was one of the most popular and well-known individuals in China. The most desirable graduate degree is the Master's of Business Administration, or MBA. Indeed, "MBA" was listed in a survey of the ten most popular expressions used on the Internet in China.[28] At the same time, and perhaps paradoxically, the more they have learned about the outside world the more patriotic, even nationalistic, they have become. Finally, they are marked by a strong tendency toward self-interest, if not individualism. Surveys have shown that this generation acknowledges the increasing importance of money in social, economic and personal life, even rivaling friendship and ideals. What is particularly striking about this generation is the ability to hold simultaneously the contradictory values of nationalism/patriotism on the one hand, and pragmatism on the other. However, these values exist in a continuing tension with each other, although this tension has thus far been handled successfully by the Communist Party. After the American bombing of the Chinese Embassy in Belgrade, Yugoslavia in May 1999, Fifth Generation college students saw no real contradiction between their participation in violent demonstrations against the United States and their continuing desire to work for an American joint venture company or study in the United States. Not surprisingly, the interviewees in this volume are often quite openly critical of the value orientations and beliefs of the young generation.

The reader will notice that this brief overview of Chinese generations does not discuss one of the major events in PRC history: the student demonstrations in the spring of 1989, followed by the military crackdown on June 3–4. Unpublished public opinion polls conducted in China on the eve of the millennium that asked respondents to list the most important events of the past 50 years reveal that "June 4th" (*liu si*) – as the military's "retaking" of Beijing is commonly known in China – remains one of the five or six most salient events to Chinese citizens, particularly those in Beijing. Not surprisingly, the subject is seldom addressed in the open press in China, except to reiterate the "correct" decision made by the leadership to restore order out of "turmoil." Moreover, given the sensitivity of the issue, it is difficult to gauge accurately current attitudes about this period. Fortunately, a number of the interviewees in *Mao's Children* do address this issue and their views will be discussed in the next section.

As suggested above, it is common in China to think in generational terms and to compare one's own generation to those that came before or after. This is not particularly new. A traditional saying had it that "Each generation is worse than the last" (*yidai bu ru yidai*). Generational conflict is therefore not unusual. For example, members of the Fourth Generation have referred to their Second Generation counterparts as "the gray or gloomy generation" (*huise de yidai*) because they were – and, allegedly, in many cases remain – overly cautious, fearful of breaking political and social taboos, and "completely worn out" (*pibei bukan*). In its turn, the

Second Generation criticizes the Fourth Generation for having no sense of mission or sense of responsibility. Indeed, they fail to see anything wrong with being cautious or with careful thinking. They criticize the Fourth Generation for being too much like western youth of the 1960s.[29] There is some evidence that they may be correct in this assessment. For example, a 1988 study of university students in Beijing found that 60.4 percent designated themselves as "the generation that pays no attention to authority" (*moshi quanwei de yidai*), while 76.7 percent demanded independent thinking. Only 7.5 percent said they were willing to obey authority.[30]

Chinese publications also reveal conflicts between the Third and Fourth Generations. Many young Chinese are critical of the Third Generation because they feel that the former Red Guards obstinately persist in defending their actions ("We were idealistic and enthusiastic") and claiming the status of victims ("We had no choice"; "we suffered in the countryside"). They are accused of an inability to reassess their past objectively or admit their mistakes and criminal acts.[31] The Third Generation is also attacked for its arrogance and conceit. Critics assert that this generation thinks of itself as the best and the brightest. Former Red Guards allegedly dismiss the oldest generation as good fighters in war but unsuccessful in constructing the nation. The Second Generation is regarded as too conservative and traditional, with no real ideas. The younger generation is seen as ignorant and naïve. Only the Third Generation, to hear their critics tell it, claims that it learned how to turn struggles into survival and suffering into maturity and flexibility.[32]

This harsh assessment suggests that some larger issues may be at play. In her thoughtful and highly entertaining book on Chinese urban popular culture, Jianying Zha, herself a member of the Third Generation, notes that "memory has generational gaps."[33] She feels that her generation may be fated to carry a heavier burden than their parents or younger siblings. Their parents often went to their graves with their faith in the revolution intact; the Red Guards lost their faith before reaching middle age. Their younger siblings, by contrast, often have little recollection of the Cultural Revolution. Their children may have no memory of the events in Tiananmen Square in 1989. Zha then provides an answer for critics of the Third Generation, such as those cited above. Her words are worth quoting directly:

> This is a country where nobody confesses sins. Massive destructions have occurred, atrocities have been committed, millions have died of starvation and persecution, children have turned in their parents, husbands have denounced wives, people have sold friendships for a casual nod from a Party secretary – yet it has *never* been popular to acknowledge openly the wrongs you have done to others. The venerable form of "self-criticism" is practiced only when individuals

apologize to the Party: you may say you're sorry to the system, even if you aren't really sorry. Other forms of confession or self-analysis, however, are neither encouraged nor expected. In fact, it's hard to talk about psychological issues in Chinese – the language just isn't well-equipped with words and expressions to discuss your inner demons. The common attitude is to leave the demons alone.[34]

The Third Generation assesses itself: viewing the mid-1990s while looking back to the past

Mao's Children in the New China, as the title suggests, tells the story of the first generation that grew up completely in "New China," after the founding of the People's Republic in 1949. Most were between the ages of 40–50 at the time the interviews were conducted in the mid-1990s. They were in the prime of life, at an age that often elicits self-awareness and self-reflection. Whatever youthful dreams they may have harbored, their lives were now anchored in hard realities. Having witnessed the entire history of the PRC, this generation has certainly earned the right to speak, and their reflections reveal a great deal, both about the Cultural Revolution years and about current conditions. Sorting through the memories of these twenty-seven ordinary citizens, the reader may find a China that looks different from what conventional wisdom – and many other sources – may have led us to believe. Particularly fascinating is the interplay between their experiences in the Cultural Revolution and the outcomes of their lives in subsequent decades down to the present. Thus, the individual stories about the Cultural Revolution era and life in the countryside are often at least as compelling as those from the present. What does the student of China learn from these interviews? Considering that the study was conducted in Shanghai, China's most "modern" city, with a unique political tradition, can we generalize beyond these cases to also say something about other parts of China?

First, we find a populace that feels quite free to complain and express open disappointment; both with the way their own lives have turned out, and with the current state of China more generally. Even those with good jobs often seem to be dissatisfied. In part, interviewees have revealed their honest opinions because they were simply talking to another Shanghainese. They were not told that their reflections would appear in a book published in the West. If they had been, they almost certainly would not have been so forthcoming. Should one conclude from their stories that most Chinese from the Third Generation are unhappy, particularly if they happen to live in Shanghai? While there is no clear answer to this question, it appears evident that Chinese citizens, at least among themselves, feel rather able to speak freely.

A second theme that resonates in a number of the interviews is the option – even in the highly politicized atmosphere of the Cultural

Revolution – to ignore the call to "make revolution," and instead pursue one's individual interests. Ironically, to a certain extent, this appears to have been most possible for those of bad class origin. Certainly, the picture presented is far more complex than the familiar one offered in popular memoirs, novels and films that center on the life of one individual or family, and far more subtle than the generalized accounts that have appeared in overview histories and textbooks on this period. For example, there is the fascinating case of interviewee no. 6, a case study that offers several unexpected surprises. As someone from a wealthy – and even counter-revolutionary – family background, one would expect him to have suffered greatly in the past. Indeed, some of his story does echo familiar themes from this period, such as the constant danger of betrayal by a friend. Yet, despite the better conditions today, he reports that the Cultural Revolution years were the most fulfilling of his life. Although he was unemployed, he was left alone to write poetry and pursue ideas freely. Other interviewees – for example no. 10, whose father had been imprisoned in the 1950s and who used the Cultural Revolution years to study languages – reveal that, for an undetermined number, the "ten wasted years" were not really being wasted.

A third theme, one that spans the entire period, from the Cultural Revolution down to the present, is the possibility of "negotiating" with the regime to pursue individual interests. One perhaps is not surprised to find this today, nor is one surprised to discover that these "negotiations" are permeated with corruption. What *is* surprising is to encounter the same practice at the height of the Cultural Revolution, when "reason" was a more important negotiating tactic than bribery. A few examples from these interviews are illustrative. Interviewee no. 6, mentioned above, despite a bad class origin, refused to cooperate with the authorities in registering to leave Shanghai when job assignments were being handed out in 1968. He describes how he was able, when necessary, to raise his blood pressure so he could avoid being sent out of the city. Interviewee no. 10 recounts how his copy of Rousseau's *Confessions* was confiscated when a Workers' Patrol Team saw the words "Oh, Eternal Beauty," and concluded that the book was referring to God. However, by bringing his copy of Engels to the police station and showing the officers that Engels praises Rousseau, he was able to get the book returned. Interviewee no. 19, from a petit bourgeois background – his father owned a tailor shop before 1949 – took the initiative to visit the Job Assignment Work Team before they had made any decision about his future. Showing them a paragraph from Mao's "Analysis of Social Classes in China" that lists his particular family background as "half proletarian," he successfully argued that if Mao's thinking was correct – and who could possibly question that? – he should not be put in the same category as children from the bourgeois class. In the end he was sent to a factory rather than the countryside.

This suggests a fourth point: the arbitrary nature of the political system, marked more by the rule of individuals in official positions than by the rule of law. One example of this comes from interviewee no. 13, who was unable to get herself reassigned from the countryside back to the city because the petty official in charge of the Educated Youth Office in Shanghai insisted on exacting revenge for her sister's refusal to accept her assignment. It was only when this official was replaced that she could return legally. Nor could families plan strategies to keep their children in the cities. Policies shifted from year to year without warning. Interviewee no. 9 reveals how a shift in policy in 1968, requiring every graduate to go to the countryside, made it impossible for her family to plan on which of their five children they would try to keep at home.

As many of the interviewees suggest, the biggest difference between the Cultural Revolution and the 1990s may be the replacement of power by money as the main commodity governing social and political life. There is widespread condemnation of the corruption and lack of morality that exists today. What is particularly striking is how the 1990s, in the course of providing many more options for Chinese citizens, has created precisely the kind of social stratification that the Cultural Revolution was designed to prevent. Interviewee no. 17 notes casually how he and his wife bought a signed document of financial sponsorship through a dealer for 15,000 yuan on the black market so she could get a student visa to Japan. Several interviewees, including a high school principal (no. 18) and a college professor (no. 11) reveal details on the corruption of the educational system by money. As the latter notes, in his son's district key middle school only one in three students are there because of their test scores. The rest are sons and daughters of district government officials, rich merchants, army officials and others with privileges.[35] At the other extreme, the principal describes his difficulties at a school where neither the students nor their parents are concerned about education: 20 percent of the students come from broken homes and most students realize early on that they are not destined for university, only vocational training. Interviewee no. 4 provides details on how insiders manipulate the Shanghai stock exchange.

As money has become more important and social stratification has become more pronounced these informants offer a decidedly mixed assessment of "socialism with Chinese characteristics," as Chinese-style socialism is now characterized. Certainly, to many, there appears to be more emergent capitalism than remnant socialism in China. The large increase in foreign investment – expected to rise still further as China moves closer to membership in the World Trade Organization – the effects of globalization, and the resurgence of Chinese nationalism have all been major topics in the western press. How has the Third Generation responded to these developments? On the evidence of this book, the responses reveal the same kind of ambivalence that characterizes their attitudes about the reforms more generally. Interviewee no. 5, for example, studied in England and now works for a western company. However, he feels uneasy, perhaps even unpatriotic, about protecting his employer's interests in China. Like many others, he finds it difficult to reconcile Chinese national interest with the penetration of foreign capital and foreign products into the country. Interviewee no. 22, a local entrepreneur, is far harsher. He blames government concessions to foreign capitalists for the destruction of China's state-owned enterprises. He has refused offers from Japanese and Taiwanese companies because he "won't work with compradors and opportunists." Interviewee no. 24, a well-to-do lawyer, is particularly critical of the United States. He suggests that Americans "are too stupid" to realize that Chinese criticize their government because they're affected by its policies, contrasting this with American criticisms of China, made "to preserve its own cultural and political hegemony."

Indeed, the harsh views of interviewee no. 24 regarding the United States suggest the attitudinal change that appears to have occurred in China since the events that riveted the world in 1989.[36] He is one of five interviewees who briefly discuss their assessment of the "Beijing Spring." However, aside from interviewee no. 14, who was a graduate student in Shanghai at the time, interviewee no. 24 is the only one who acknowledges supporting the students. His view today – "another revolution wouldn't have done China any good" – is broadly similar to the comments offered by other interviewees. They note that there was too much turmoil during the Cultural Revolution and that China needs to concentrate on economic development now (interviewee no. 22), or that the ordinary working people will be the first to suffer if the country once again falls apart (interviewee no. 23). Even the former graduate student finds the events of 1989 a distant memory. The market economy, he notes, has dissolved the unity that existed then and ended the commitment to social causes.

There is a strong flavor of poignancy that pervades this volume, particularly as we read of the growing number of middle-aged residents confronted by unemployment as the reforms go forward. Interviewee no. 25, a member of the Shanghai Writers' Association, expresses this sentiment best, noting that history has singled out her generation to play a cruel joke. She contrasts her own "lost generation" to the Second Generation, using her mother – a former high-ranking official – as an example. Her mother doesn't like the present and doesn't pretend to understand it. Yet she's serene, has no regrets, and is content in knowing that the great challenges and crises of her life are all behind her. As for later generations, they're not out of place either. These times are custom-built for the young. She concludes that the members of her generation are "phantoms caught between two worlds. The shards of idealism are lodged in our hearts. But the world's not for idealists anymore." It is fitting that hers is the last interview in the book.

As the editors tell us in their introductory remarks, these interviews have been conducted in Shanghai, and most of the participants are natives of Shanghai. Since Shanghai is clearly not a "typical" Chinese city, it is useful to discuss how the choice of location for these interviews has influenced the results. In other words, what should the reader know about Shanghai that will help to place these stories into a proper context?

The name "Shanghai" is associated in the West with a variety of images, not all of them positive. As the metropolis with the largest foreign penetration, it became the center for China's modernization effort before 1949. It has always been a city of paradoxes. In the 1930's it was known as "the paradise for adventurers," and had the wealthiest members of society living alongside a large underclass of fringe members of urban society, including beggars, prostitutes and other members of the lumpenproletariat. It was a port city fraught with dangers, hence the term "shanghaied," which has entered the English language to describe the situation where a man is made unconscious with drink or drugs and then carried off to be a seaman on an outgoing ship. It has been a major center for industrialists, as well as literary figures and intellectuals. Leading political figures such as Sun Yat-sen and Chiang Kai-shek started their careers in Shanghai. It has also been the locus of China's working-class and revolutionary movements, serving as the birthplace of the Chinese Communist Party in 1921, the great strike waves of 1924–1927, and the base of the radical faction – later known in popular parlance as the "Gang of Four" – during the Cultural Revolution.[37] More recently, with some of China's most prominent national leaders – among them Party General Secretary Jiang Zemin and Premier Zhu Rongji – rising to the top as a result of their successful performance at the helm of Shanghai, it has become common to refer, perhaps only half-jokingly, to a so-called "Shanghai *bang*," or "Shanghai Mafia" running the country. Shanghai's seeming ability to accommodate such a varied political history suggests the first attribute that characterizes the city: a high degree of tolerance.[38] Yang Dongping, in his bestselling book contrasting the cultural spirit of Beijing and Shanghai, identifies six distinctive characteristics of the Shanghainese. As other writers have often noted these characteristics, they are worth citing in some detail:

(1) "shrewdness," being capable, concise, excellent, flexible and clever; (2) "practical benefit," emphasizing concrete material interests (first estimating gain or loss, then judging people's value according to everyone's actual gains); (3) "rationalism," requiring everything in life to be as fair and reasonable as possible, e.g., reasonable prices, reasonable attitude toward life; (4) "standardization and etiquette," which attaches a great importance to regulations, rules, and order (this is a reflection of "the contract consciousness" in daily life necessitated by commercial actions); (5) "secularization," which means that because of the establishment of the basic value of a commodity economy, the political and ideological activities that once controlled society have gradually been replaced by new standards of the actual effect, achievement, popularism, and rationalism of the modern society; and (6)

"westernization," which is defined as a synonym for civilization and enlightenment.[39]

Can we see this distinctiveness in the experiences and attitudes of the subjects of this book? First, we must strike a cautionary note. As Yang Dongping suggests, during the pre-reform period Chinese national identity was fostered and regional identities were suppressed. People were expected to follow the "revolutionary center," which was located in Beijing where Chairman Mao resided. Thus, prior to the late 1970s, there was considerable tension between Shanghai and the central government, as the latter bled the city of resources, capital and skilled workers. With the onset of reform one begins to see the proud reassertion of these regional identities marked, for example, by the appearance of books "explaining" the differences between individuals from different regions. Books about the denizens of Shanghai – such as Luo Shuang's *"Dissecting" the Shanghainese*[40] – appear to have become particularly popular examples of this genre of literature.[41] At several points in these interviews the reader is aware that the comments offered reflect the situation in Shanghai rather than the country as a whole. For example, interviewee no. 4 discusses the workings of the Shanghai stock market. Currently, China has only two functioning stock markets, one in Shanghai and one in Shenzhen. A second difference is the number of college graduates in the sample – thirteen – and the number of respondents who studied abroad, or refer to friends who studied abroad. Indeed, interviewee no. 24, the well-to-do lawyer mentioned above, reflects the amazing changes that have occurred in Shanghai just in the 1990s. He starts the interview by noting how in 1990 a former classmate, the dumbest of their group, returned to Shanghai for a visit from abroad and regaled those left behind with stories of his "astronomically high salary" of US$28,000. Everyone was suitably impressed. When he returned again in 1996, his Shanghai friends were all doing so well that no one paid him any notice. In fact, we are told, "people in Shanghai have started making fun of students coming back from abroad." Self-confidence and perhaps a bit of arrogance are returning to China's most modern city. But the advanced nature and future potential of Shanghai is expressed best by interviewee no. 7, the general manager of a government-sponsored project, when he relates how he came to return to Shanghai. A friend convinced him that if he wanted to accomplish anything he would have to return to Shanghai. As his friend put it, "Don't go back to Anhui; Shanghai is China's America."

Notes

I would like to thank Mark Selden for his helpful comments on an earlier version of this introduction.

1   For some of the earlier examples of such works, see Liang Heng and Judith Shapiro, *Son of the Revolution* (New York: Random House, 1983) and Nien

Cheng, *Life and Death in Shanghai* (New York: Grove Press, 1987). More recent works have provided even more harrowing accounts, as in Zheng Yi, *Scarlet Memorial: Tales of Cannibalism in Modern China* (Boulder: Westview Press, 1998).

2   Jung Chang, *Wild Swans: Three Daughters of China* (New York: Simon and Schuster, 1991). The quotes are from the back cover of the paperback edition and derive from the *Washington Post Book World*, *The New Yorker* and Mary Morris, the author of *Wall to Wall*. They are very representative of the critical commentary that greeted this book.

3   Anchee Min, *Red Azalea* (New York: Pantheon, 1994). The quotes were taken from the Amazon.com website for this book. In June 1995 *Red Azalea* was released in a mass-market paperback for US$7.50. It has also appeared as an audiobook, read by actress Nancy Kwan, attesting to its success among western audiences.

4   Roger Ebert, "Hearts of Darkness Revisited: A Stark Portrait of Life in China," *Chicago Sun-Times*, July 30, 1999, p. 30. In the film Xiu Xiu is sent off to the countryside with hundreds of other teenagers from Chengdu, the capital of Sichuan province. After a year of boring labor in a small town near the Tibetan border, she's ready to return to her family. Instead, however, she is sent even further away, to the Tibetan grasslands. Again, she expects to return home after six months, but no one comes for her. Various men pass by the lonely outpost and promise to use their connections to help her leave in return for sexual favors. She becomes an object of complete humiliation and scorn, repeatedly used and abused by any man who chooses to drop by. To virtually everyone else in the area this innocent and naïve young girl has become a shameless slut, an object of ridicule even to the local female medical staff, worthy of no sympathy. The home video version announces on the front that the film was "banned in China for political and sexual content."

5   See the interview with Joan Chen in Scarlet Cheng, "Applying the Hard Lessons: Actress Joan Chen Didn't Let the Chinese Government Derail Her Acclaimed Directing Debut, 'Xiu Xiu', " *Los Angeles Times*, June 23, 199, Calendar, p. 1.

6   See, for examples, Shi Weimin, ed., *Zhiqing riji xuanbian* (Selections from Zhiqing Diaries) (Beijing: Zhongguo shehui kexue chubanshe, 1996); Shi Weimin, ed., *Zhiqing shuxin xuanbian* (Selected Zhiqing Correspondence) (Beijing: Zhongguo shehui kexue chubanshe, 1996); Jin Dalu, ed., *Kunan yu fengliu* (Hardship and Heroism) (Shanghai: Shanghai renmin chubanshe, 1994); Jin Yonghua and Jin Dalu, eds, *Dongfang shiritan* (The Oriental Decameron) (Shanghai: Shanghai renmin chubanshe, 1996); and Jin Dalu, *Shiyun yu mingyun* (World Destiny and Individual Fate) (Shanghai: Shanghai renmin chubanshe, 1998). This latter book, a study of the *zhiqing* today, perhaps comes closest to the present volume. Also see *Zhiqing dang'an 1962–79* (Zhiqing Case Files) (Chengdu: Sichuan wenyi chubanshe, 1992); Deng Xian, *Zhongguo zhiqing meng* (The Dream of the Chinese Zhiqing) (Beijing: Renmin wenxue chubanshe, 1993) and the five-volume fiction collection entitled *Zhiqing wenxue jingdian* (Classics of Zhiqing Literature) (Lanzhou: Dunhuang wenyi chubanshe, 1998). I would like to thank Professor Richard King, chair of the Department of Pacific and Asian Studies at the University of Victoria, for bringing these sources to my attention. For translations of *zhiqing* literature in English, see Richard King, ed., "There and Back Again: The Chinese 'Urban Youth' Generation," *Renditions* Special Issue 50 (1998). Twenty-six writers of the *zhiqing* writers are interviewed in Laifong Leung, *Morning Sun: Interviews with Chinese Writers of the Lost Generation* (Armonk, New York: M.E. Sharpe, 1994). There is also some useful material in

Sang Ye and Zhang Xinxin, eds, *Chinese Profiles* (San Francisco: China Books and Periodicals, 1987), which contains interviews with 100 ordinary Chinese citizens, some of whom are from the Red Guard generation. One of the earliest works of this type was B. Michael Frolic, *Mao's People: Sixteen Portraits of Life in Revolutionary China* (Cambridge, MA: Harvard University Press, 1980). The interviews for this book were conducted with Chinese émigrés in Hong Kong in the mid-1970s.

7   For one recent example, see "Jiu ti xin lun: zhongguo zhiqing de zuotian, jintian he mingtian" (A Fresh Approach to an Old Topic: The Past, Present and Future of China's *Zhiqing* Youth), *Zhongguo qingnian yanjiu* (Research on Chinese Youth), no. 6, 1999, pp. 45–49.

8   Jung Chang won a scholarship to Britain and left China in 1978; Anchee Min ends her story after the death of Mao and the disgrace of Jiang Qing. Although she spent another six years in China before moving to the United States, she summarizes those six years very briefly, providing few details on how the post-Cultural Revolution period affected her.

9   Ma Bo, *Blood Red Sunset: A Memoir of the Chinese Cultural Revolution* (New York: Viking Penguin, 1995). This work was originally published in China in 1988 by the Workers Publishing House. Liu Binyan, in his review for the *New York Times Book Review*, noted that the book "echoes the realities of contemporary China." By the time the book had appeared in the West, Ma Bo was a writer-in-residence at Brown University.

10 Zhang Lijia and Calum McLeod, *China Remembers* (Oxford: Oxford University Press, 1999), as cited in *Far Eastern Economic Review*, November 4, 1999, p. 65.

11 William Strauss and Neil Howe, *Generations: The History of America's Future: 1584 to 2069* (New York: William Morrow, 1992).

12 All members of this group are sometimes called the "thinking generation" because they were the first to gain broad experience and a broad knowledge of Chinese society under conditions that provoked many to question the ideology they brought to the countryside.

13 There are many books and articles published within China analyzing generations and generational differences. This section draws most heavily on the following sources: Wu Junping, *Di wu dai ren* (The Fifth Generation) (Tianjin: Tianjin jiaoyu chubanshe, 1998); Zhang Yongjie and Cheng Yuanzhong, *Di si dai ren* (The Fourth Generation) (Hong Kong: Zhonghua shuju, 1989); Song Qiang, Qiao Bian *et al.*, *Di si dai ren de jingshen* (The Spirit of the Fourth Generation) (Lanzhou: Gansu wenhua chubanshe, 1997); Xu Sihe, "Qudong xin zhongguo lishi nianlun de si dai ren" (Four Generations that Have Moved China), *Qingnian tansuo* (Youth Studies), no. 4, 1994, pp. 12–14; and Liu Shaolei, "Xin de daigou: 60 niandai daxuesheng ji qi zinu" (The New Generation Gap: 1960s University Students and their Children), *Qingnian yanjiu* (Youth Research), no. 4, April 1996, pp. 24–28.

14 The expressions "Rebel Heroes" and "Loyal Soldiers" are drawn from Wu Junping, note 11.

15 See Zhang Yongjie and Cheng Yuanzhong, note 11

16 See Xu Sihe, note 11.

17 Ibid.

18 Su Shaozhi was formerly the Director of the Institute for Marxist-Leninist Studies at the Chinese Academy of Social Sciences.

19 Liu Binyan, a reporter for *Renmin ribao* (People's Daily), was China's most famous muckraker and greatly admired and respected for his exposés of corruption.

20 Yang Xiguang was a secondary school student in Hunan during the Cultural Revolution who became famous for writing an "ultra-leftist" critique of China's leadership and society. It was entitled "Whither China?" and criticized some of the country's top leaders as "red capitalists."

21 The Li Yizhe group took its name from the three main participants: Li Zhengtian, Chen Yiyang and Wang Xizhe. Their wall posters on the streets of Guangzhou (Canton) in the mid-1970s, promoting socialist democracy and the development of a legal system, created national and international attention. For translations of their writings, see Anita Chan, Stanley Rosen and Jonathan Unger, *On Socialist Democracy and the Chinese Legal System: The Li Yizhe Debates* (Armonk, New York: M.E. Sharpe, 1995).

22 Yu Luoke was a high school student during the Cultural Revolution. His most important work was entitled *Chushen lun* (On Origin Theory) in which he questioned the emphasis on a person's class origin as the key determinant of his likely behavior. He was executed during the Cultural Revolution, but he has not been forgotten. Recently, some members of the Third Generation have compiled a book of his writings, along with critical commentaries from his enemies at the time, reminiscences and current assessments of his thought. See Xu Shao, Ding Dong and Xu Youyu, eds, *Yu Luoke: Yizuo yu huiyi* (Yu Luoke: Works and Recollections) (Beijing: Zhongguo wenlian chuban gongsi, 1999).

23 For a recent collection of Professor Zhu's writings, see Zhu Xueqin, *Shuzhaili de geming* (Making Revolution from Within my Studio) (Changchun: Changchun chubanshe, 1999).

24 Hu Ping was a graduate student in the philosophy department at Beijing University specializing in Kant. He took a prominent role in the local National People's Congress election in 1980 and won his seat. However, he was denied work and eventually pressured into going abroad for further studies in 1986. He is perhaps best known for his article promoting freedom of speech, although he has written widely on events in China down to the present.

25 Fang Zhiyuan was among a small group of student leaders at Beijing University who had been active in the April 5, 1976 Tiananmen protests and at Democracy wall in the late 1970s. Like Hu Ping, he was also a candidate for election to the National People's Congress in 1980.

26 For the great intellectual opening of the 1980s and the origins of these translation series see Chen Fong-ching and Jin Guantao, *From Youthful Manuscripts to River Elegy: The Chinese Popular Cultural Movement and Political Transformation 1979–1989* (Hong Kong: The Chinese University Press, 1997) and Edward X. Gu, "Cultural Intellectuals and the Politics of Cultural Public Space in Communist China (1979–1989): A Case Study of Three Intellectual Groups," *The Journal of Asian Studies*, 58(2), May 1999, pp. 389–431.

27 Because this generation has not yet received the detailed analysis accorded the first four generations by Chinese authors, I draw on my own forthcoming article entitled "Chinese Youth in the Year 2000" for many of the ideas in this paragraph.

28 See *Beijing qingnian zhoukan (Beijing Youth Weekly)*, 29, 1998, citing reports from the Internet survey network of Horizon Research, the leading private Chinese public opinion agency.

29 See Zhang Yongjie and Cheng Yuanzhong, note 13.

30 Cited in Stanley Rosen, "The Effect of Post-4 June Re-Education Campaigns on Chinese Students," *The China Quarterly*, 134, June 1993, pp. 310–334.

31 This paragraph is based on Song Qiang, Qiao Bian *et al.*, cited in note 11, pp. 211–214 and interviews with Chinese youth in their twenties. It should be noted that the authors of this book had previously become widely known for

their nationalistic tract, *The China that Can Say No* (*Zhongguo keyi shuo bu*), so their views perhaps do not represent the majority of Chinese youth.

32 For other contemporary comparisons of youth from different generations, see Xu Meng, ed., *Guanjian shike: dangdai zhongguo qite jiejue de 27 ge wenti (Critical Moment: The 27 Problems that Urgently Require Solutions in Contemporary China)* (Beijing: Jinri zhongguo chubanshe, 1997, pp. 538–556), which compares 1980s and 1990s youth, and Shi Chaoge, Zhang Meng and Zhu Min, "Dangdai daxuesheng dui qibashi niandai daxuesheng de kanfa" (The Views of Today's University Students about the University Students of the 1970s and 1980s), *Beijing qingnian zhoukan* (Beijing Youth Weekly), no. 41, October 13, 1998.

33 Jianying Zha, *China Pop: How Soap Operas, Tabloids, and Bestsellers are Transforming a Culture* (New York: The New Press, 1995, p. 17).

34 Ibid., p. 18.

35 For a confirming account, based on data from Beijing, as well as more details on educational stratification and the role of money and power in choosing schools, see Stanley Rosen, "Education and Economic Reform," in Christopher Hudson, ed., *The China Handbook* (Chicago: Fitzroy Dearborn Publishers, 1997), pp. 250–261.

36 For some evidence of this attitudinal change among youth, see Rosen, "Chinese Youth in the Year 2000," cited in footnote 27.

37 The revolutionary nature of Shanghai's working class has been documented most effectively in the works of Elizabeth J. Perry. For example, see *Shanghai on Strike: The Politics of Chinese Labor* (Stanford, CA: Stanford University Press, 1993) and Elizabeth J. Perry and Li Xun, *Proletarian Power: Shanghai in the Cultural Revolution* (Boulder: Westview Press, 1997).

38 This point about the tolerance of the Shanghainese is also made in Yang Dongping, *Chengshi jifeng: Beijing he Shanghai de wenhua jingshen* (City Monsoon: The Cultural Spirit of Beijing and Shanghai) (Beijing: Dongfang Press, 1994). Chapter 9 of this book, "Shanghainese and Beijingese," has been translated in Cheng Li, ed., "City Monsoon: The Cultural Spirit of Beijing and Shanghai," *Chinese Sociology and Anthropology*, vol. 29, no. 2, Winter 1996–1997. Chapter 8, not translated, is entitled "New Beijing and the Third Generation," and discusses the characteristics of the "lost generation" and its impact on the new culture of Beijing. I have drawn on Cheng Li's excellent introduction to this issue, pp. 3–17 for several of the ideas in this section.

39 This passage is quoted from Cheng Li's introduction in "City Monsoon," pp. 10–11.

40 Luo Shuang, chief editor, *"Pouxi" shanghai ren* ("Dissecting" the Shanghainese) (Beijing: Zhongguo shehui chubanshe, 1995). By October 1997 the book was in its third printing and the print run had reached 31,000 copies.

41 One could, however, also argue that some of the stories about the Cultural Revolution are influenced by the locale. For example, the ability to "negotiate" with officials who will listen to reason may be a reflection of Shanghai's vaunted tolerance and a higher educational level. It is likely that such "negotiation," particularly by those of bad class background, would not have been possible in less developed parts of the country.

Acknowledgments

We would like to acknowledge the help we received from Mark Selden, Jonathan Unger, Anita Chan, Jiangmin Xin and Liping Jiang, and from Yarong's parents and her brothers – Xiangming Jiang and Jianan Jiang.

Part I
Authors' introductory remarks

The interviews that form the heart of this book are with twenty men and seven women, nearly all of whom participated during their student years in the Cultural Revolution and subsequently in the Up to the Mountains and Down to the Villages movement in which nearly 18 million young people were sent to serve in the countryside. By 1974, 890,000 students from Shanghai alone had been mobilized to go to rural areas.[1]

The initial idea for this study emerged during a six-month stay in Shanghai in 1994 as we directly experienced perhaps the most dramatic economic revolution of the twentieth century. Shanghai had recently experienced economic growth rates that were restoring its lustre as China's most dynamic city, prompting an extraordinary construction boom. We were simultaneously caught up in what the Chinese media called "a great wave of remembering the past" (*yijiu*).[2] Among other things, this involved numerous newspaper articles and features in Shanghai, Tianjin and Beijing periodicals about the experiences of millions of student-settlers who had gone to the countryside twenty-five years earlier. These reminiscences triggered hundreds of responses, many of them published in *Qingnian Xuezhe* (Young Scholars) and *Tianjin Ribao* (Tianjin Daily) and elsewhere. In addition, retrospective works by ex-Red Guards such as "Youthful Days with No Regrets" and "Suffering and Glory" also focused attention on the not-so-distant revolutionary past.[3]

Our study attempts to convey a sense of how members of "New China's" Third Generation (the first to grow up in the People's Republic of China) view the past and cope with the present. We have tried to let our interviewees speak for themselves. We assume no responsibility for how they see the world or what they have to say about their own experiences during the Cultural Revolution and today. Our goal merely has been to give voice to their diverse recollections and conclusions about the tumultuous times through which they lived.

All of the people in this book are members of "the Three Old Classes": the cohort that would have graduated either from middle or high schools in 1966, 1967 and 1968 had the Cultural Revolution not impinged on their lives with such dramatic and far-reaching effects. With a few exceptions, members of the Three Old Classes were all born between 1946 and 1953.

The interviews that follow were conducted exclusively by Yarong Jiang, who grew up in Shanghai in the years 1955 to 1987 and who retains many close ties with the city. Our subjects were contacted either by Yarong directly or through third parties who knew her well and could provide appropriate introductions. We thought it important that interviews be conducted in an informal and open-ended fashion and that our subjects feel confident that they could talk candidly as one Shanghainese to another.[4] Interviewees were told that Yarong was researching the Three Old Classes, but, with the exception of Professor Zhu (interview no. 8), they were not informed she was gathering data for a book that would be published in the West. We did not want people to feel that they had to present a suitable "face" to a western interrogator or that they were addressing a western audience.

Five of the interviews (nos 1, 2, 7, 20 and 25) were conducted in May or June 1994; the other twenty took place in November or December 1996. All interviews were taped and later transcribed and edited. Our subjects were promised confidentiality to encourage them to speak as freely as possible about frequently painful and conflictual subjects. In essence, we gave our interviewees the anonymity each of us would request if asked to speak frankly about our bosses, colleagues, jobs, private lives and so on. But that anonymity was all the more important given the contested character of the events discussed here and our wish to have respondents discuss issues in ways that might be at odds with official perspectives. As a result, many of our subjects were willing to speak critically about Party policies and their own actions during the Cultural Revolution and later.

We have chosen to provide through our interviewees a cross-section of Shanghai life as experienced by the Red Guard generation. Shanghai's importance in the late 1960s stems from the role it played as a storm center of Cultural Revolution activity, which was, itself, but a continuation of a long tradition of working-class militance. Equally important, Shanghai has more recently played a major role in fomenting business growth in the New China and has also become a center of international banking, finance and high technology in an economy that has globalized rapidly. Accordingly, with but one exception ("Zhang Aixiang", interview no. 15), all of the interviewees we have selected grew up in Shanghai. The twenty-seven people we chose for this book (out of forty-two who were interviewed) are better educated and many are unusually knowledgeable about China and the world. Thirteen have a college degree, eleven are managers or administrators, and nine are teachers, writers, researchers or editors. Four are jobless, three are private businessmen – one quite wealthy. The group is fairly representative of relatively well-educated residents of their generation in China's largest metropolis.

Most of our subjects discuss their involvement in the Cultural Revolution, but this is not a book about the Cultural Revolution. More exactly, it is about more than the Cultural Revolution. What we wished to explore was how members of the Red Guard generation perceive and cope with the consequences of the economic and social reforms that have transformed China and reshaped their lives since the late 1970s. We also hoped to learn how members of this generation reconcile their present situation with the quite different experiences of and values espoused during their youth. Finally, we wanted to discover how our interviewees view their own roles in Shanghai's and China's future.

In the last ten to fifteen years, some ex-Red Guards have published memoirs in the West. Many of these were written by the privileged offspring of high-ranking Party officials or by children of members of the pre-revolutionary political or business elites, who were able to leave for the West at a very early stage.[5] Invariably, these memoirs tell how the various authors both played an active role in the Cultural Revolution *and* were victimized by it. Written and edited for western readers, it is hardly surprising that they rarely challenge dominant western (and, often, Chinese) perceptions of the Cultural Revolution as one of "ten lost years." Moreover, because the authors of such books left China nearly twenty years ago, they have little or nothing to say about Deng Xiaoping's economic reform or its consequences.

Whereas the reminiscences of ex-Red Guards published in the West tend to follow a narrative form best described as generic, our subjects, by contrast, develop themes that are contradictory, complementary and critical in discussing both the Cultural Revolution and the subsequent era of economic reform. And in telling their story to a fellow Shanghainese, they have, perhaps, been better able to capture the youthful passions that guided their experience at the time, and to allow the more jagged edges and contradictions of those experiences to remain in the narrative.

In setting off the voices of those who have profited from economic reform against those who have suffered from it, and in including respondents from upper-class as well as working-class backgrounds, we hope to capture a measure of the diversity of experiences and perceptions that are representative of this revolutionary generation of Shanghainese both in their Cultural Revolution years and since. We believe that the stories told by our interviewees illustrate perspectivism: the idea that each conscious entity views the world from an orientation peculiar to itself, but that such orientations are themselves part of a social matrix that can only be grasped holistically.

Regardless of obvious differences in perspective, our subjects nonetheless exhibit certain commonalties of feeling and perception. These include:

1   deep ambivalence toward Mao and the Mao Period (1949–1976) –
    particularly the Cultural Revolution;
2   a strong sense of collective identity that emanates from a shared
    history and the memory of a more idealistic past;
3   a sense of alienation from today's society, and a feeling of detachment
    from a younger generation that has no memory of the Cultural
    Revolution;
4   the belief that members of the Three Old Classes were not so much
    passive victims as active participants in a social movement that posi-
    tively helped to shape what they and China are today;
5   criticism of many but by no means all of the social consequences of
    economic reform including class polarization and official corruption;
    and
6   strong criticism of the Chinese Communist Party (CCP) for failing to
    implement its stated ideals – but not, it is important to note, a whole-
    sale rejection of the ideals themselves.

The Cultural Revolution and the Red Guard movement

From the perspective of our respondents, the cultural revolution era was
divided into two distinct phases: (1) a rebellious political insurrection associated with the Red Guards that lasted from 1966 to 1968, and (2) a
demographic movement involving the resettlement of urban students to
rural areas that for many in this generation began in 1968 and continued
until the mid- to late-1970s.

First phase

In the late spring of 1966, Mao created a Cultural Revolution Group to
spearhead the new movement. The Chairman proceeded to topple many of
the top leaders of Party, government and army, simultaneously calling on
the nation's revolutionary youth to join him in rebelling against what he
would now brand a crystallization of illegitimate authority at every level of
party and society. The first Red Guard group was formed in Beijing on
May 29, 1966. From June 1, when Mao broadcast his approval of philosophy teacher Nie Yuanzi's "Big Character"[6] poster attacking the
entrenched Party leadership at Beijing University, student rebels swung
into action throughout the country. Within a year, the majority of high
school and college students, together with many younger workers, had
joined Red Guard or other rebel organizations.

As defined in Mao's "Sixteen Articles,"[7] in August, 1966, the rebels'
political opponents were "those power holders in the Party who were
taking the capitalist road" and the "Four Olds": viz., "old thinking," "old
culture," "old customs" and "old habits." The septuagenarian Mao
sought both to eliminate his enemies in the party and to shake up its orga-

nization and society generally with the rebellious spirit of youth. Rejecting one of the cornerstones of orthodox Marxism, and looking back to the youth of his own generation, Mao targeted revolutionary youth, rather than the proletariat per se, as the new revolutionary vanguard.

Schools and colleges in the PRC ended formal classes as early as June of 1966, and, as competing loyalist and rebel factions vied for power throughout the summer of that year, schools and campuses across the country were blanketed with Big Character posters attacking school authorities and teachers who had followed a "'bourgeois" line. The move- ment quickly moved beyond school and campus walls, and, with Mao's support, Red Guards took to the streets in August 1966 to oppose both the "Four Olds" and those categorized as "class enemies." They directed their attack both against the power holders now branded as "Capitalist Roaders" (*zouzipai*) and the hapless victims of "class struggle" – in actu- ality all those who had been branded as capitalists, landlords, or rightists in previous campaigns. All regions of the country – not only the cities but also rural areas – were deeply affected, and much private and public prop- erty was vandalized as the allegedly "bad elements" were subjected to humiliation, physical abuse, arrest, torture and even death.

Between August 18 and November 26 Lin Biao's army organized and provided the logistics to mount eight Red Guard rallies in Beijing's Tiananmen Square. Approximately 1 million students who traveled by train to Beijing from all over the country jammed into the square to be reviewed by, and to catch a glimpse of, the Chairman. During this period approximately 9 million students engaged in the "Great Exchange" (*dachuanlian*) by which young people traveled all across China to "spread revolution," and to visit the capital to be received by the "Great Helmsman" himself. Millions of youth also took the opportunity to ride the trains free (all that was required at the time was a Red Guard armband, a school identification or simply adequate bluster) and visit China's great cities and cultural and revolutionary centers as a tightly organized society suddenly opened its doors to youthful idealists and adventurers.

By 1967, with verbal and physical clashes between loyalist and rebel forces on the increase, the nation was at the brink of civil war. "Loyalist" groups tended to include cadres' children and were more respectful of reigning authority. By contrast, the more rebellious activists, many of whom came from working-class families, often were eager to strike at established leaders.[8] Before long, the situation became chaotic, and, with Mao's reluctant acquiescence, the People's Liberation Army (PLA) was called in to restore order. At this time some of the more radical leaders were arrested, and the military – which was, itself, rent by divisions – took power on a scale not seen since the early years of the People's Republic. The first phase of the Cultural Revolution had ended.

Second phase

In February 1968 a group of Red Guards from Beijing traveled to remote regions in southern China and petitioned the Cultural Revolution Group to permit them to settle in the remote region of Yunnan province. The request was granted. Shortly thereafter, in spring 1968, the Party – now moving aggresively to restore order – officially disbanded the Red Guards, ordered all of them to return to their schools or units, and actively promoted the "Up to the Mountains and Down to the Villages" campaign. In 1968–1969 alone, some 4 million urban youth were permanently resettled in the countryside to take up a life of farming. This brought to an end the radical and anarchic phase of the Cultural Revolution. It also constituted an official response to the dilemma created by the closure of higher education opportunities for educated youth, and particularly to the shortage of state sector jobs in an economy that was just beginning to recover from the Great Leap Forward-induced economic collapse and mass starvation of the early 1960s.

Initially portrayed as an opportunity for "educated youth" to "learn from the peasants" and contribute to rural development, the Up to the Mountains and Down to the Villages movement, which had attracted youthful volunteers in its initial incarnation going back to 1964, now entered a new phase. With mounting state pressures on youth to give up urban residence and settle permanently in the countryside, the movement lost its idealistic and pioneering spirit in the decade after 1968 and, beneath its high-flown rhetoric, took on the character of forced migration. The tensions were not limited to those between urban youth and the state. There were also formidable material and cultural problems. Many rural communities resisted relocation of urban youth who had no knowledge of, or experience in, farming, no familial or historic ties to their communities, and who, in many instances, scorned the "backwardness" of villagers. Typically, students either ended up in state-run farms – often in underpopulated areas such as Mongolia, Yunnan and Heilongjiang – or they established "educated youth households" (*zhiqing hu*) in remote villages in some of the poorest frontier areas. Most were desperate to find ways to return to their homes and families in the cities.

The Three Old Classes constituted the core of the "sent-down" students. Beginning in 1972, some of these students were able to find work in local factories or as accountants in their villages, and a very small number were among the elect chosen to become "Worker-Peasant-Soldier students" (*gong nong bin xueyuan*) in reformed and vocational programs of higher education. Some became village teachers, "barefoot doctors" (*chijao yisheng*) or propagandists. Others became local cadres.

Beginning in 1973, some student-settlers were permitted to return to the cities. In order to qualify, students either had to have aging or sick parents, be single children or provide certification that they were physically unfit for rural labor. In one way or another, by the end of 1976 about half of the 18 million "sent-down" youth had either left the countryside or no longer worked as manual, rural laborers.

The Cultural Revolution officially came to an end in 1976, when Mao died and the members of the "Gang of Four" were arrested. In 1979, sent-down youth mounted a powerful political campaign to permit their return and, this time, with a fragile new regime in power, the student-settlers were allowed to end their protracted rural exile.

Shanghai in the Cultural Revolution

Shanghai figures prominently in the history of the Cultural Revolution – both as a center of one of the most radical challenges to the entrenched Party apparatus and as the political base favored by Mao to undermine entrenched communist leaders in the nation's capital and to challenge others elsewhere. Beginning in the fall of 1966, rebel Red Guards and worker organizations, such as the Shanghai Workers' Revolutionary Rebel Headquarters under Wang Hongwen (1935–1992), tried to wrest control of Shanghai municipal government from long-time local cadres and loyalist Red Guard supporters. In January 1967, the rebels launched a "January Storm" against the existing authorities, and, under the leadership of Zhang Chunqiao (1917–1991), they declared on February 5, 1967, the founding of the short-lived "Shanghai People's Commune." Although Mao eventually rejected that political organization in favor of a "revolutionary committee" of recently deposed Party and government cadres, military officers and rebel youth as the primary institutional vehicle for forging a new revolutionary order, Zhang and his allies retained control of Shanghai, and the city continued to be a center of revolutionary activity.

At the Ninth Party Congress in 1968, Zhang Chunqiao became a member of the Politburo in Beijing, together with Yao Wenyuan (b. 1931), his Deputy on the Shanghai Revolutionary Committee. Yao, a literary critic had caught the eye of Mao and Jiang Qing (1913–1991), Mao's third wife, with his pyrotechnical attacks on "revisionist" writers. The same Congress appointed Wang Hongwen, the fast-rising Shanghai labor leader, as a member of the Central Committee, and in 1973, at the Tenth Party Congress, he became Vice-Chairman of the Chinese Communist Party. Shanghai leaders and activists thus advanced to center stage in the course of the Cultural Revolution, dominating not only China's leading industrial city but assuming principal roles in the cultural and ideological spheres through their strong position in control of the press and key theoretical journals. Together with Jiang Qing, an actress who had spent some time in Shanghai, Wang Hongwen, Zhang Chunqiao and Yao Wenyuan made up the "Gang of Four" – or the "Gang from Shanghai," as they were some-times known. The members of this "Gang" constituted Mao's power base in Shanghai. As mentioned earlier, their arrest and imprisonment in 1976 marked the end of the Cultural Revolution.

China since Deng Xiaoping's reforms

Mao called for the creation of an egalitarian utopia and for common sacrifice for the collective good, but since his death China has pursued quite different goals. Since the end of the 1970s the social relations of production in China have changed beyond all recognition.

In the 1980s and 1990s, economic reforms associated with Deng Xiaoping have transformed China's economy and society, accelerating economic growth, spurring foreign trade and investment, dismantling the communes, stimulating markets and expanding freedom of movement for villagers. The same processes stimulated the rise of a class of wealthy cadres and businessmen including a plutocratic ruling class, which combines political power and personal wealth. If many have prospered under Deng and his successor, Jiang Zemin, reform has also led to new forms of social dislocation. These include the layoff of millions of state sector workers, the dismantling of urban and rural social welfare, environmental degradation, growing health problems for many people and a range of new social problems associated with rapid urbanization, financial and real estate speculation, and the transfer of public resources to private hands.

According to an official report in the Chinese press (and, therefore, not likely to be an exaggeration) about 2 million surplus workers were laid off in cities in 1996 alone, and total unemployment in all urban areas stood at over 15 million people.[9] In order to accelerate cutbacks in once profitable but now hemorrhaging state-owned enterprises, lifetime employment was replaced by term contracts, and early retirement policies have been implemented in many enterprises. With women over 45 and men over 50 targeted for layoffs, members of the Red Guard generation are now experiencing the consequences of these reforms directly. Moreover, as a result of the 1997 Asian financial and economic crisis, touched off in part by the decade-long Japanese recession, and China's own internal economic problems, the pace of economic growth has slowed and the prospects for workers – notably middle-aged and laid-off workers – is grim.

The reform economic program of Deng and Jiang brought an end to the radical mobilization policies of the Mao era. If this has not produced a democratic breakthrough, it has given rise to a more relaxed intellectual and cultural atmosphere. Yet, although the Party tolerates some diversity of personal expression, it continues to act aggressively to crack down on any signs of organized political opposition – as was shown by its brutal suppression of the independent worker and student movements of May–June 1989. The Party's sensitivity to organizational challenges was strikingly revealed in 1999 by its repression of the Falungong, a sect practicing Qigong exercise and meditation techniques that is said to appeal particularly to elderly and unemployed workers.

It is nonetheless striking that neither the 1989 movement nor subsequent political or intellectual crackdowns have derailed the reform economic agenda. Indeed, the bloody resolution to the conflict on June 4, 1989 may have helped clear the ground for a broader and more rapid expansion of capitalist commodity production and for a greater incursion of foreign capital. After a brief pause, foreign investors showed even greater confidence in China's business environment following the crushing of the 1989 rebellion. From 1988 to 1993 foreign direct investment in China increased eighteenfold.[10] Throughout much of the 1990s, Chinese domestic product continued to grow in the range of 10 to 12 percent per annum, slowing to 6 to 8 percent only in the final years of the decade.

During the Deng era, authoritarian rule in China did not wither away. Instead it changed its nature. Whereas Mao sought to impose cultural integration and ideological control, the CCP now anxiously monitors and polices an increasingly privatized workforce. According to China's political leaders, the market economy will continuously improve everyone's standard of living. Official ideology is silent about the thorny issues of exploitation and economic domination.

Deng's reforms mean different things to different people; but one thing is clear: in China, the Communist Party no longer is an immediate or vital part of people's everyday life. In this sense, at least, the Mao era truly is dead and buried.

This is the context within which our interviewees tell their stories. As one of them explains, these narratives are less about the past than about the problems of living in the present. Indeed, through the experience of a generation the stories that follow express important links between the period of our subjects' youth and the stunning transformation of contemporary China in an era of commodification, privatization and uneven development that many now see as the triumph of capitalism in China.

Notes

1 Victor F.S. Sit, *Chinese Cities: The Growth of the Metropolis Since 1949* (Oxford: Oxford University Press, 1985), p. 109.
2 For more on the "Mao Craze" of the early 1990s, see Geremier R. Barmé, *Shades of Mao: The Posthumous Cult of the Great Leader* (Armonk, New York: M.E. Sharpe, 1997).
3 *Qingchun Wuhui* (Youthful Days With No Regrets), edited by Wang Su (Chengdu: Sichuan Literature Publishing House, 1991); *Kunan yu Fengliu* (Suffering and Glory), edited by Jin Dayong (Shanghai: People's Publishing House, 1994). Both works contain more than a hundred essays each, all written by Red Guards.
4 There are two exceptions to this rule. Wang Xiaoying, a novelist (interview no. 25), did not request anonymity, and Professor Zhu Xueqin (interview no. 8), who read and approved the edited transcript of his remarks in 1998 while he

was a visiting scholar at Harvard, did not believe it was necessary to disguise his identity.

As well as providing pseudonyms for most of our interviewees, we have changed minor details about their past or present lives that might be used to identify them.

5 For representative examples of the genre, see Zi-Ping Luo, *A Generation Lost: China Under the Cultural Revolution* (New York: Henry Holt, 1990); Zhai Zhenhua, *Red Flower of China* (New York: Soho, 1992); and Rae Yang, *Spider Eaters: A Memoir* (Berkeley: University of California Press, 1997).

6 "Big Character" posters, which made use of traditional Chinese calligraphy, were often used as a means of political expression during the Cultural Revolution. On August 5, 1966, Mao's own "Big Character" poster, urging his followers to "Bombard the Headquarters," appeared at the Party Leaders' Compound in the Forbidden City. This effectively sanctioned the widespread use of "Big Character" posters during the following period of struggle.

7 Published in all Chinese newspapers on August 8, 1966.

8 The fights among Red Guard factions in 1966 and 1967 have often been characterized in the West as non-rational, crazy or mindless. However, the basis of much of the conflict among the various factions was difference in social position and even class background. For a detailed analysis, see Anita Chan, Stanley Rosen and Jonathan Unger, "Students and Class Warfare: The Social Roots of the Red Guard Conflict in Guangzhou (Canton)," *China Quarterly*, vol. 83, 1980, pp. 397–446, and Anita Chan "Dispelling Misconceptions about the Red Guard Movement: The Necessity to Re-examine Cultural Revolution Factionalism and Periodization," *Journal of Contemporary China* 1, 1998, pp. 61–85.

9 Hu Angang, "Keeping Down the High Unemployment Rate is the Primary Task for the Future," *Liaowang*, no. 31, 1997, pp. 12–13.

10 In 1988, direct foreign investment in the PRC was US$6.2 billion. By 1993, it had risen to US$114 billion (*Zhongguo Tongji Zhaiyao* (Statistical Abstract of China), Beijing Statistical Publishing House, 1994), p. 110.

Part II
The interviewees

1 Lu Xin, female: novelist

I was a simple-minded child.

My grandfather traded lumber in Nantong, Jiangsu province. The business was prosperous enough to support six children. His son – my father – left for Shanghai when he was very young and became an accountant. My mother was a *taitai* – a housewife with some status. She never worked outside the house until my father died from an illness in 1953. Then our lives suddenly changed.

My mother was a traditional Chinese woman with a very strong will. She came from an old family in Hunan and had attended school. After my father died she sold some of her jewelry so she could support the family while she trained as a nurse. Later, she found a position in a factory clinic. We moved into a poor residential area close to the factory where my mother had found her job.

The memories of my childhood are associated with a big dark room with old, creaking floors, situated on a noisy, crowded lane. Mother raised four children – my three brothers and me – by herself. She made no attempt to remarry. I suppose the responsibility of bringing all of us up was just so overwhelming she forgot herself completely.

Because of the absence of adult males in our family we were untouched by the purges of the 1950s and 1960s. The political struggles that left such a mark on others passed us by.

When I was young I believed everything the Party said. During the 1950s and 1960s, the government did make mistakes. But its policies also tried to give the working classes some security. Because our family lived in harmony with the new society we were supportive of government programs. I was seen as a very "progressive" kid – the term we used in those days. I was a student leader, a model child.

When the Cultural Revolution began I immediately became a Red Guard. Many accounts of Red Guard activity that circulate today are distorted. Most Red Guard organizations – particularly the ones in Shanghai – were not violent or monstrous. My friends and I were not hooligans. We saw the Cultural Revolution as an ideological struggle between right and wrong. I really believed that the Principal of my school was a bad person. To criticize him was to defend the highest ideals.

I was taught the most honorable way of living was to be a member of the working class. Xing Yanzi and Hou Juan were role models for the rest of us to follow.[1] Some now claim that the Up to the Mountains and Down to the Villages movement was Mao's attempt to get dangerous elements out of the cities. But Mao's policy was consistent with his attitude towards knowledge and education. He always believed intellectuals should serve workers and peasants.

Today, the Cultural Revolution is often characterized as a political movement designed to stir up infighting among the masses. It's untrue. The Cultural Revolution gave the masses the power to punish those who misbehaved. Although corruption and the bureaucracy in the Party were minor then compared to today, problems nonetheless existed. In those days people had high expectations and demands of Party officials – nothing like today's cynical attitude. We all took it for granted that the Party was good and that bad people didn't belong in it.

In the 1960s, many young students responded enthusiastically to the call to serve the less privileged because it seemed as natural to them at the time as it does now for students to go to college. But this attitude didn't start with the Cultural Revolution. It sprang from many years of education.

In 1968, I went to Heilongjiang province.[2] I could have waited another year, but I was determined to go to the countryside and wanted to leave as soon as possible. My eldest brother was one of those idealistic students who left to serve peasants in Xinjiang province before the Cultural Revolution began. When he got tuberculosis he had to return to Shanghai for treatment. After he recovered he persuaded several unemployed young people from our neighborhood to return to Xinjiang with him. He was a great influence on me. I thought I was going to change the backwardness of our countryside and transform the whole world. I was, of course, very innocent.

When millions of educated young people moved to the countryside they did begin to stimulate some changes, no matter how small these were. The students were the losers because they sacrificed their education. The countryside offered no hope of personal advancement. But we willingly adjusted to the harsh conditions.

All our energy was consumed by the primitive, endless labor. In winter, the temperature could fall to minus 40° centigrade. I didn't have a pair of boots or a sheepskin coat. My cotton-filled coat was useless because, after a couple of years, the cotton hardened into big lumps. The cold was unbearable, but we still had to work outside or in an unheated room. I was not spoiled as a child, but, before I joined the peasants, I'd never experienced real hardship.

Our farm, close to the border with the Soviet Union, was a militarized production corps administrated by army officers. Because the soldiers didn't really know how to operate an agricultural enterprise it was reorganized later as a non-military state farm. I worked at various occupations, such as laborer, tractor driver, unit secretary and reporter for the farm's Public Affairs Department. Unlike many others, I made no attempt to return to Shanghai. The city no longer had any attraction for me. In any case, my younger brother – the only one of my siblings who had remained in Shanghai – needed our family's room.

During the Cultural Revolution I believed that the "Gang of Four's" ideology and policies benefited families and social classes such as mine. When the members of the "Gang" were overthrown I was bewildered. Our generation had grown up under their influence. They had become part of my body and soul. Some of the radicals on my farm couldn't take it any more and committed suicide. For the first time in my life I was forced to question some of my deepest beliefs.

In early 1976, I published a short story in one of the country's leading literary magazines. Overnight, I became famous. Everyone wanted to know who Lu Xin was. In high school, I'd not been particularly interested in literature – I'd wanted to be a scientist. But, at the farm, people spent a lot of time reading, and classical Chinese literature was often cited to help make a point. After I published that short story I was immediately moved up to the provincial Bureau of Public Affairs. My life as a professional writer began.

Just before the "Gang of Four" was arrested, the magazine that had published my short story recruited me as its editor representing peasants. After the arrests I assumed that the appointment would be retracted since the political situation in the country had changed. But I was told that, because I was a temporary employee, the appointment would stand. So I moved to Beijing at the end of 1976.

At the farm in Heilongjiang I'd "talked love" (*tan lian ai*) with one of my fellow students – a boy I'd known since middle school in Shanghai. In 1977, we were married. In those days, when you were attracted to someone you first began to "talk love" with them and then you entered a relationship that led to marriage.

I didn't know anything about sex or how a child was born. I thought that if a man touched a woman's private parts in a bus this could make her pregnant. Sexual desires were something dirty. I remember that words like "rape" and "adultery" in the posters about convicted criminals always confused and embarrassed me. When I was married at the age of 28 my mother, the nurse, had to tell me how a child was made. During my time in Heilongjiang I was psychologically and emotionally – as well as politically – frozen. I'd been stored in a freezer. A decade passed as if it were one day in my life.

After we married, my husband entered Fudan University in Shanghai, and I continued to work on the literary magazine in Beijing. The magazine wanted to give me a permanent position, but my registration as a rural resident couldn't be changed to that of a city cadre. I decided to go back to the farm and prepare for the College Entrance Examination, which had just been reinstated. In 1978, the Central Drama School in Beijing accepted me. I didn't have high scores on my exams, but my publication and work experiences were taken into consideration.

My new life at the university was a revelation. It was as if I'd awakened from a dream. I watched western movies, and I was stirred by a portrayal of emotion and behavior that previously had been suppressed. I read many Chinese and western novels that were unavailable in the past. I went to the Xidan "Democracy Wall" to read the Big Character posters, and I discussed political reform with my classmates. I felt like a newborn child.

I also attended dance parties. For the first time in my life I was hot and excited about being so close to strange male bodies. Like an adolescent, I was deeply confused by emotional and physical excitement. I'd previously lived in a shell that had protected me from the sexual confusion felt by normal adolescents. That's why I said I was like a child at the age of 30. Human sexuality is disturbing. Maybe I was lucky to have been so protected at an earlier age.

Even though my husband and I had to part immediately after we married I wasn't particularly upset. I don't know why. Perhaps, because I was tough. I know I wasn't sentimental. Not like now when I'm sensitive to everything. When life gets easier you become spoiled. Maybe it was because sex wasn't a major part of the marriage. I didn't worry my husband might be unfaithful. I just took it for granted we'd always be together.

After he graduated from the university my husband was assigned to Beijing as a corespondent for *Wenhui Daily*. We still couldn't live together though. I stayed in the university dormitory, and he lived in his work unit's dormitory. We visited each other at weekends. We were two native Shanghainees living in Beijing, where everything depends on political connections – more so than anywhere else in China.

I had my baby when I was 32 – a year away from graduating. Because I'd had two miscarriages already we decided to keep the child, not have an abortion. At the time, my husband was assigned to report the activities of a Chinese expedition team to the North Pole, so I was alone. My mother came to Beijing to help with the birth. We rented a room from a peasant in the suburb. I didn't know how to look after a child. When my son was two months old he fell off the bed and broke his arm and leg. Even today, the guilt still bites at me whenever I look at him.

My baby was small compared to the other children. I think this is because, when I was pregnant, I didn't eat properly. You know what the food is like in student dining rooms. My friends sometimes criticize me about being too protective towards my son, but they don't know my past. The child had a hard time.

I know that westerners think it's normal for people to change their love and feeling towards one another, but this wasn't acceptable to me. I thought that once a man and a woman marry the most important thing is for both of them to work hard and be responsible towards one another. I never asked what my husband wanted from me as a woman. When he started an affair with someone else I was totally lost. I was so humiliated I couldn't even tell my mother and friends.

Why did this happen to me? The question tortured me. I'm the type of person who gets along well with everyone. I didn't demand anything special from my husband. Instead, I put him first in every single matter. I never thought I should be treated differently because I was a female – that it was all right for me to be a little weak or a little spoiled. All I wanted was to do everything I could for him and for our child. I was deeply wounded. The only way to escape the pain was to divorce him.

During many sleepless nights I returned again and again to the realization that my husband now belonged to another woman. Once we had been in the same middle school and high school; then we went to the farm together; finally, we made this child. A strange woman came. She knew how to talk in a sweet voice, and she knew how to use feminine guile to get what she wanted. My husband said he left me because he wanted some romance in his life. He told me I didn't understand what a man wanted. My devotion meant nothing to him.

After we divorced, my ex-husband wrote me letters saying he felt guilty that, all those years, he'd taken it for granted that I should wait on him. But he'd wanted it both ways. On the one hand he was happy when I played the role of servant and substitute mother, but on the other I was expected to be his fantasy lover. He was satisfied with me as the mother substitute but unhappy with me as the fantasy lover. But how could I have satisfied him? No one ever took the time to spoil me. My husband let me to do all the work, and then he turned around and told me I wasn't a proper woman. He once told me that a woman who doesn't know how to take care of herself couldn't expect to be loved by others.

I asked him whether he felt ashamed that he had betrayed me. He told me that what I'd done for him could have been done by a common house-keeper. My kind of love has little value today. Communist education always taught us to put others before ourselves. That kind of morality wasn't so different from traditional Chinese morality. I always subordinated myself to my husband. I'm a typical traditional Chinese woman.

I hate what he did to me. However, in a way, I'm thankful about what happened because it made me re-examine my life. After I recovered, I became a stronger person.

I don't want to get married again. First of all, I don't trust anyone to ignore my past or treat my child as his own. Second, I overcame a great deal of pain to get out of one marriage. I won't enter another as easily.

Once I was told that marriage is the biggest punishment God places on human beings.

Many of my friends' marriages aren't happy. But as long as both partners make money and raise the family together you don't ask whether a marriage is happy or not. Why bother? In any case, when you get old you don't want to be alone. You start to worry about many trivial things.

The official divorce rate in Shanghai doesn't reflect reality because many people can't afford to divorce. What about their apartment, which was so difficult to obtain? What about their careers? Divorce is still a black mark for officials.

As a single, divorced woman the only relationship I can have with a man is as his "lover," not as his wife. I once believed that marriage alone could justify a sexual relationship between two people. But I have changed because society has changed. Now I, too, have a boyfriend or "lover." It was hard for me to take this step. I still have some reservations about what I've done.

Many people have complimented me on my independence. But they don't know how I feel. Many nights I cannot get to sleep. I long to have someone lying beside me, cuddling me and loving me. I miss the presence of someone who can share my concerns and help me make decisions. In China, very few women live by themselves. If I'm a heroine, I'm not one by choice.

Today, I'm often invited to give speeches about the "new modern female" (*xiandai nüxing*) – meaning a woman with "progressive" ideas that fit our new society. What a joke! The deformed capitalism we have in China has made things worse for women, not better. People spout nonsense about the "new" women who have become so "open-minded," so "cosmopolitan," so "well-educated," but all I feel are sadness and pessimism. When men gain wealth women lose ground.

Women who are strong and independent are now more isolated than ever. Society doesn't accept them. It's more accommodating towards females who are playmates and decorative companions. Today, we have a new type of career woman – the "Public Relations Miss" [*gongguan xiaojie*]. What's "new" about her is that she's the newest kind of prostitute. Her job is to accompany men and make sure their social and business activities are enjoyable. Between these two extremes are the majority of Chinese women. They're commonplace. Change doesn't touch them.

Under socialism, women's independence was valued. Women were treated equally. It's nonsense to claim that, after reform, Chinese women attained a higher status. But change was inevitable. We had to catch up with the rest of the world. However, we run too fast in no particular direction. The gap between the rich and the poor has become so wide. The privileged class is made up of the Party bureaucrats plus the rich businessmen. They make incredible amounts of money.

Then you have intellectuals such as me sitting here talking to you, emoting about "sentiment" and "humanity." Most Chinese people don't have that luxury. They're hard pressed to make a living. It's a continuous struggle. Few women have the time to talk about "rights" or independence. The more material society becomes the less independence women actually have. Money is everything today.

What became of the spiritual aspirations of my generation?

Let me tell you the hottest news in Shanghai media circles. It's about the man who used to be the Vice-Director of the municipal government's Overseas Chinese Affairs Office. He had a position anyone would envy because he traveled abroad frequently, socializing and doing little else. This man is now in jail for murdering his lover, and may soon be executed. Because he's a high-level Party official his crime is not reported, and it's forbidden to interview him. I heard he wrote a novel-length confession about his life. My journalist friends love him. He writes beautifully, and can give wonderful speeches. He was one of the rising stars of our generation: someone who recently achieved very high office.

This man's story reflects the tragic characteristics of our generation. He had a love relationship with his mistress that lasted many years, and she wanted to be with him forever. But he had to end the relationship. The woman had become a liability. I heard he offered her money and a two-bedroom apartment, but she refused. All she wanted was him.

It's sad isn't it? Most modern girls would have grabbed what they could and run to the next man. But this woman wanted her affair to lead to marriage. She expected to be treated equally. She'd had several abortions because our society doesn't permit illegitimate birth. If she'd had a child things might have been different.

I can understand why she couldn't step aside and let him go. The only way he could get free of her was to kill her.

Our generation is tragic. I've just finished a novel about the end of a heroic period. The teacher in my story is one of our generation and still has idealistic and revolutionary dreams. But when he tries to live up to his principles he fails every time.

Of course, there are those among us who've made a good adjustment. There'll always be the opportunists. But let me tell you something: the best officials today are worse than the most corrupt cadres of the past.

Our generation – the Red Guard generation – cannot catch up with this world. Our thoughts are out of date. What we learnt in our childhood soaked into our bones. You'd have to install a new brain in us to change our way of thinking. Even if we move to the United States we're still the same. Many of my expatriate friends have told me that, although they understand American culture, they're still, at heart, "Chinese peasants." They cannot change their belief system or their mode of behavior – no matter how long they live in America.

You married a foreigner. Have you changed a lot?

Notes

1 Two "educated youths" who went to the countryside to live as peasants a few years before the Cultural Revolution began.

2 Heilongjiang or "Black Dragon River." A province in the far northeast of China. During the 1960s the government encouraged people to settle in this relatively under-populated region. In part, this was because of its proximity to the Soviet Union.

   Students who ended up on state farms in Heilongjiang tended to be from "good" family backgrounds, i.e. from working-class or cadre families.

2 Wu Shanren, male: private businessman

I come from a family of intellectuals. My mother was the principal of an elementary school. She had the reputation of being very strict. She was the same way at home. However, I am the first child – also the only son – and I always did very well in school, so my mother never scolded me. In fact, she was extremely proud of me.

In primary school I developed an interest in Chinese water painting. Because of my skill I was recruited by Datong Middle School – a key [selective] middle school, specializing in the arts. I won several Chinese water-painting competitions. One of my paintings was given an internationally prestigious award and was reproduced in *Wenhui Daily*. So I was kind of famous. My life was full of sunshine. I expected to go to the best art school in China: the Central College of Visual Arts in Beijing.

I was not in the Youth League and not "progressive" politically. But I became a popular leader because I was well known as a talented painter.

When the Cultural Revolution began I was just a month away from graduation. Was I disappointed because the movement interfered with my dream of becoming an artist? No, not at all. The Cultural Revolution opened another world for me. My painting and calligraphy skills were immediately put to good use.

All the excitement was very infectious. My political ambitions were awakened. Soon my Red Guard organization emerged as an influential organization. I don't think I had any individual ambition – such as knowing what I wanted for myself. I was just a young, hotheaded follower of Mao.

Most of the members in my Red Guard organization were drawn from the oldest students [i.e. from the senior high-school class of 1966]. We had a deeper political awareness and a wider range of activities than most of the others. We were also closely allied with the Red Revolutionary Association (*honggehui*) at Fudan University.[1] On three separate occasions I participated in the "Firing at Zhang Chunqiao" campaign. Later, when Zhang became a member of the Small Group of the Cultural Revolution, I realized immediately we were all in trouble. Before long, I was "separated and investigated" (*geli shencha*). After the organizations that supported

Zhang got control of Shanghai municipal government I was forced to confess my counter-revolutionary activities. I realized I'd picked the wrong side, but I also knew I wasn't a counter-revolutionary. On the contrary, I was, at the time, very revolutionary.

Some soldiers put a gun to my head and ordered me to confess where I'd hidden some documents. They said I'd been seen carrying some boxes away from a house occupied by a leader of the Red Revolutionary Association. They told me that if I didn't make a confession I could go see God with my granite-like skull. I was very scared, but I didn't give in. I don't think I could be so brave today. At the time, I was very young – 18 years old, and full of hot blood. I saved that Red Guard leader, who later became a close friend of mine. It was he who got me started in business.

It was only later that I learnt that our organization had had an association with Lin Biao's faction.[2] Because I was only a minor figure I was released with an "inconclusive" evaluation but also with a notation on my record that I'd had a "serious political problem." Of course, when Lin Biao was shot out of the sky over Mongolia I was separated and investigated again. Anyway, from very early on in the Cultural Revolution I was finished politically.

In 1970, I was given a factory job. I had two younger sisters, both of whom were in middle school. My mother wanted me to stay in Shanghai. As soon as it was clear that at least one or two of us had to go to the countryside she sacrificed her two daughters. This guaranteed I'd be given the "unquestionable category" (*yingdang*) and assigned a job near home. I felt guilty, but I couldn't disobey my mother.

Now, I regularly give money to my sisters. One of them still has her residence registration in Anhui, but now works for me in Shanghai. She married a local man. They sacrificed for me, and now it's my turn. I've promised my sisters I'll support my two nephews until they get married.

Life in the factory was easy. Even though I was classified as someone with a "serious political problem" I was still asked to make posters and banners. Half the time I wasn't doing any physical labor. I was well liked. However, I was only used as a hand. I wasn't going to get remunerated for my artistic services.

In every political purge – such as the campaign to clear up the "May Sixteenth Elements"[3] – I would be hauled in again for questioning. The Party Secretary in my factory got to know me better than my wife because he talked to everyone I'd known since elementary school. My wife worked in my factory. She's not interested in anything political.

What was my reaction when the "Gang of Four" was overthrown? Neither happy nor sad. I was tired of the endless turmoil and deeply despised politics. Still, I'd once been a rebel – a Red Guard, and, in one way or the other, I identified with them, or with that clique. In any case, after Mao died, people like me with no educational qualifications were simply dropped into the garbage bin.

In 1981, I managed to get a job at a newspaper for elementary school students. I'd been drawing cartoons for them for several years. To others, this move must have seemed a good one. My duties, which were to draw pictures to go with headlines and stories, took up two days of the week. I had lots of spare time. However, I was unhappy. First of all, there was no chance I'd ever become an official. Politically, I was dead. Second, I was too old to pursue an academic career. I'd been given no chance to develop the skills of my youth. I was forced to acknowledge I'd failed the dream of my childhood. I was nearly 40 years old. Because I had no credentials I was the lowest-paid employee at the newspaper. To tell you the truth, I felt inferior all the time.

In 1987, I quit my job and started my own business. I decided to do this when I was taking care of my sick mother. She broke her leg and then got a serious attack of uremia. She was a teacher, and you know that these workers don't have good healthcare coverage. She couldn't get the expensive medicine and decent hospital care she needed.

I had to take her to the hospital on my bicycle. One day she was too weak to sit on the seat, so we had to stop every 10 minutes or so to take a rest. We sat on the sidewalk. Looking at her – old, pale and weak – I almost cried. I told myself I'd failed her. I couldn't arrange for decent housing or care. I'd done nothing to repay her devotion. That same day I told my brother-in-law I wanted to make money. Money buys power.

Soon after I quit my job, my old friend from the Red Revolutionary Association called me from Shenzhen. He wanted me to help him produce Chinese New Year pictures and calendars. He told me he could use my artistic expertise. That first year I made 60,000 yuan profit [US$11,500].[4] It's now been six years since I "jumped into the sea" (*xiahai*) [quit my regular job to try something uncharted and risky]. I own several companies – private ones and, also, joint ventures with foreigners. I've just purchased a piece of land and opened a trade company in Pudong, Waigaoqiao tax-free Zone. I rent four office rooms in a first-class hotel in Shanghai. I bought a house for US$600,000 near Xijiao Park. I have a Lexus and a chauffeur to take me around. Most people would say I'm a very successful man.

Am I happy, and enjoying my new life? No, I'm exhausted. I built up this fortune with my bare hands. I was a nobody – with no money and no support from the government. All they did was certify my business. Now I have to pay "fraternal duty" to the bureaucrats. When you enter such a relationship you never get free of it. I must keep my businesses going to pay all my expenses. It's an endless, stressful life.

I moved my business base to Shanghai this year. Shenzhen is different from Shanghai. Business is much less restricted there. From bottom to top everyone is doing business of some sort. No one in Shenzhen makes unnecessary trouble for you. Shanghai has too many regulations and restrictions. They check up on all your taxes and wrongdoing. Frankly, what's called an "economic crime" in Shanghai is treated as nothing in Shenzhen. I moved my business here because, after this year [1994], Shenzhen no longer will enjoy special trading privileges and tax-free advantages. Also, I know Shanghai is going to be much more important than Shenzhen. It's got the biggest industrial base in China.

It's confusing, isn't it? The same country, but two different sets of rules. Even the rules passed by the People's Congress can be changed by a simple pronouncement from the State Council. Chinese laws are like a rubber band – you can stretch them at your will, according to your powers. In America, ordinary people such as me can use laws, but, here, law is used chiefly for the benefit of high-ranking officials. This is why so many people are getting passports. They don't trust the government. But I haven't had any problems yet. I'm a member of the Three Old Classes – not the same as the young generation. I'm not wild or reckless.

It's not easy doing business today. Everyone wants to make money fast. If the Cultural Revolution was a period of political frenzy, now we're living through a period of money frenzy. What the old Chinese bourgeoisie possessed was nothing compared to the wealth rich people have today. In fact, the old capitalists are poor again. They must have long since spent whatever compensation they received after the Cultural Revolution.

People "sitting on a seat" (*zaiwei*) [holding an official position] make the most out of the situation. If an official cannot do business himself he can let his wife, sons, daughters or in-laws do it. I've no objection to this system. I'm sure it's the same in America. But if you're an official you should do something good for society as well as for yourself.

No, I don't have any objection to the leadership of the Communist Party. We don't have any alternative. The model we should follow is Singapore – an authoritarian, one-party government with a market economy. Such a huge country needs a strong center.

I fly over different parts of our country a lot. What I see makes me sad. You know, most parts are just bare earth. People are so poor. It's a dilemma for the Party. It had to make some changes, but it really doesn't know how to solve our problems. I'm carping as usual. We Chinese do have this fault. We like to chew on others. But why don't the people who complain take some responsibility? Are they sure they can do any better? Don't spend half a day complaining and the rest of your time squatting and watching! Do something instead!

China is a peasant country. Deng Xiaoping is a great man. Do you know why? Because, although in nature he's a communist and peasant, he managed to bring the country to this stage. It's not easy; he has lots of courage. People shouldn't have unrealistic expectations. I agree that there are lots of bad things around today. But is there really anything unusual about this? America, European countries and Japan were often in a mess during their history. Don't worry. China has 5,000 years of civilization. We'll make it.

It's not my business to criticize the government. I just want to follow the rules and do my best. I made money, therefore I help my friends. I don't concern myself with larger social responsibilities. My family and my friends are my beneficiaries. I do all sorts of favors for them. I've helped lots of people out of my own pocket. People should remember their own humble past and not become self-important and selfish. I've told my old friends I'm still the same person inside.

But I've changed too. I'm more flexible now, no longer quite so stubborn. But the biggest change is that I feel nervous and uncertain all the time. Every morning I wake up in a sort of panic, knowing I have to deal with lots of things alone. I keep looking for some relief. It's like a rock rolling down the mountain; it keeps rolling down. You can't stop it. I'll never escape.

I think the Cultural Revolution was the happiest period of my life. There was something special about that time: the loyalty, the sense of solidarity, the confidence and the certainty. In difficult times, my friends were always there for me. I don't trust people now – especially in business, no one can be trusted. For instance, I run an advertising company. After I trained someone they immediately quit and began to compete with me.

I do business mainly with Chinese in Hong Kong. I do them a favor and they return one to me. I feel at ease with Chinese businessmen. Foreigners are different. If you do them a favor they think it means you're stupid.

My wife is a wonderful person. She married me when I was very low. She was attracted to my ability and I was moved by her kindness. But my marriage is dead. The gap between us is wide. Basically, my wife is a housewife who's uncomfortable with social activities. We don't share any interests. Sometimes I long for a new life with someone else. However, I would never divorce my wife against her will. I have my duty toward her. I'll never abandon her. This is my determination. Marriage and divorce are serious matters. Any decision affects another person's life. I've made up my mind, and I'm not going to change it. Chinese still care about face. For westerners, it's simple – if you no longer have feelings for each other you get a divorce. But I'm Chinese. In China, we're not yet that modern. After all, my wife married me when I was nobody. She gave me all she had.

I gave my wife a big sum of money so she could play the stock market. She's one of those big investors (*dahu*) who have their own monitors in the stock exchange. She spends all day there.

My wife knows about my girlfriends. I overcome my embarrassment to tell you the truth. I've had several mistresses. The last one just broke off with me. I'm not bitter about it. I gave her an apartment. She's young and pretty and wants the best out of life. She had another chance, and I let her go. Don't delude yourself. Young girls today only want money. I would never take this kind of relationship seriously unless someday I really fall in love with a good girl. But that's not likely. [His cellular phone rings]. Sorry, I have to take this call.

I've been to Hong Kong many times. In June, I'm going to America, and, in July, to Russia. Russia has more appeal for me than America. I learned Russian in middle school. I love Russian literature. Whatever you learn at that age you never forget. I'm much closer to Russia than to America. I'm very excited about the trip. Not like the young generation – they come to know America first. They like America best.

Am I bothered about the rumors of Russian gangsters? No. It's all propaganda. You know it's like people today who talk about the Cultural Revolution – did we really feel we were in danger all the time? Propaganda exaggerates things. Anyway, I want to see the Great Russian homeland.

Our generation is unique. We grew up in a different era. The Three Old Classes are made up of good people. What marks our generation is that we're all responsible and hard working.

My son is my pride. He's in a key boarding school, a year away from the College Entrance Examination. He's first in his grade. The only place he goes is the bookstore. He looks after himself and takes care of his schoolwork. I don't have time to be with him. I donate money to his school to show I care about him. We don't talk much. But I don't talk much to my father either. I go to see him twice a month. Chinese fathers and sons are like that – still a bit feudal in their relationship.

Unfortunately, my mother died before I could do any more for her. My dear mother always loved me the most. She gave me financial support even after I got married. At least I was able to get the best doctors and the best hospital for my father after he got sick. It saved his life.

I'm planning to buy some property abroad – probably in Vancouver. One day, if it becomes necessary, I can emigrate. It's not that I want to live in a foreign country. Obviously, it would be nice to have a place to which I could retreat. But foreign countries have no great attraction for me. I'm too old now to settle in a strange place.

I've some distant relatives in America. The old couple live on government money. Their children are too Americanized to take care of them. This uncle and aunt play mahjong day and night. Their letters are full of complaints. What's so great about that kind of life? However, there's no harm in having a foreign passport. It doesn't stop you from staying in China if that's what you want.

[His phone rings again].

Notes

1   The Red Revolutionary Association at Fudan University in Shanghai opposed Zhang Chunqiao, who later became one of the "Gang of Four."
2   Lin Biao, Vice-Chairman of the Central Committee and Mao's designated heir, was the second most important figure during the Cultural Revolution. He died in a mysterious airplane crash fleeing China on September 13, 1971. Many Chinese at the time believed that his plane was shot down on Mao's orders.
3   "May Sixteenth Elements" refers to followers of the Lin Biao faction.
4   Before June 1993 the Chinese renminbi was worth about US 17 cents to the yuan. The exchange rate in 1998 was approximately US 12 cents for 1 yuan.

3   Wang Chen, male: cadre in charge of a ferry company, and Wu Qing, male, his friend: private businessman

WANG: Wu and I are both from the high-school class of 1967. Our class was the second to be affected by the Four-Facing Policy.[1] The first was the class of 1966.

I was the eldest child in my family so it seemed unlikely I'd be allowed to stay in Shanghai. But I wasn't afraid to go to the countryside.

Mother always depended on me to fetch our family's rice supply. So the day before I was due to get my work assignment I lugged home a 100 jin [110 lb] sack of rice – a two-month ration. I took it for granted I'd be sent out of the city.

WU: Wang was a bully-looking kid. Don't be fooled by his nice suit and by his elegant appearance today. The first time I saw him he was a head taller than I, with plenty of muscles. We were 17 years old and had just become new members of the working class in Shanghai.

WANG: As it happened, I wasn't sent to the countryside. Instead, I was assigned to the Inland River Transportation Bureau in Shanghai. Altogether, sixty boys and sixty girls were sent to this Bureau. All the girls became mechanics, and all the boys were sent to work the boats on the Huangpu and Suchou Rivers. In old China, dockers and boatmen were the hardest working –and some of the poorest – people in Shanghai. I wasn't too pleased to discover that, since liberation, working conditions hadn't changed that much.

Our job was to transfer cargo, such as coal, timber, and various construction materials, from the big ships in Shanghai harbor to the factories along the banks of the Huangpu. Our steam tugs towed eight to ten barges each trip. It was eight days of continuous work followed by four days of leave. At work, we lived and slept on the boat.

WU: The living area in the junk was a tiny space, just big enough for two cots. We cooked on a portable coal stove on deck, shat in the river, and then used the same river water for washing and drinking. In the evening, we used oil lamps for illumination. Looking at the electric lights on the banks of the river, we often used to wonder what part of the world we lived in: the most developed city in China or the primitive countryside?

There were no great skills or techniques to be learned in our job. All we had to do was ride that boat up and down the Huangpu. For me, the most difficult thing was to live in such close quarters for eight days and nights. I was clumsy and physically frail and didn't get on with the others. No one wanted me in his tug, and I was kicked off two before I met Wang. He took me in and treated me like his younger brother. I'm still grateful to him for looking after me. I couldn't imagine anyone else doing what he did. He took care of all the cooking, washing and cleaning. He even mended my clothes. We lived in the same boat for five years. It was like being a married couple, wasn't it?

WANG: Well, I wouldn't put it quite that way. But we had to cultivate the habits needed for a successful marriage. Luckily, Wu and I had interests in common and we talked a lot.

Life on board was extremely boring. One of my friends came to stay with us for two days. He enjoyed himself. He thought it was romantic, lying on deck in the evening reciting Tang poems. Of course he wasn't there during the winter nights when all you wanted to do was to get into bed as early as possible because it was too cold and dark to do anything else.

We passed our time reading anything that was available. Books were scarce. I read lots of Marx's and Engels' works. When you read the Bible you don't ask whether it's correct or not – you just try to understand it. I sometimes spent half a day thinking about a sentence from one of Marx's or Engels' books. I became totally absorbed in their work and wrote lots of study notes.

I still believe Marx was the greatest thinker that ever existed. No one in the past or present can compete with him. What he said about capitalist society is right. What he said about socialist society didn't actually work out. But he couldn't have foreseen this, could he?

WU: See! He's still a good Communist Party member!

WANG: It's unfashionable today to say you still believe in Marxism because this suggests you are out-of-date and a knuckle-headed fool. But truth is truth.

I also think Mao was the greatest Chinese leader that ever existed. Do you know the following saying: "Mao (Zedong) created the world" (*kaitian pidi*); "Zhou (Enlai) was a moral giant" (*dingtian lidi*); "Deng (Xiaoping) turned the world upside down" (*fantian fudi*); "Jiang (Zemin) rules without vision or responsibility" (*huntian hudi*)? Today's leaders have no sense of morality. I still have deep feelings for Mao.

WU: That's just some residue left over from the past. I don't think you want to claim that Mao is relevant to your life today. If there were another Cultural Revolution you'd be one of the first targets. You've become a "king of the bush" (*caodouwang*) [in charge of a unit with autonomous powers]. You wouldn't claim you had "deep feelings" for Mao if you came under attack from your own workers.

WANG: I agree Mao made mistakes – especially later in his life. By the end of the Cultural Revolution the country's economy was near to collapse. At least, that's what we were told later. But, at the time, we didn't know anything about this. We didn't think things were coming apart. Maybe this is because Shanghai was always under control. The only chaotic political event I can recall here was the fight between the United Command Workers' Organization (*liansi*) and the Red East Workers' Organization (*dongfanghong*) in August, 1967. Many people were involved and there were heavy casualties on both sides. Ultimately Red East, backed by Wang Hongwen [one of the "Gang of Four"] crushed the United Command. After this, the Cultural Revolution was conducted here in an orderly fashion. Other parts of the country weren't so fortunate.

I do think that the Cultural Revolution was the biggest mistake Mao ever made. My father was a playwright. He joined the Party before liberation. He was so intent on being a good Party member that he never once questioned the endless political strife – not in front of me at least. He kept out of trouble. However, when the Cultural Revolution began he warned me not to get involved. During the Great Exchange he ordered me not to go to Beijing. I had to sneak out when he was in his workplace.

WU: Perhaps Shanghai wasn't as disorderly as other cities. But there was a lot going on under the surface. Maybe Mao didn't intend to unleash such strife, but this was an inevitable consequence of the political movements he launched.

After several years on the boats, I was "borrowed" by our Bureau's "One-Attack-and-Three-Against" (*yidasanfan*) team.[2] My job was to guard the prisoners who'd been detained and held for investigation. It was a pretty horrible job, let me tell you. It didn't take too long for me to figure out that the Cultural Revolution was a chance for the people who'd gained power to strike out at those who'd lost power. Over the years, many bloody accounts were left unsettled. Now was a chance to get even.

WANG: Few people got personally involved in these kinds of political struggles. But, after several campaigns, most work units contained a few people with questionable political records. These became "veteran athletes" – individuals who could be picked on whenever a new campaign was launched. We called these "athletes" "dead tigers" (*silaohu*) too because they were "dead" from the moment they first got hit. When the Party bosses had to respond to initiatives from above they would schedule a meeting, call their "tigers" out of retirement and "honor" them once more. No one took these escapades too seriously.

The students who remained in Shanghai had different experiences from those who went to the countryside. It was relatively easy for us to adjust. By the end of the Cultural Revolution most of us were getting married. We saved up equivalent amounts of money, bought the same set of furniture and arranged for the same wedding banquet. Everyone was equal. What one family could afford, others, too, could purchase. Therefore, our hearts were at peace.

When I got married my work unit gave me a one-room apartment with a kitchen and bathroom that was shared with three other families. This room had just enough space for the standard set of furniture. But there was only one place where you could put your bed and still leave room for the other things. So every family set their bed in the same spot. Sometimes, during the night you couldn't help hearing the noise overhead. Then you'd start worrying about the couple downstairs. That's about the furthest equality can go. Maybe it was a bit too far.

By the way, I still live in that room but now I have new furniture.

WU: The man is absolutely foolish! He must be about the only person in his position that hasn't yet been given a two-bedroom apartment. He's a boss in charge of six ferries and 200 employees. Perhaps he's trying to get himself a medal as a "Model Party Member."

WANG: No. Don't make fun of me.

Our company is state-owned. In fact, the transportation sector has not been touched by privatization. It was only recently that the government allowed foreign money to be invested in roads, railways and river transportation. I heard that the Japanese JR Company and the French TGC Company are competing for the chance to build a high-speed rail service between Beijing and Shanghai. The Japanese train is smaller and is capable of reaching 500 kilometers per hour. If this line is built it will take six hours to get to Beijing. Now it's a trip of more than seventeen hours. Japanese companies also want to begin a new passenger line from Japan via Shanghai to Chongqing. This would be a very important step for the Japanese. They've never been allowed to sail up the Changjiang River.

Our unit is responsible for ferrying cars and trucks across the Huangpu River between Shanghai and Pudong. I started working at this particular job in 1983, and was put in charge of our unit in 1993, the year the Yangpu bridge was completed. Because of the bridge our business dropped off considerably. However, since late 1994, the business has been coming back because there are often traffic jams at the bridge. About 50,000 vehicles a day now use the Yangpu bridge, which is about the maximum amount of traffic it can handle.

Our company increased its profit from 7.2 million yuan in 1994 to 10 million yuan in 1996. I think I'm doing a good job. But I'm just a worker hired by the Party. They can reward me if they want. But they don't have to because I'm just doing my duty. All I care about is avoiding accidents. In my line of work if you make a mistake it's likely to be a big one. I try to treat my workers fairly. I tell them I'm a "father-and-mother" official (*fumuguan*) who will look after them. In return, I expect them to do their duty.

WU: I don't believe what I'm hearing! A "father-and-mother" official? Is this why you were visiting one of your workers at home today on Saturday?

WANG: [ignoring Wu] You ask me to compare being a cadre before and after reform. It's a lot easier now. Today, you have the freedom to get rid of employees, and you don't even have to come up with a reason for firing them.

During the Cultural Revolution, if you wanted to punish a worker you had to be careful. They could fight back and get into a shouting match. But no worker would do this now. The government's policies have made them fearful of losing their jobs. There are 600,000 people who have lost their job in Shanghai this year [1996]. At least, that's the official figure. The real number is probably much higher.

When Deng Xiaoping said, "let a few get rich first" I think he acted in good will. China is so big it wasn't likely that everyone would get rich at the same time. Because of Deng's policy, however, we now have a few very rich people and many others who are left behind and who will never catch up.

I think the living standards of ordinary people have improved a lot but inflation is a big problem. I remember the first time food prices were adjusted was in November 1979. It was a big thing back then and officials had to make a lot of speeches to justify the decision. Now, inflation is growing too fast. People might have a better diet but they feel tense and insecure all the time.

I do see good signs for the future. In 1995, there were 336 registered foreign companies in Waigaoqiao tax-free zone in Pudong. This is a 22 percent increase over 1994. As long as Pudong is developing our work unit will do all right.

WU: I would describe China like this: in economics, the Party follows a Westernization movement (*yangwu yundong*), but, in politics, it moves toward a constitutional monarchy – the only difference being that the king is replaced by the Party. Wang is like a good-hearted Chinese official from the Qing dynasty. He wants change but remains loyal to the past. I envy his relaxed attitude. He claims that yesterday was not too bad and today is better. My position is that yesterday *was* bad and today's no better. The more the economy develops the more society disintegrates. Wang and I still are good friends but now we see things slightly differently.

After I left the One-Attack-and-Three-Against team I was sent to our Bureau's Department of Public Affairs to help produce a newsletter. I'm good at Chinese water painting and calligraphy. That's why they wanted me to work on the newsletter. In 1980, the Bureau ended production of this newsletter, and I was given the job of managing the car pool. It was a nice job because I was another "king of the bush."

One day, a former driver, who had left us to go to university years ago, came to visit me. He'd graduated and had started working for the Shanghai Elderly People's Association. He told me that the Association was looking for people to help start a newspaper. He told me that if I wanted the position he could get it for me. I took the job without a second thought. Officially, the Association had "borrowed" me from the Inland Transportation Bureau.

This is how I got to know people in sociology. Because of my new job I started to do some research on elderly people. This was a new area of investigation without much of a history. It was easy for someone like me with no sociological training to become an "expert" on the elderly.

In 1991, I was "borrowed" again by the State Statistical Bureau in Beijing to work on the population census. My job was to take demographic samples. Frankly, I didn't have a clue what I was doing. I saw my assignment as "mixing glue" (*daojianghu*) [performing a task perfunctorily]. But I was given pretty good insight into how the State Statistical Bureau actually operates.

It's difficult for Shanghainese to work in Beijing. It's so political there. In any case, I didn't want to stay in Beijing. By 1993, the city was full of college-educated people looking for work. I had no degree.

So I returned to Shanghai and decided to "jump into the sea." But I didn't know anything about business and didn't even know what kind of enterprise I wanted to start. I went to Shenzhen to make money. But, like many others there, I had no idea how to do this.

I'd been in Shenzhen before and knew some people there. So I began my "business" by calling on these friends and by throwing dinner parties for them. Everyone said they would help me, but I couldn't even tell them what kind of help I was looking for. Before long, I'd spent all my money but my "business" was still in the talking stage. On my last day in Shenzhen I had 29 yuan left in my pocket – not enough, even, to buy a ticket home.

When I finally got back to Shanghai I had far less money than when I'd left home. My wife told me I should view my losses as the "tuition" I had to pay to learn something new. I learned my lesson. I took time out to think about what I wanted to do.

I formed a partnership with a Chinese overseas student who had a "green card" [US residence permit]. Unfortunately, he had no money. But I needed a "foreign investor" as my partner in order to qualify for tax breaks and other subsidies.

Now I'm doing all right. Once you get started you start building up a network. Then things get a bit easier.

I'm not like Wang. I have a monkey's ass. I can't sit still for long. Of course, my future is hardly secure.

WANG: [laughing] You're a born businessman. You'll be all right.

Notes

1   The "Four-Facing Policy" (*sige mianxiang*) originally urged graduates to serve in (1) industry; (2) rural areas; (3) frontier areas; and (4) grassroots organizations. Later, the policy was used to give work assignments to the high-school classes of 1966 and 1967. At the time, service in rural and frontier areas was stressed.

2   The One-Attack-and-Three-Against Campaign asked people to: Attack Counter-revolutionaries! Oppose Corruption, Extravagance and Profiteering!

4 Jie Qian, male: director in a securities company

Until 1991, I never said no to the Party. When I finally did it changed my life. That's why I'm here. I did the right thing.

In 1969, I went to a farm in Heilongjiang. I've a younger sister, and I agreed to go to the countryside so she could secure a job near home. However, her class was "Completely Red" (*yipianhong*) [they all had to go the countryside] so she ended up going to Heilongjiang too.[1]

I'll never forget my life on the farm – the grueling labor and the terrible food. I worked in the fields for four years. The worst time was the harvest. We worked day and night, almost non-stop. The rice paddy was vast. By the time you'd finished a row your back was in such pain you thought you'd never straighten up again. When it rained hard it was worse than anyone could imagine. We were up to our knees in muck, and we had to transport the rice stalks on our backs. Mechanical devices were useless in that kind of situation.

Winter was spent on irrigation projects. We were sent to the construction site for weeks or months. Every day our lunch was two plain sorghum buns, one piece of pickled turnip and a bottle of water. By the middle of the day the buns were frozen like rock and the water had turned to ice. We had to build a fire to melt the water and heat the dumplings. The surface of the buns was burned; the inside was rock hard.

In summer, we suffered from thirst. Most of the time we worked miles away from farm headquarters. We never had enough drinking water. Often, I had to lap up the muddy water left in tire tracks. I could see larvae swimming in these stagnant pools. The girls were a bit more careful. They used rice straws to skim from the surface.

After four years' hard labor I was put in charge of the dining room. We had no cooking oil. A piece of fatty pork skin hung above the stove. When we cooked vegetables we greased the wok with this skin.

In 1971, we suffered food shortages. The leader of our team had given our rice to the government as "faithful heart grain" (*zhongxinliang*). It was unnecessary because state farms worked by students were not required to make this gesture. From spring until summer that year we had only potatoes to eat.

After I was put in charge of the dining room I tried to improve our diet. I managed to trade some of our beans for cooking oil from Shandong. When two barrels of oil arrived at the farm everybody got very excited. That evening we enjoyed our first fried vegetables for many years.

These kinds of experiences have given me a tough outlook on life: whatever the hardship I can endure it; whatever the pleasure I'm not going to miss it. That's my philosophy now.

I was among the last to be sent to university as a Worker-Peasant-Soldier student. I studied physics for three years, and then I was assigned to a factory as Party Secretary. From 1981 to 1991 I was promoted step by step and ended up with an important position as Party Secretary of a big industrial sector.

In order to be a Party official you've got to let your head follow your ass – in other words you act according to the seat you occupy. In the end I was fed up with my job. All I ever did was give speeches in meetings, mostly lies.

In 1991, I heard that this newly established Securities Company wanted to recruit some officials to run the company, so I applied for a position. My superiors tried to stop me, but, for the first time in my life, I said no. I passed the written test and was selected for an interview, where I was given ten sealed envelopes and told to pick a question. Mine asked how the Shanghai stock market could help development in Pudong. I got the job.

I'm the head of a division that helps prepare new stock issues. We do the paper work for preliminary offerings (*yuanshigu*), and we distribute shares to institutional investors and to other important clients before the rest of the offering officially goes to the public. Institutional investors own three-quarters of all stock in China.

Who are these institutional investors? Let me put it like this. Except for Party organizations, every other organization in China is involved in the stock market. From workers' unions to women's federations to youth leagues, many government organizations gamble in the market. A lot of state-owned enterprises have employees who do nothing but trade stock. Some local government organizations use the funds the government gives them to purchase grain to play the stock market. So when the peasants bring in their grain all they are given for their efforts are IOUs.

We keep a certain percentage of the money raised in offerings as our fee. This year my division made a profit of 16 million yuan. I have 14 people under me, so that's more than 1 million yuan's worth of earnings per person. I can't tell you how much each of us take home. But I can tell you that you have to be in the financial sector today to make a real killing. It's called "making money out of money" (*kaoqian zhuanqian*).

I've visited America several times. I was told repeatedly how unregulated and how risky the Chinese stock market is. I said: "Look, you're all missing the point. Because of the lack of regulations there are unbelievable opportunities. Remember the old saying: 'It's easier to catch fish in muddy water' " (*hunshui moyu*).

Well, I agree, there are no easy pickings for individual investors. Small investors in China are not like their counterparts in the West. In America, individual investors are long-term investors. They put savings away to build a more secure future. Chinese small investors are desperate "get-rich-quick" gamblers. They invest their money for TVs, VCRs, their kids' college education, maybe a new apartment. Now, 21 million small investors have a part of themselves in either the Shanghai or Shenzhen markets. The cash they put in represents every bit of income they've managed to accumulate over the years. So they bet their life dreams on the stock market and desperately monitor every fluctuation in price. This kind of fever makes it easy for corrupt parties to manipulate and to control the market to their advantage.

What you've heard is correct. *Zhengquan Bao* (Securities) [a newssheet aimed at small investors] is the most corrupt newspaper in China. In fact, it's a tool used by powerful insiders to spread misleading information so that investors can be lured into traps. For instance, this year [1996] it was pushing the so-called "97 concept," telling everyone that 1997 will be a boom year because of Hong Kong's return.[2]

Small investors have no way of getting accurate information. Their decisions are based either on guesswork or on faulty information. Some companies release deliberately falsified financial reports in order to force down the value of their stock. Then they conspire with big investors to buy the undervalued stock. By continuing to manipulate information they can lure small investors back in again and push up the value of the stock. After this happens they pull out.

There's little relationship in China between industrial performance and price. There are many enterprises that should never issue stock to the public. They've no investment value and no potential. They just need money to fund their operations. We call this kind of stock "hooligan" or "garbage" stock (*lajigu*).

You ask why so many people believe that all new offerings are an opportunity for a quick profit, and why it is that every company desperately tries to get permission to sell stock. Up to now there are about 9,000 enterprises in China with joint-stock limited liability. But these enterprises comprise only a small proportion of all businesses. Moreover, among these 9,000 companies only about 500 sell stock directly to the public.

Why is that? Because the government has a policy of "limited offerings." Every year, the State Planning Commission restricts the amount of new stock available for public offering. For instance, new offerings this year are limited to stock with a total face value of 5.5 billion yuan. Stock offerings are parceled out among the provinces, and the political leadership in each province is responsible for choosing those enterprises allowed to issue stock. Nearly every large enterprise wants to offer stock, so the opportunities for bribery and corruption are endemic. To cope with "too little porridge for too many monks" the provincial governments try to divide what's available into as many portions as possible. As a result, one of the characteristics of the Chinese stock market is that the majority of companies are "small bird" companies with capital stock that barely reaches the minimum requirement of 50 million yuan.

Typically, when a company sells stock for the first time the value of its shares soar immediately after the offering. That's what we call "pushing new stocks" (*cao xingu*). This summer, all the new stock offerings increased by more than 100 percent immediately following their launch. Why does this happen? The demand for stocks is much bigger than the supply – that's the root cause of over valuation.

Why does every company want to sell stock? Because it's so profitable you can't lose.

All initial public offerings are priced at five or six times more than their face value. In some cases, they trade at nine or ten times face value. For instance, this September, one Shanghai Company with capital stock of 200 million yuan issued 60 million shares to the public. Each share's face value was 1 yuan, but it sold at 5.8 yuan. When the initial offering was all sold the company showed a paper debit of 60 million yuan. But in less than a day it had collected capital gains of 288 million yuan, with no interest payable and no debt obligation.

Don't ask me where the supervisory institutions are. As I told you, some people are making money. The government's making a lot of money too. It owns nearly half of all stock.

You've seen how much public infrastructure Shanghai has acquired in the last several years. Where did the money come from? Not just from the profits the government made leasing public land to foreigners. Every time a stock is traded the government collects a 1.4 percent commission. The average daily trading volume for the "A" Market this year was over half a billion.[3] On some days it was closer to a billion. Shanghai people look at the Yangpu bridge and say to themselves: "The cut taken by the government from the 'A' market alone was enough to fund this bridge." There's some truth to the claim.

I'm in the business. I know what goes on. What I told you was part of an off-the-record, dinner table conversation.

Let's change the subject.

I'll recite some popular doggerel since you're so interested in what people are talking about today. Are you writing it down?

First, a verse celebrating China's "new socialites":

> Playing mahjong – one night, two nights, sleepless.
> Dancing at night – three-steps, four-step, flawless.
> Drinking liquor – five glasses, six glasses, endless.
> Screwing girls – seven girls, eight girls, tireless.[4]

Here's another verse celebrating the so-called "qualifications" of Party officials. [In the following, the last word of every sentence has the sound "ping," so it's called the "Nine Ping" verse.]

College degree – good talker, poor worker.
Left hand with wine bottle; right hand with flower vase [girls].
Control the ones who work for you; please the ones above you.
Manage the ones below you; have in your heart Deng Xiaoping.[5]

The third verse is about Beijing, Shenzhen and Hainan Island [known for prostitution]:

Only in Beijing you realize how few connections you have.
Only in Shenzhen you realize how little money you have.
Only in Hainan you realize how strong your body is.[6]

The fourth verse is about people in different age cohorts:

Ten years old: controlling the whole family.
Twenty years old: spending every penny.
Thirty years old: getting quite wealthy.
Forty years old: waiting for promotion.
Fifty years old: accepting bribes.
Sixty years old: going to Babaoshan.[7]
Seventy years old: playing mahjong day and night.
Eighty years old – time to work for the "Four Modernizations."[8]
Ninety years old – ready to revive the Chinese nation.[9]

Are they making you laugh?

I don't invest personal feelings and emotions in my business relations. The people I'm closest to are the buddies from my old farm. Because there were 108 students in our team we called ourselves the "108 Bandits." Now, we're not in such great shape. Some of us died, got serious illnesses, lost our jobs, became street peddlers and so on. I can only help out in emergencies. One of my old friends is paralyzed. I bought a wheelchair for him.

I took my daughter to my farm one summer and tried to teach her some lessons. I don't think she got them. I still have strong feelings about the place. Last year I donated 100,000 yuan to the village so they could build a "Hope" school. There's still no sign of the school. I've no idea where the money went. By now I should know better than to do this kind of foolish thing.

I have to go a meeting now. I can give you a ride in my car. I like to drive it myself. It's really fun to drive.

Notes

1   The middle-school and high-school graduate classes of 1968 and 1969 were all sent to the countryside. The Four-Facing Policy was re-established for the classes of 1970 and 1971.
2   In March 1999, Yarong was told by one financial journalist in Shanghai that she had made a considerable amount of money over the previous five years taking bribes from various companies to write positive articles about their stock.
3   In other words, the government collects about US$1.265 million a day in fees from the Shanghai and Shenzhen stock markets.
    The "A" markets in Shanghai and Shenzhen trade in renminbi. At the end of 1996 they listed shares issued by 537 joint stock enterprises. Their total market value was about US$118 billion.
    In 1993, the government began to offer stock on the Shanghai "B" market, which trades in US dollars. After Hong Kong's return to China on July 1, 1997 the "B" market stock index plunged more than 70 percent from a high of 91.05 in mid August 1997 to 26 a year later.

4   搓麻将, 一夜两夜不睡.

    跳夜舞, 三步四步都会.

    喝白酒, 五杯六杯不醉.

    玩女孩, 七个八个不累.

5   大学文凭, 说话水平, 工作平平,

    左手酒瓶, 右手花瓶, 左右关系摆平,

    上下关系烫平, 下面也要摆平, 心里放着邓小平.

6   在北京才知道关系少

    在深圳才知道钱少,

    在海南才知道身体好.

7   The cemetery in Beijing reserved for high Party officials.
8   Industry, Agriculture, Science-Technology and National Defense.

9   10岁统治全家, 20岁有钱就花, 30岁飞黄腾达,

    40岁等待提拔, 50岁贪污腐化, 60岁八宝山火化,

    70岁整日麻将, 80岁大干四化, 90岁振兴中华.

5 Wang Xiaozhi, male: deputy manager for a western company

A few days ago a journalist wrote a story about me. I didn't like the article. He exaggerated my concerns and made me look like an arrogant man who complains a lot. I did tell him about some of the difficulties that I'd experienced since I returned to China. But that was only a small part of our conversation.

In 1988, I went to England to join the woman I planned to marry. She'd left Shanghai the previous year. Before I left China I'd worked for a company under the jurisdiction of the Central Military Committee [he names it]. I guess you know about it. It specializes in arms sales. My work there was classified as a state secret. For security reasons I had to vacate my position a year before I could apply for a passport.

I'd been among the first to grab the opportunity to go to university after the Cultural Revolution, and I graduated from a university in Shanghai with a degree in international politics. After this, I enrolled in the Academy of Social Sciences for a three-year graduate program in Chinese history. But I'm not really the academic type.

Although I had an advanced degree in history I welcomed the opportunity to work for the government as a manager of one of their newly established export companies. The job offered good opportunities and material rewards. I speak good English. That's probably why I was offered the position.

I wasn't that interested in going abroad. However, my girlfriend, who was seven years younger than I, was eager to take advantage of an English friend's offer to help her get to Britain. After she arrived in London, every letter she wrote urged me to join her. She even saved up some money to prepare for my arrival. A little more than a year later I was on my way to enroll as a graduate student at the University of London.

My life in a new country didn't begin well. When my girlfriend picked me up at the airport she was with a fair-haired young man. They dropped me at an apartment. That was when I found out I was going to live by myself. After the man left, my girlfriend confessed. "He's my new boyfriend," she admitted.

"How long has this been going on?" I asked, hardly believing what I was hearing. To me, the boy looked like someone she'd just picked up in the street.

"About a year," she admitted. "I won't lie to you. I know you're probably very angry with me. But I trust you enough to believe you'll take it well. I couldn't control what happened. I just fell in love with him."

I asked her why she hadn't given me this news earlier and saved me a lot of trouble. She said she'd be in the wrong no matter what she did. Besides, she wanted to do something to repay me for all I'd done for her. So, she had paid six months advance rent on my flat and stuffed the refrigerator full of food. When I began to question her about her boyfriend she started to look embarrassed. So I stopped asking.

She was right about trusting me. I was very upset, but I accepted her change of heart. There was nothing I could do about it, in any case, except get on with my own life. I stayed at the University of London for about a year. For some reason, I lost interest in studying Chinese history.

After I got the offer of a scholarship from a university in the North of England I left London without a second thought. The university's East Asia Program was very interested in my background in China. They told me my proposed dissertation on Taiwanese investment in Britain was very promising.

I returned to China in 1994, without finishing my dissertation. After I passed my comprehensive examination at the end of 1992 I seriously considered quitting my studies. My research was not going well because I got little assistance from Taiwanese companies. Every time if I tried to get information from one of these businesses they'd treat me as if I were some kind of spy. I closely followed what was happening in China, and I began to feel I was missing out on a lot of opportunities.

What made me finally board a plane back to China was the fear that if I didn't act quickly I'd miss my chance. I'd be one of those sad people who're lost between two worlds – a stranger at home and a stranger abroad.

By then, I'd become engaged to a woman from Hong Kong. She was in England to get a degree in education. She supported my decision but wanted me to take one step less and go to Hong Kong. Instead, I took *her* one step farther. We were married in Shanghai the year I arrived back in China.

I thought that, with my education and work experience, I would have no difficulty getting a job in a state-owned enterprise. I wanted to work in the state sector because I believe that here you find the greatest potential as well as the greatest risk. I did get two serious offers from state-owned enterprises, but, when I tried to bargain for a higher salary and better benefits, they backed off. Obviously, they wanted me but they weren't desperate.

After searching fruitlessly for nearly a year for a satisfactory position with a Chinese company I finally gave up. About eight months ago I walked into the offices of a western company with a recommendation from my ex-teachers in England. I was given a job as a market analyst. I thought this would be a temporary position that would tide me over until I found something more permanent. Last month, however, I was told that I would be appointed as Deputy Manager of this company's Shanghai office. I'm now negotiating for better pay.

I'm confident about our future. I believe that economic development is on a healthy path. Since reform began we have experienced bold moves followed by retrenchment. As a consequence, we saw periods of chaos punctuated by stagnation. "Give it its head, it's chaotic; try to control it, it dies" (*yifangjiuluan*; *yizhuajiusi*) – that's how I would describe our experience of reform. People would take bold steps and start to stumble around in the dark. Then they'd get scared and refuse to budge.

There used to be many misconceptions about the market economy. Today, one thing, at least, is clear: a market economy (*shichang jingji*) isn't the same thing as a free unplanned economy (*ziyou jingji*). The market economy doesn't give people license to grab whatever they can regardless of the consequences for others. In the past, our leadership didn't appreciate this distinction.

No western capitalist society has a pure market economy: it is always the market plus planning. We should preserve state-owned enterprises. All capitalist countries have economic sectors owned or managed by the state. Often, these are among the most important parts of the economy.

There isn't anything intrinsically wrong with public ownership. What needs to be changed in state-owned enterprises is the culture of "cradle-to-grave" responsibility. But it would be wrong for our government to relinquish its planning role. Actually, during this critical period of transition, it's vital to consolidate central economic management.

In the past, we debated whether a particular policy was a step towards capitalism or socialism. For Mao, everything was either "right" (capitalist) or "left" (socialist). There was nothing in between. Mao would ask: "Does this serve the people or the enemy?" All our energies were absorbed trying to think in terms of these stupid dichotomies.

Today, our leadership has liberated itself from Mao's way of thinking. No one cares any more about whether this or that policy follows "socialist" or "capitalist" principles. China now has government without ideology. That's good. We no longer flip-flop over the direction we should take. Instead, we have a consistent policy. That's the advantage of having a one-party state.

The economic situation today is good but not stable. Over the next five to ten years, government will face the serious challenge of having to reform state-owned enterprises, more than half of which are heavily in debt. The government has developed a "merge and restructure" policy (*hebing chongzu*) to try to save these enterprises.

Last week, I met with Shanghai municipal officials and told them we should be careful. The merge and restructure policy is intended to slow layoffs and ease some of the problems experienced by state employees. Millions of people have already lost their jobs. However, if the policy is politicized too much, state-owned enterprise will not be strengthened. So, as I argued in the meeting, the correct policy towards state industries should be an economic policy that also serves political purposes.

Mergers should not be "forced marriages" between healthy and bankrupt enterprises. They should occur only when healthy enterprises will benefit from a growth in investment and size. Mergers should also be seen as a way to produce more efficient forms of management. I fear that if we are too rash we will overcorrect one defect and end up with another. As I said to the Shanghai municipal authorities: "Please proceed cautiously! Don't be in too much of a hurry."

I do feel uneasy about being the employee of a foreign company. My duty is to protect my employer's interests in China. Of course, I would rather work to further the interests of my nation. But I have to provide good service in order to secure employment, promotions and so on. Still, my heart's not in it. When the opportunity arises, I will definitely quit and work for the Chinese side – no question about it.

We need foreign investment. But the capital flowing into China didn't come here on a charity mission. Foreign companies want to make a big profit. I think this is one of the most effective, yet cruelest, forms of exploitation. But China is desperate for capital. So we must take whatever we can get.

Of course, it's contradictory! How can we reconcile national interest with the penetration of our society by foreign capital and foreign products? People get upset when domestically produced goods with well-known brand names lose out in competition with foreign products. Huasheng is one such example. Their electrical products had been in production for more than eighty years. Their appliances had a very good reputation. But where are these products today? The factory's gone. People ask: "Why did our government surrender a national industry?"

Western countries used to advocate "free and equal trade." Now they're more likely to be protectionist because they don't like it when Asian countries achieve a trade surplus. What we're talking about here are power relations. An imbalance of power reinforces unjust economic relations. Western societies still want to impose their will on Asian countries. The United States and some European countries have their own agenda. They don't like China when it's unwilling to be their little brother.

Face it. That's the reality.

You ask if five years in England changed me a lot. I guess it's only after an expatriate returns home that you can tell whether he was affected by his travels. There's no doubt I've changed. During my first year back in China I was frustrated much of the time. But I settled back into a familiar environment. The most beneficial consequence of being abroad for several years is that I now see things from a different perspective. I'm no longer an extremist. I've learned to be more moderate and more tolerant.

Although I complain less about life in China, my wife has become more critical. She thinks that I've changed into a different person – not the one she knew in England. She doesn't like Shanghai. She cannot speak the dialect. When people hear her talking Mandarin with a Cantonese accent they assume she's one of those less-educated southerners. She's not at all happy. Now, she spends more time in Hong Kong than in Shanghai. She says this is because I spend more time at work than with her. You met her yesterday. I know she was complaining about me. I admit I stretch myself a bit thin. But I've so many things to do, and there's just not enough time.

I'm sorry I really have to leave. We should try to meet again.

6 Yang Yinzi, male: factory technician

I've always loved *Dream of the Red Mansions*.[1] I've read the novel so many times. It has a special meaning for me because it's about a wealthy, influential, upper-class family that was ruined. My family's history resembles the story in this book. The difference, though, is that, whereas the Jias brought themselves down, our family was destroyed by historical events we couldn't control.

When I was very young my grandmother used to tell me stories about our family's past. At the time, I didn't understand much. Now, of course, I wish I could listen to her one more time. She died when I was 12 years old.

My great-great-grandfather was a high ranking Qing mandarin. During the reign of the Jiaqing Emperor [1799–1821] he was awarded the degree of *Jinshi*.[2] Later, in the Daoguang period [1821–1850], he was appointed Governor General of Jiangsu, Anhui and Jiangxi provinces. After the defeat of the first Opium War, he and the Manchu Commissioner Qiying represented the Emperor at the Treaty of Nanjing. So my great-great-grandpa's name is in the history books as the man who signed the first humiliating treaty with the British.

In 1851, the Emperor sent my great-great-grandfather to prevent Taiping rebel forces from crossing Hunan. Because my ancestor failed to stop the insurgents he was dismissed from imperial service and exiled to Xinjiang. After he'd served his seven-year sentence of banishment he came home and died the following year.

My family owned several mansions on Lake Poyang. Grandmother used to tell me all about them. She said we needed a room just to store all the keys. During the 1930s our estates fell into disrepair. Burglars broke holes in the walls and carried away whatever they could.

My grandfather sent his children to St John's College in Shanghai so they could get a western education. But he was the traditional Chinese intellectual. He spent his time drinking wine and writing classical poetry.

Grandfather served in the Nanjing Guomindang government but later quit, disappointed with all the corruption. He moved to Shanghai late in his life. Most of his friends and associates were writers, historians and actors. His brother was ambassador to France.

I remember the chest in which grandfather stored his published and unpublished writings. I didn't recognize the value of these materials when grandmother first showed them to me. The old-fashioned verses were meaningless to a small boy.

All I now recall about grandfather is that he was an old man with a long gray beard and an old-fashioned robe. The only keepsake of his I still have is the painting with his inscription you can see on that wall.

Two years ago I received a letter from a local historian in Jiangxi. The government had listed grandfather's name in *Who's Who*. He was described as a "well-known scholar and gentleman" who was executed during land reform in 1952.

No matter how apolitical he tried to be grandfather recognized that liberation augured a coming storm. His visits to our house became short and secretive, and he left quickly as if he didn't want the neighbors to notice him. But he always remembered to bring me some sweets.

Grandfather was indicted in Jiangxi province, where he owned his estates. He went into hiding. Understandably, he tried to keep our family out of trouble, and he broke off all communication with my father. Even grandmother, who, meanwhile, had moved in with us, didn't know what had happened to him. The news of his death didn't reach us until months after he'd been executed. Later, we learnt it hadn't taken long to track him down.

Grandmother was always bitter about grandfather's friends because she believed they'd betrayed her husband. But I don't blame them. In those days no one could afford to be loyal. Grandmother, herself, lived long enough to see her own son get himself and his family into trouble for trying to help a friend.

My father was an economist. He went to work for a bank in Nanchang, but lost his job during the civil war. When Shanghai was liberated he was working as a private English tutor. He disguised his qualifications, claiming he was only a primary school graduate. I think grandfather told him to do this.

At the time, my family still had quite a bit of money – enough to keep us going anyway. My parents didn't look for work until 1954, when the Shanghai unemployed were ordered to find jobs. Then, they took work as book-keepers.

During my childhood I lived in constant fear. I vividly recall the nights we sat around our table waiting for my father to come home. Whenever he was late we all assumed the worst. Finally, in 1958, our fears were realized.

Mother had cooked eggs and rice for father. It was late. We'd finished our dinner and our homework, but father still hadn't returned. I'd begun to read a book and was soon absorbed in it. Suddenly, father appeared under a dim light. Because his face was so grim we jumped up in alarm.

"Eat first," my mother told him as she led us out of the room. Later, we learned father had been sentenced to three years in Dafeng labor camp.

Father's "crime" had been to assist a "counter-revolutionary fugitive" – an old friend. This man didn't live in Shanghai, and he'd had no contact with father for some time. One day he appeared at our door and asked if he could stay for the night. Of course, father said yes. He and father talked until midnight. I believe that next day father gave his old friend some money and took him to the railway station. Half a year later this person was arrested, and father was taken in for questioning. The authorities claimed that, by helping his old friend, father had revealed his "true face."

At my school, a young, stupid and insensitive teacher came up to me and asked: "Is your father going to Dafeng?" I nodded dumbly. The teacher seemed pleased: "He's got his iron bowl now" he noted. I felt as though ice water had been poured over me. My whole body went numb.

After my father left, my mother decided to take my elder sister and brother out of high school. She sent them to my aunt's home in Nanchang. So, my family was split three ways: mother, grandmother, my second sister and I were in Shanghai; two of my siblings were in Nanchang; and my father was in Dafeng.

I felt terribly lonely and depressed. I'd been very close to my elder sister and brother. I was their "little tail." They both liked reading and had spent all their allowance on books. They kept these books in a locked bookcase and had even made a "library card" for me to sign if I wanted to borrow anything. After they left home the house became quite different: it seemed large, empty and strange.

Every morning, my mother got up at four o'clock. She had to travel more than two hours to get to her workplace in Wusong. She was transferred there after my father got into trouble – obviously as punishment. Mother never got home until after seven. I sometimes woke up late at night to find her sitting under the dim light, writing letters to father, sister and brother or sewing or mending something.

Father served his term in the labor camp. During these "three years of natural disasters"[3] food was in short supply and mother worried constantly. Father's letters said he got enough to eat but mother wasn't convinced. So she decided to send father some dried rice powder. However, she was afraid the postal officials wouldn't permit it. They checked all packages before they could be mailed.

Mother asked me to help. At home, we measured out a quantity of rice powder that weighed exactly as much as a thick dictionary. When we got to the post office we showed the clerk our package with the dictionary in it. After the clerk inspected, weighed and stamped this parcel he gave it back to us so we could sew it up. That was our chance to switch the book for the rice powder.

Father's time at the labor camp wasn't too bad. I think the authorities treated highly educated people leniently, and they made father keeper of the tool storage room. Father's co-worker in the storage room was once Sun Zhongshan's [Sun Yat-sen's] secretary.[4] He'd known grandfather's brother – the Ambassador to France. Father never complained much about prison. I think he found it less stressful there. He returned to Shanghai in 1962.

Because of my family's background, I was, during my school years, very much the outsider. But I accepted the situation. Unlike my schoolmates, I had the freedom to make of my world what I wanted.

I had a very close friend in middle school. Before liberation, his father had been a rich merchant. His family still lived in a big house with a servant. He had lots of books. On Sundays, I would often walk a long distance to borrow some of them.

One day, I went to this friend's house, but he was not at home. While I waited for him to return, I started looking through some of his books. I came across a note written by him to the Youth League Organization at my school. It was about me. My friend had listed the books I'd asked about and had claimed he'd refused to help me. The books he'd cited – Dante's *Divine Comedy*, I remember, was one – weren't banned. But a good student wouldn't seek them out. If you were drawn to this kind of literature it indicated you probably had anti-social tendencies.

The report was only a draft. I suspect it was never handed in. But I left my friend's home before he returned and I never went back.

The incident scared me. It also hurt me dreadfully because one of the few friends I'd ever been able to make was planning to betray me.

When the Cultural Revolution began in 1966 I was in the second year of high school. You can imagine my fear: my father was an ideal target. Before long, people came to search our home. They stayed two days and nights.

Mother had prepared us. She gave me a Swiss watch and some money. She said the watch was a gift she'd planned to give the first child who went to university. She told me that, since this wasn't going to happen, I might as well have it now. She also told me to keep out of the house as much as possible.

We didn't know when the search team would arrive, so, for two weeks, I left home very early and didn't return until late. During this period I walked the streets aimlessly, with the watch strapped to my wrist. By the end of the day I was tired and hungry. My legs were as heavy as stone. But I defended my tiny watch as if I were guarding a kingdom of treasure.

In 1968, all Shanghai students were told to report to their schools for job assignments. Those with a "bad" family background, such as mine, were often sent to farms on Chongming Island.[5] But a few others and I refused to cooperate. Weeks passed and the number of students remaining in Shanghai dwindled. Finally, only two of us were left – a friend and I. Before long, we received an official letter telling us we had one week to go to the Security Bureau to cancel our Shanghai resident registration. That scared us a bit. We walked to the dispatch station with our registration books in our pockets. Reluctant to give in, my friend suggested that we draw a card to determine whether we should enter the building. We decided that if we picked the King of Clubs this would mean we should go in. Of course, the odds were against drawing that particular card. After we picked something else we let out a sigh of relief.

Now, I had to come up with an excuse for not going to the countryside. After discussing the problem with my parents I told the authorities I had chronic high blood pressure.

Obviously, this was a lie. I was ordered to report to the hospital for a test. People told me if I held my breath long enough while I was being checked the pressure would go up. I tried it but it didn't work. Then, a friend let me smoke one of his father's cigars until I felt my head spin. But that didn't raise my blood pressure either. Next, my mother was advised to give me lots of fatty pork – especially pig's head. So I started stuffing a large bowl of fat down my throat as often as I could. By the third day, just looking at the meat made me want to throw up.

I'd tried everything. No one in my family could get any rest. The situation was unbearable. I wanted to give up.

Mother said to me: "What I fear most is that if you go to the farm you may stay there forever, whereas other kids with good family backgrounds might have a chance to come back some day. If you stay at home at least we'll be together."

Finally, we found the solution to our problem. It was a medicine that temporarily raised blood pressure when taken in large enough quantities. Immediately, I swallowed some and went to the local district hospital to be tested. Before long I'd established a history of abnormally high blood pressure. When the doctor arrived at my home for an unannounced check my parents kept him talking downstairs while I rushed upstairs to swallow more medicine. After several such checks the authorities decided I wasn't malingering after all. I was left in peace.

Gradually, I settled into my life as an unemployed youth. You might not believe me if I tell you that the happiest and most fulfilling years of my life were spent during the Cultural Revolution. But it's true.

I was the complete outsider – both mentally and in every other way. I didn't belong to any organizations, and I had the freedom to do as I wished. I read, wrote and painted. Most important of all, I had a few very close friends. Every day we would meet and talk for hours. I used to look at other people in the street with pity. I thought my life was superior to theirs – even though I was supposedly the lowest in the society.

During the Cultural Revolution I wrote more than 300 poems. I had a lot of emotion bottled up inside me and this was the only way I could express it. I was very influenced by the poets of the 1930s. That was the only period we Chinese were able to pursue ideas freely. I used to go for long walks and stay up all night composing my verse. It was an intense, absorbing and exciting time for me.

No, I don't have those poems anymore. I burnt them. The finished verses were copied into little notebooks. I never anticipated that one day I'd have to destroy them.

What happened was this: I had an acquaintance not one of my close friends – with whom I shared books. He was particularly interested in aesthetics. He used to talk about girls – their shape, and the way they walked. I remember this because this kind of talk was unusual back then.

This man and I later fell out. He stopped returning the books I'd lent him. He even stole some books from my home – including a volume of poems I'd borrowed from someone else. That was the end of our relationship.

This acquaintance lived in half of a big room. The other half was a neighborhood inoculation station. It was separated from his living quarters by a thin piece of board with a small window in it. So, he and the nurses in the front room had few secrets from each other.

At that time, I was temporarily working in a neighborhood workshop. I polished razors on primitive machines in a cold, damp room for 70 cents [US 12 cents] a day. One morning, I was ordered to go to the Public Security Bureau. My heart raced like a crazy horse's. I couldn't think of anything I'd done that might have caught anyone's attention.

The police immediately asked me whether I knew the acquaintance I just mentioned. Then, they ordered me to confess the counter-revolutionary activities I'd committed with him. After a day's interrogation, they finally released me at nine in the evening. When I was in the station what worried me the most was the poems I'd written. I knew that if the authorities got hold of them I'd definitely be in trouble.

I promised the police that, if they released me for the night, I would return home, think about the conversations I'd had with this man and return the next morning to report anything I thought might be significant. As soon as I got home I burnt my notebooks. Fortunately, it was winter, and I could let the smoke out of the house without attracting any attention.

Next day I went back to the Security Bureau, no longer afraid. I'd turned my poems into ashes. The police finally explained why they'd pulled me in. The nurses at the inoculation station had told them my friend was listening to enemy radio broadcasts. The nurses had told the authorities they'd seen me visit him.

In the end, the police found no evidence a crime had occurred, and they gave up. But that was the end of my career as a poet. I tried to remember some of my verses and start writing again, but, somehow, it was different. I was always afraid I'd be found out.

During the Cultural Revolution father made good use of his spare time. I think the Dafeng experience taught him how to survive. He never much reacted to anything. When he was ordered to sweep the lanes or clean up sewage he did what he was told, without comment.

Later, after things quieted down, he began work on a Chinese–English dictionary. I know this meant a lot to him. He would spend a certain amount of time on this every day. The dictionary was written on the back of desk calendars. He didn't have the money to buy paper. I'll show you what I mean.[6]

I don't think his work was original enough to be published. However, it's worth millions to me. When father left China he asked me to throw his dictionary away. I couldn't. I'll show it to my child. It's part of my father's life.

In 1978, I took the College Entrance Examination. I did it for my parents. They wanted at least one of their children to get a degree. I was accepted by a university, graduated, and found work as a technician in a photographic paper factory. I've been in this factory since 1982 and now I'm head of a technical department.

The job's for making a living. I don't like it, and never will. I've no passion for numbers, which are what I deal with daily.

It's strange I miss the past so much. I view the time I spent during the Cultural Revolution as my golden period. Life since has become increasingly boring. I always feel I'm doing something I don't want to do. My real life was elsewhere.

On a superficial level, things are much better. I've got more possessions. Books are widely available. But I no longer feel there's any substance or intensity to my existence. My routine is colorless and without texture. Every morning when I wake up I feel the rush of depression.

Our factory isn't doing well. Secretly, I hope it'll close down. If it does I can end this kind of existence. It's not that I'll be better off leaving my job or that I have something else planned. It's just that I feel trapped and I don't have the courage to end things myself. I'll be relieved if events are taken out of my hands.

My brother and his family left for the United States. He found work in a factory in New York. Later, he sent for my parents. At last they have a better life. Now, they're US citizens, so I might get a chance to emigrate also. But I'm not that interested. It's too late for me now.

Notes

1   *Dream of the Red Mansions* by Cao Xueqin (1715–64) has been described as the greatest masterpiece in traditional Chinese literature. English trans., 3 vols, by Tsao Hsuch-chin and Kao Ngo, San Francisco: China Books and Periodicals, 1978.

2   *Jinshi*, the highest degree awarded by the Chinese civil examination system, was given to just one candidate out of 10,000.

3   This refers to a period of economic retrenchment (1959–1962) during which bad weather and the disastrous consequences of "The Great Leap Forward" led to severe food shortages. Millions of people died of famine during these years.

4 Sun Zhongshan (1866–1925) was founder of the Republic of China (1911–1949).

5 Chongming Island, the third largest in China, is situated across the mouth of the Changjiang River, a short ferry trip away from Shanghai. It was easy for the authorities in Shanghai to keep a close eye on students sent there.

6 He produced a sheaf of notes about a foot thick. These were written on the backs of calendars from 1970–1974. There were about 3,000–4,000 English words or idioms explained in Chinese, together with examples.

7 Wan Jinli, male: general manager of a government-sponsored project

I tried to make arrangements for you to talk with one of my friends who's just come back from America with a PhD in genetic biology. But she's involved in a dispute with her neighbor. Her family lives in a third-floor apartment of 20 square meters. An official in the District's Housing Management and Maintenance Office gave her permission to add an attic to her apartment. She spent 20,000 yuan on it. Now, her neighbor is threatening to take her to court because the attic overlooks his bedroom. She knows he'll win. He's rich and well connected.

My friend is just a university professor. I tried to help her by telling people that her father-in-law used to be a high official in the Shanghai municipal government. But, it was no good: *xianguan buru xianguan* [a distant magistrate is no match for an immediate boss]. Her father-in-law's no longer an official, so no one gives a damn. The official to whom she spoke won't back up his words. Now, he says he only agreed to think about the extension. My friend's being made to demolish her attic. She's very upset, and is trying to find someone who can help her. This is why she didn't want to talk to you.

This friend chose to come back to China. She could have stayed in America, because, after the 1989 Tiananmen Square incident, all the Chinese students in the United States were given "green cards." Her university promised that she would be given her own lab, but there's no sign of it. Scientific research today is not as important as making money. She's having such a hard time. I'm sorry I couldn't get her to talk to you. She's more interesting than I am.

I'm from a working-class family, and was taught to value work. In school, I was a member of the Young Pioneer Committee. I was put in charge of labor activities because I had a "correct" attitude and wasn't afraid of physical labor. Like most of the other students I participated in all kinds of activities at the beginning of the Cultural Revolution. I didn't want to be left out.

However, I felt lost. There was no authority anymore. Previously the teachers and the school authorities had always praised me. In return, I respected them and took pride in myself. Now, my teachers no longer could give me the sense of purpose and identity I needed. I think this is why I was so excited by the Up to the Mountains and Down to the Villages movement. At once, I knew this was the direction in which I wanted go. The only decision I had to make was *where* I should go.

At one meeting I attended I heard a speech by an official from Anhui. He told us how much we were needed in those poor regions. In my mind, I saw myself as a new type of peasant transforming the countryside, and I assigned myself to Huaibei region [the northern region of River Huai]. You see, I was very serious. I was 16 years old.

I had the full support of my parents. Before they'd arrived in Shanghai they'd been simple farmers. So they weren't offended when their son became a peasant. When I left home my teacher gave me a whole set of books about agriculture. He'd been attacked during the Cultural Revolution, and I don't know why he gave these books to me. Later, though, they were very helpful.

Nearly 4,000 students from Shanghai were sent to Nanqin County in Anhui province. Almost every commune received 200–300 students. Each production team had at least 30–40 new settlers. By the end of the 1980s, however, only 44 of the original students were still living in the county. They'd stayed because they'd married local peasants and were assimilated. Life there is hard, but no doubt they're used to it by now. Of course, in comparison to what we found when we first arrived in the countryside, conditions today are much better.

A full day's labor then was worth only about 8 cents [US 3 cents]. We used to joke about it. A day's work wouldn't pay enough to send a letter home. Domestic mail cost an 8 cent stamp but you had to buy an envelope as well.

My production team was the Little Autumn Village, which had more than 100 residents. Before we arrived the only person who could read was the production team's Accounts Recorder. He'd had about three years of schooling. We had to adjust to an entirely different environment. The peasants never brushed their teeth, and they bathed annually, just before the New Year celebration. They would heat the water in a huge cauldron. "Let the educated youths go first," they always used to say.

The best building in the village was the storage barn, parts of which were constructed with brick. The peasants' houses were made of mud and straw. No one in the village had as much as 5 yuan to touch in their pocket. It was bare poverty. Everyone was shocked by what we found. It was a scene of desolation.

Obviously, we weren't going to get much material help from the peasants. We had to figure out for ourselves how best to survive. The government asked the students to be self-sufficient in three ways. I can't remember now what they were. Basically, we were expected to cope.

All the students got 180 yuan as a settlement fee. This was spent on food and furniture during our first year. But it took some time for the money to arrive. In the meantime we had to rely on what we'd brought from home. Some of us brought rice, whole cases of dry noodles – coal even. You don't believe me, do you? In that region, the main food was corn [maize], and the fuel was the stock of the plant. So, the same plant served two purposes: food and fuel.

We lived on corn for two weeks. We had three days to organize our "educated youth" collective households, which typically consisted of three or four students living together in one small cottage. Then we joined the peasants in the field.

I had two close school friends in my collective household. We knew nothing about horticulture, but the first thing we did was to study those books on agricultural technology. The peasants in the village had been planting the same crops and the same vegetables for generations. I asked our team leader to give us a piece of land for a scientific experiment. At the time, this request was politically charged. Who would dare refuse such a revolutionary suggestion? We got a piece of uncooked [uncultivated] land.

During our first year we grew eggplants, beans, melons, tomatoes and Shanghai-style cabbage. It was a big success. For us, it was very interesting experience. We read the books, put the knowledge into practice and saw the fruit of our labors. Our student household also raised chickens and pigs. We did better than the peasants. We could read, you see – that made a hell of a difference. Local people were accustomed to the familiar ways of doing things; they were attuned to the rhythms that connected them with all the past generations. But we brought some revolutionary culture into their lives and really stirred things up.

I've always believed that the Up to the Mountains and Down to the Villages movement served to bring the fresh culture of educated youth into the countryside. This was a very good thing. For the first time ever, local people who had never even seen a city had some contact with urban culture. We often visited Shanghai, and we brought back all kinds of goods and gossip.

After our first year's success, my collective household was named a "Model Household." The second year, I was elected team leader. Local people began to trust me. I wasn't an ambitious person but a leader made by circumstance. If the peasants hadn't been so poor I wouldn't have felt such a pressing need to do something.

After I became team leader the next project I wanted to complete was a drainage system. The village flooded frequently. However, the local people thought that digging ditches wasted land. They loved their land. I pointed out to the peasants that, if they sacrificed one stretch of land, they could save the whole field. They listened. We didn't go back to Shanghai for three years. We spent the winters on irrigation and drainage projects. New roads and new ditches – it was a beautiful sight in my eyes. In 1974, I joined the Communist Party. I was 20 years old.

I became increasingly interested in scientific farming, and I visited model villages to learn from them. We developed new techniques designed to get as much as possible from the land. Low-and-High-Planting, for instance, took advantage of row arrangements for different crops. We would plant wheat next to corn, which has a different planting and growing season. After we harvested the wheat we would sow cotton while the corn was still growing. Then we would plant peanuts where the corn used to be.

Why do plants by roadsides grow best? Because they don't compete so much for sunshine and for space. Low-and-High-Planting creates a similar environment for many rows of plants. It's like extending the sides of a piece of land from four to many. This helps increase production.

Knowledge creates results. Manual skills aren't difficult to learn, but an educated mind makes a great difference. After I'd been in the village for four years the members of our production team made more than 1 yuan for a full day's labor.

I was promoted to be a leader of the Zhuda Production Brigade, and put in charge of twelve production teams. Four years later, in 1979, I became Second Party Secretary in Xianshen Commune. But the promotion didn't release me from field labor. In those days, cadres were "not-relieved-from-production" (*bu tuochan*). I got 100 jin of grain, 50 jin of beans and 50 jin of noodles. If I needed cash for anything I had to sell my grain or my beans back to the government.

Back then I took it for granted that the future would be as the Party had planned. Before too long the two lowest levels of the collective system – the small and big brigades – would be abolished. Then we would enter a more advanced stage, where cooperatively governed and self-sufficient communes would become the primary unit of organization. As leader of the Zhuda Brigade I planted the first fruit farm and developed its May Seventh factory.[1] I believed I was constructing the kind of future envisioned by the Party.

However, I was aware of a very fundamental problem. After we increased production we were obligated to submit more to the government. Peasants got only a tiny share for their hard work, so they were not enthusiastic about increasing productivity. But we still did the best we could. For instance, we changed the way we cultivated cotton. Instead of creating large spaces between plants to let as many healthy flowers grow as possible, we densely planted seeds and kept only two or three of the biggest flowers. This meant we continuously had to prune back new growth. This was very demanding because we had hundreds of plants to take care of. However, bigger flowers could withstand the rain that frequently came during the cotton-flowering season. So we increased cotton yield significantly.

In 1977, when I was still in the Zhuda Brigade, I knew that areas in southern China were experimenting with the "responsibility system." I tried to get permission to implement the new system in my area but didn't succeed. However, the attitude of the Party boss was that he'd just shut his eyes. So my brigade was the first to start the responsibility system in Anhui province.

After 1980, I moved up quickly. In 1982, I was made First Party Secretary of my district. After a year in that position I decided I wanted to go to university. The Party Committee was against the idea. However, the Prefecture Authority told the Party Committee to let me go because I was a "third echelon" candidate designated for office. I went to Anhui College of Agriculture and studied agricultural economy for two years. After graduation, I was given a job as the Director of the Agriculture and Industry Bureau in Nanqin County.

I married a local girl, who died of cancer some years back. She left me a son. When student-settlers started moving back to the city my parents and friends hoped I'd leave too. But I didn't. Once, some of my friends arranged to meet with me, and they told me one by one that I should return to Shanghai. I knew they were right, but I also recognized things weren't quite that simple. After nearly twenty years in the countryside I was no longer a Shanghainese.

In 1990, I got engaged to a woman in Shanghai. She agreed to move to Anhui to be with me. One day, as I was on my way to the Public Safety Bureau in Shanghai to cancel my fiancée's city registration, I ran across an old friend. I hadn't seen him in years. He'd worked in Anhui with me ten years earlier and had also attained a leadership position. He asked what I was doing and, when I explained, he told me I was crazy. He dragged me into a little restaurant and, over dinner, persuaded me to change my mind. He told me about a position his office was trying to fill and said I was the ideal person for the job. If I wanted to accomplish something, he said, I'd have to return to Shanghai. "Don't go back to Anhui," he implored. "Shanghai is China's America."

It was a fateful occurrence. If I hadn't run across him that day I'd still be in the countryside.

The main factor that persuaded me to return was my son's education. He's definitely better off in Shanghai. For me, it was like starting over again for the second time in my life. When I came back to the city I felt as if I were in a foreign country. It's been stimulating; I've learnt a lot. But it's also been stressful. As you can see, I've lost most of my hair.

Since my return I've had to cultivate new relationships. In the countryside there was a network I could rely on. There, it was much simpler. Everything was on the surface, and I knew the rules of the game. I had enough confidence to play well. In Shanghai, though, you have to learn how to grasp "hints." I've learnt to penetrate the surface, to understand the hidden language. For instance, if you deal with an official who tells you he has to ponder something you know it's time to give him a gift.

I started working here in 1994. I'm General Manager of this project.

[He names the company for which he works, and he explains that the son of one of the most powerful men in China planned the project he manages.] I cannot give you all the details. The fact is that the initial plan for this site came to nothing. A lot of money was put into the project and then the Hong Kong investors pulled out. I was given the task of picking up the pieces. I've just submitted a proposal to turn this site into a first-class club for foreign businessmen and high-level officials. I'm going to turn this place into an international club.

The site is very special. It's outside Shanghai and reserved for top Chinese leaders. It already has a number of unique facilities. [He describes them, and talks about the well-known people who have used them.] Several years ago the government added a restaurant, a health resort, a spa and a small hotel. If the Party leaders are not in residence, foreigners and private businessmen can pay to use these facilities. When the leaders arrive from Beijing the whole place is sealed off.

My club would provide a place for foreign businessmen and officials to exchange information and have some fun in the process. I want to supply the best facilities and the best food. I'll build an organic farm in Anhui to supply the club with the freshest vegetables and meat. We won't use those polluted products you find in Shanghai markets. Members will be able to take a shower massage that shoots water right into their acupuncture points. Everything will be the very best – the best Shanghai can offer anyway.

There are already ten exclusive clubs in Shanghai. The Number One Club charges an annual membership fee of US$110,000. It's like buying a royal title. You ask what kind of person can afford this. Well, foreign businessmen understand that if they get to meet high-ranking officials it's worth the price. Of course, our officials don't pay anything out of their own pockets.

My club's going to be different. It will be a center of politics and entertainment. I'm going to combine politics with entertainment – I will integrate officials and businessmen. Foreign businessmen have to learn Chinese political affairs and government policies. This will be the place.

This piece of land is a Treasure Island. Because of all the trees you see here the temperature in summer is about 3° or 4° [centigrade] lower than it is in the city. I'm very excited about the proposal. I've already got backing from municipal authorities. They're extremely interested in my idea. They'll have free access to the club. Why wouldn't they be interested?

I'm not sleeping well these days. I've been given this place in order to do something with it. I want to succeed. I've another ten years to do something with my life. This is my project. This is the last chance of my life. I want to succeed. Next Monday they're going to have a meeting to discuss my proposal. I lost several nights of sleep worrying about it.

Note

1   On May 7, 1966, Mao issued a directive calling on soldiers, workers and peasants to study politics, the military, culture and production. This directive became the rationale for the May Seventh factories, colleges and cadre schools started during the Cultural Revolution.

8 Zhu Xueqin,[1] male: college professor

The article you mention focuses on a subgroup of Red Guards I call "1968ers" (*liuba nian ren*).[2] These Chinese 1968ers were unique in modern Chinese history. Like the 1968ers in Europe and North America, however, their influence was short-lived.[3]

My essay was written in response to the recent interest in the Three Old Classes. Frankly, I was disappointed at the naïveté of all those who participated in the discussion. But, at the beginning of the 1990s, everyone in China was hopelessly confused.

I think the chaos caused by the new market economy is responsible for the renewed interest in the past. Today, we have become nostalgic. "When the journey ahead is uncertain return to the shore" (*qiancheng mangmang, huitou shi an*). It's not just ex-Red Guards though. Many others, too, are in a mood of mourning.

My article was a requiem for the Chinese 1968ers, who've long since disappeared from the scene. These rebels were opinion-shapers who recognized that the Maoist dream of mass democracy was never realized in the cities.

The 1968ers were the first insurgents to challenge the Cultural Revolution. By 1968, most of them had been Red Guards for a couple of years. Typically, they were high-school students from key schools – very different from the brutish, mindless, thugs who were later portrayed in movies, TV shows and books. The 1968ers joined the Cultural Revolution as moral idealists, not as mob leaders. Their struggle and their critical attitude were genuinely spontaneous and largely unsupervised.

What was significant about 1968 was that this was the year the Up to the Mountains and Down to the Villages movement took off. Before long, hundreds of thousands of students found themselves in the countryside. This nurtured a unique environment that encouraged autonomy and self-reliance. These urban kids were removed from the political center. I would describe the rural settings in which they found themselves as decentralized "free-thought villages." I, myself, discovered the work of Hegel, Kant, Rousseau and Belinsky[4] when I was in a remote village in northern China.

In spirit, the Chinese 1968ers followed the heritage of traditional Chinese intellectuals: "Be the first under heaven to worry about social and political matters; be the last under heaven to enjoy what the world has to offer." They cared more about spiritual than material issues. They were willing to question everything.

They were nurtured by Marxist political thought – particularly by Marx's earlier more humanistic writings – and by Mao's belief in the value of continuous revolutionary struggle. Slowly, the discrepancies between Marxist thought and Maoist dogma became increasingly apparent to them. They dug deep into German philosophy, Russian eighteenth- and nineteenth-century literature, and French Enlightenment thought. All these works had some bearing on the Chinese Revolution, but at a distance, and, often, through the prism of official Party dogma. Of course, these kids were also the creatures of their own time and place.

Basically, the Chinese 1968ers were amateur intellectuals. During the daytime they were workers and farmers. At night, they were enthusiastic students of history, philosophy and politics. Not surprisingly, they had more questions than answers or solutions. The 1968ers were not academically sophisticated. They were – let's not forget it – teenagers. I would say they were stuck at a stage of revolutionary populism.

Unfortunately, these amateur philosophers were quickly pushed aside by the corrupting materialism of the post-revolutionary period. You will not find many critical thinkers in China today. They've all disappeared, swallowed up in our current back-to-mediocrity campaign. History, of course, wields a sharp knife. It's not sentimental about having to dump you into the trash can. A culture of mediocrity does not, of course, foster any serious or painful historical inquiry.

I know that some commentators like to describe New China's Third Generation as the backbone of contemporary Chinese society. Many people claim that this generation now plays a major role in politics, the economy and intellectual life. This assertion is nonsense, however. First of all, in the political arena the Red Guard generation has been excluded from office. The so-called policy of "recruiting 'over-the-next century' people" (*kua shiji*) is designed to favor those who were born in the 1960s and educated in the 1980s. The members of this generation will reach the pinnacles of their careers at the beginning of the twenty-first century.

In other words, the up-and-coming leaders are members of a younger generation. They're also likely to be those petty bureaucrats who rose in the system by doggedly adhering to all the rules. This cohort is young and has no collective memory of the Cultural Revolution. Its members are very different from those born 1946–1953.

I'm not suggesting this is a conspiracy, but one thing for sure is that Jiang Zemin and the other top political leaders are nothing but careerists and bureaucrats. Naturally, they fear the Red Guard generation. There were two generations in China this century that had any first-hand revolutionary experience: one is the May Fourth generation and the other is the Red Guard generation.

May Fourth [1919][5] produced a generation that altered the course of Chinese history and managed to dominate Chinese social, political and cultural events for nearly half a century. The second revolutionary experience [the Cultural Revolution] didn't produce anything that lasted because it was imprisoned in the wrong body: the Chinese Communist Party. However, this second revolutionary experience left a legacy of "suspect-everything-and-down-with-everything." This rebellious inheritance makes a difference. High officials today believe that the members of the Red Guard generation can't be trusted with too much power.

In academic circles, too, the Red Guard generation has been passed over. I'm not suggesting that there are no outstanding scholars and scientists from that generation. But, in general, they missed the opportunity to reach the levels of scholarship attained by the older generation. Now they cannot compete with a younger generation. If you look at universities and colleges in China today, people in their thirties play a more important and visible role than those born around the time of liberation.

In the economic arena there are many people from the Red Guard generation who occupy middle-level managerial positions in state-owned enterprises. But the state-owned sector is in decline, so these people are stuck in positions of increasing irrelevance.

I don't believe the Red Guard generation has a significant role to play in contemporary China. They've outlived their era.

You raise the question of the Tiananmen Square demonstrators, which is an important one. At the beginning, I hoped the torch would be re-lit, and I was very much involved. I do believe there was a hand reaching out from the past, trying to reach the students. But, the connection wasn't made.

The 1989 movement was a complicated event. You cannot call it a "Movement for Democracy" just because "democracy" was painted on some banners. It was a marriage made of many parts. Some people from my generation tried to contact the student leaders and give some depth to their demands. Personally, I was disappointed.

Last year I was in the United States, and I saw a documentary about some of the student leaders who had fled China. Chai Ling made the worst impression on me. Her face had been cosmetically altered. As she flirted with the TV camera, she stroked a puppy dog on her lap and told her audience: "Don't just think of me as an activist; I'm a woman too." With the casualties of 1989 fresh in my mind, I felt deeply insulted and quite a bit nauseated.

Let's talk about history some more.

There were two movements around the time of May 4, 1919: the New Culture Movement of the pre-May Fourth period and the National Salvation Movement of the post-May Fourth period. The former movement aimed to establish a new civic culture. The latter was a political movement that tried to transform the state.

Those who led the New Culture Movement tried to change Chinese intellectuals from state bureaucrats to social critics. This created a new ideal for those who traditionally had been both associates and wards of the state. As reflected in Hu Shi's writings,[6] the spirit of the New Culture Movement was "a new attitude: one of faultfinding." Hu asked people to struggle for individual freedom. He thought only free individuals – those liberated from the patronage of the state – could create a decent society.

However, history never allowed the New Culture Movement to develop. During a period of national crisis it was far more important to rescue the Motherland from ruthless imperialist rape than to defend individual freedoms. Therefore, the post-May Fourth nationalist movement took precedence over the pre-May Fourth cultural movement. From that point on intellectual activities in China were dominated by power politics. In Mao's words, if you were not with "Yan'an," you were for "Xi'an."[7] Either Red or White! There was nothing in between.

What I am suggesting is that, under Mao, Chinese intellectuals played a traditional role. Their social participation once again was defined by how they could serve power and the interests of the state. Unfortunately, Chinese intellectuals have always lacked autonomy and have never really been able to act as social critics. The role of social critic has always been the most important and difficult one for them to assume.

Let me now answer your questions about the controversy caused by my writings on the French Revolution. As you know, many Chinese academics were surprised that I would try to make a comparison between events in France in 1789–1794 and the 1966–1976 Cultural Revolution

My study shocked people because Chinese intellectuals are expected to accept the French Revolution as an exemplary moral narrative. Of course, if you find similarities between what people were taught was "good" [i.e. the French Revolution] and what they now see as "evil" [i.e. the Cultural Revolution] you are likely to be accused of denigrating the first or praising the second. At least, that's the kind of comment I get from my colleagues.

I don't believe the French Revolution was morally uncompromised. Nor do I see the Cultural Revolution as unambiguously evil. Serious historical research recognizes ambivalence. It doesn't favor one-dimensional forms of condemnation, nor can it be a simplistic accolade.

Two very different forces make human history. One represents the optimistic side of human nature. It's conformist and represents positive attitudes and constructive behavior. The other force is negative and represents the pessimistic side of human nature. It's critical, and suspicious about order. It recognizes the need for a complete structural revolution.

Most people are influenced by the first force. Only a few have sufficient ambition to try to reshape human society. Mao was one of them.

Towards the end of his life Mao claimed he had accomplished two great things. The first was to overthrow Jiang Jieshi [Chiang Kai-shek]; the second was to launch the Cultural Revolution. Mao was a revolutionary nihilist. His colleagues never realized how much he subconsciously suspected and distrusted established Chinese institutions. It's no coincidence that his favorite works of literature were *Water Margin* and *Dream of the Red Mansions*. The first is the story of a band of outlaws who fought against the political establishment in Song. The second ends with the exhausted hero of the story turning his back on the established cultural order.

In my work, I compare Mao's political thought with that of Jean-Jacques Rousseau. There are many similarities. Rousseau contrasted the "noble savages" with the corrupt individuals of the civilized world. Mao equated "the noblest with the stupidest; the most humble with the most intelligent." Not surprisingly, he ordered educated youths to go to the countryside to be re-educated by the peasants. Rousseau believed that science and art led to the decline of human moral life. Mao concurred. As he phrased it: "When the satellite is in the sky the red flag falls to the ground." Like Rousseau, Mao placed moral values above all else. He believed that the pursuit of material wealth was dangerous. Materialism would only stifle spiritual satisfaction.

Mao was a revolutionary purist. He couldn't compromise. What he wanted was moral perfection.

As well as looking at political ideology I also studied the similarities between the political activities of the Red Guards on the one hand and the Jacobins on the other. Anyone who knows about the French Revolution could easily make a connection between the bloody events in Paris of September 1792, and the terror in Beijing and Shanghai during July and August of 1966. Many of the Red Guards studied the French Revolution. The Jacobins certainly inspired their utopian idealism. The example of Jacobin cruelty and revolutionary violence was important to all those who believed the Old World could only be smashed by force.

It's a question for psychologists why idealism and violence often go together. The more idealistic the students the more accepting they were of violence. Of course, if you're pessimistic about the existing order a refusal to compromise is the ultimate test of moral rectitude.

The Red Guards believed that the western world was demoralized and that the Soviet Union was equally decadent and corrupt. They rejected both political systems, as reflected in the popular slogan of the day: "We Oppose American Imperialism and Soviet Revisionism" (*fandi fanxiu*). In their innocent naïveté, they thought they'd discovered a third alternative – a new type of society that could save the entire world.

I'm not trying to defend the Red Guards. I condemn much of what happened during the Cultural Revolution. But, as a historian, you can't think like a moralist or a career politician, hemmed in by the need to give a "good" or "bad" slant on events. You want to understand *why* things happened as they did.

The third connection I make between the Cultural Revolution and the

French Revolution has to do with the aftermath of revolution. The Jacobin effort to use violence in the service of liberty was ultimately thwarted by the Thermidorian reaction.[8] After Maximilien de Robespierre and other leftists were executed French society suppressed revolutionary energy and revolutionary memory, and the new leaders started to construct a safe, solid, national bourgeois order. In a similar fashion, after Mao died we got the "reform" to undo the revolution.

No matter how far revolution goes, Thermidor lies in wait. Mao once boasted that he wanted to release the nuclear energy of spiritual renewal. Such creative destruction creates heavy casualties and exhausts the survivors. When people can take no more the reactionary period comes into its own.

Do I have reservations about our Chinese Thermidor? Of course I do. If our "Jacobin" period revealed our capacity for aggression and cruelty, Thermidor shows how shallow and banal we can be. Today, many people want to repress all memory of the Cultural Revolution, as if this period were a natural catastrophe best forgotten. Remember how, almost overnight, the French gave up calling each other *citoyen* [citizen] – an expression that symbolized their newfound equality. Soon, they were back to "Sir," "Madame" and "Count." The same thing has happened here. We no longer address each other as "comrade." Instead, *xiansheng* (master), *taitai* (madam) and *laoban* (boss) remind us of the persistence of social hierarchy. We do our best to erase the freedom of equality. Such liberty is what a mediocre society fears the most.

For my generation, no matter where we live, no matter what we do, we'll never escape the shadow of the Cultural Revolution. We'll live with it forever. If we reflect on its historical significance we can learn from it. If we refuse to come to terms with it we shall never be free of it.

Goethe once wrote: "I once had lofty ideals. To this day, I cannot forget them. This is my problem."

Yes. And this is my problem also.

Notes

1   Not a pseudonym.
2   Zhu Xueqin, "Of Those Missing in Chinese Intellectual History," *Dushu* (Digest), October, 1995, pp. 55–63.
3   Unlike other interviewees, Professor Zhu was given questions beforehand.
    Zhu Xueqin is Professor of History at Shanghai University. His book, *Collapse of a Moral, Ideal Kingdom: From Rousseau to Robespierre*, was published in Shanghai in 1994.
4   Vissarion Grigoryevich Belinsky (1811–1848), Russian literary critic, is described in the 1984 *Chinese Encyclopedia* as a major contributor to the Russian "national" type of socialism. Belinsky's letter to the author Nikolai Gogol was regarded in China as a classic statement of "revolutionary populism."

5 The May Fourth movement began with student demonstrations in Tiananmen Square on May 4, 1919. The protesters were outraged that the Treaty of Versailles had transferred Germany's rights in Shandong province to Japan.

6 Hu Shi (1891–1962), a writer and philosopher, studied at Columbia University with John Dewey. Hu was a leading figure in the May Fourth New Culture Movement. From 1938–1942 he served as the Nationalist government's Ambassador to the United States.

7 Yan'an, a village in Shanxi province, was the capital of the Soviet base governed by the CCP in the 1930s and 1940s. Xi'an was the capital of Shanxi province, held by the Guomindang.

8 So called because it began on 9 Thermidor, year II, of the new French calendar (July 27, 1794). The Thermidorian reaction in France led to the Directory, to the disarming of the Committee of Public Safety, and to Robespierre's arrest and eventual execution.

9 Chou Linlin, female: former head of a factory clinic

I'm so unhappy these days. When Li asked me if I could talk to you I said to myself: Why not? Let people know how miserable I feel. I've nothing to lose and nothing to do at home. I certainly have time to talk to you.

I always knew my place and obeyed all the rules. I was the same as my father. He came from a rich family and was its only heir. My grandfather was a merchant in Ningpo [a coastal region in Zhejiang province] who moved to Shanghai.

Grandfather sent my father to Shanghai Hujiang University for a modern education. But he chose father's wife for him. Mother is uneducated. She never worked outside the house. Her life was centered on husband and children. People from Ningpo tend to abide by custom and tradition. My family was always very conservative.

If a leaf dropped on father's head he'd be scared to death. Before liberation, he had owned a factory that made organic pigment. In the late 1950s, when collectivization started, he handed the business over to the government. So, he became a "Red Capitalist" (*hongse zibenjia*). Actually, in temperament, father is more of an intellectual than a businessman. He was quite happy to swap the ownership of his factory for an "iron bowl." He was, at the time, the leading authority on organic pigment in the Shanghai Bureau of Chemical Industry. Because he had the status of "expert" the government gave him a very high salary.

Before the Cultural Revolution my family lived quite comfortably. We had our own three-floor house. Father's salary, together with our family savings, gave us a higher standard of living than most urban Chinese. We had no worries at all.

When the movement began I was just finishing my first year in middle school. I had no idea what was going on. Father spent a lot of time talking with my brothers. I soon realized my family would be in trouble. I felt I was waiting in line to get a shot. All I wanted was for it to be over quickly. I secretly hoped that people would come to raid our house, the sooner the better.

Finally, the Workers' Rebellion Team from my father's factory arrived. It was a rainy day. I remember it distinctly. All five kids were taken to the upstairs spare room. My parents didn't want us to see what was going on. I listened to the raindrops on the roof. None of us talked.

The raid was carried out gently. Father had a reputation as an honest and decent man, and he had had a good relationship with his workers. The workers said they'd organized the raid so that my father would be spared a visit from the Red Guards, which, certainly, would have been a lot worse. Afterwards, they put paper seals on windows and furniture to show everyone that our house had been subjected to "revolutionary action." Luckily for us, this was the only time we had to endure a raid.

Father was demoted to the rank of worker, and his salary was reduced. He'd never performed manual labor before. It was hard for him, both mentally and physically. Although I wasn't old enough to grasp the big political picture I was aware of the effect this was having on our lives. I stayed home a lot. There were only one or two friends I could talk with. Like me, they had a "black" family background.

One night, one of these friends came to see me. Without saying a word she started to cry. I didn't ask why but just cried too.

All five children in my family were in school when the Cultural Revolution began. My eldest brother was about to graduate from Fudan University. All but the youngest sister went to the countryside between 1968 and 1970. My second brother actually had a chance to stay in Shanghai since the eldest brother was already in the countryside. But he decided to leave so I'd have a good chance of being assigned to Shanghai the following year. He told me that, because he was a boy, he was the one who should go.

However, when I graduated the following year the government's policy had changed. We were told that the class of 1968 would be "Completely Red." Everyone had to go to the countryside. The next year, the same thing happened to my younger sister.

I didn't complain about my poor luck. How could I add to my parents' unhappiness? In any case, I wasn't afraid to go to the countryside. My school had assigned me to a good rice-growing region. So about the only thing I knew about where I was going was that I'd be able to eat rice the year round.

The train – the first I'd taken my entire life – carried me through many strange places. I'd never been out of Shanghai. I was barely 16 years old, with no understanding of peasant life. Yet, I didn't worry at all. Quite mindless, right? Most of us were the same though.

There were three other students in my production team. None of us knew how to cook – not even steamed-egg soup. The commune gave us two very small cottages in which to live. They were made of mud, with no chimney. Every time we tried to light a fire we had to run outside in order to escape the thick smoke. I shared the cottage with another girl. My parents had packed everything they thought I might need – from toilet paper to a cutting board. My companion's family had done the same. So it was as if a couple of families had moved in together.

The peasants were very poor. But they were the most generous people I ever met. Often, on rainy days we couldn't start a fire because the kindling was so damp. But, when this happened, the team leader simply invited us to eat at his home or asked other families to send us food. At the beginning, we didn't realize we were getting the best food available.

Once, a family cooked us some rice cakes that they'd stored for more than a year. Of course, the cakes were moldy and tasted terrible. We threw them into the rice paddy. A couple of days later some peasants were netting small fish in the field. They caught the rice cakes instead. Before long, the whole village knew about it. Ah! Everyone scolded us for weeks.

We were very silly city kids indeed. I owe those people a great deal for the years I spent in their village. When I received my first month's salary working in Shanghai in 1979 I sent half of it back to the village. Just a small gesture of thanks.

In 1973, the other three students in my production team were allowed to return to Shanghai because they were their parents' only children. The justification was that aged parents needed at least one child to live with them. This kind of opportunity changed my perspective. I'd not been unhappy before. However, now I was left all alone in the village. I was deeply depressed. My family urged me to leave and to return to Shanghai. They thought I'd be unable to cope with the situation.

The village leader was one of those good communist members. He sent his daughter to sleep in my house, just to keep me company. In fact, he treated me as if I were his own child. I appeared at his family's dinner table more frequently than ever. Before long, he decided to make me the "barefoot doctor" for the production brigade. His support was critical in my life. I stayed in the village. But I was unsettled. I missed my family.

By 1972, many universities and local factories were recruiting "sent-down" students from the countryside. Competition for positions created hostility among old friends. Opportunity caused corruption. Things got quite ugly.

I didn't try to compete with others. Partly, this was because I was not an aggressive person; also it was because I felt my family background would put me at a disadvantage. In fact, my "bad" family background didn't mean much to the peasants. They said I was from a "high-class category" (*chengfen gao*), which made me sound rather superior. I was rather confused by the use of this flattering term. Later, I found out that many peasants insisted on calling ex-landlords and people from rich families "high class."

There were a few opportunities for me to work in local factories. But my father told me that I should choose further education rather than a factory job. In 1976, my commune informed me that I'd been selected to study in a nursing school in the provincial capital, Hefei. It was a two-year "From the Commune and Back to the Commune" program (*shelai shequ*) that was designed to train medics to serve local people. I immediately sent a letter to my family. My father wanted me to take advantage of the opportunity. "Things will change after two years," he told me. "You may not have to return to the countryside." So I enrolled in the school.

Looking back, I think those two years were the happiest in my life. I was in my mid-twenties. However, it was as if I'd begun my childhood all over again. Everyday life was simple and pleasant. The school was for girls only. I can't recall any unpleasant incidents. The teachers liked me because I always got good grades. On Sundays they invited another girl and me – the two Shanghainese – to dinners and outings.

Things didn't turn out as my father had hoped. Because the From the Commune and Back to the Commune policy was still in place when I graduated, I was supposed to return to the village. My father sent me a panicky letter. "Don't go back. Just jump onto a train and return to Shanghai." So the Cultural Revolution taught even my father something! He did something he never could have done before. He rebelled!

I did as my father asked. By 1978, there were very few city students left in the countryside. By one route or another, nearly everyone had returned to Shanghai.

I asked for "resettlement for physical reasons" (*bingtui*). There was a long waiting list for physical examinations. While I was waiting, the school telegraphed me. The government had decided to make better use of trained nurses and I'd been assigned to a big prefecture hospital. I was torn into parts. I really wanted to go. After all, what kind of future would I have in Shanghai? Even if I were eligible for "resettlement for physical reasons," which was questionable, the best I could hope for was a job in a neighborhood workshop earning 70 cents a day. Of course, if I went to the prefecture hospital I would never again be able to live in Shanghai with my family.

My eldest brother was iron firm: "You must stay in Shanghai. A family should always be together. To be with your family is better than anything else." The school sent me five telegrams. I ignored them all.

So I stayed in Shanghai. In 1979, Deng Xiaoping let all the "sent-down" students reunite with their families. I returned to the village to get my papers in order. I've never been back since.

After 1977, our family gradually was given back the property that was taken from us during the Cultural Revolution. The tenants who had moved into our house moved out again. Father's original salary was returned to him, and he was compensated for lost income. During the difficult years my eldest brother had made lots of sacrifices for our family. Because he had a university degree he was assigned a job in a provincial factory after he'd served just a short time in the countryside. But he sent most of his salary home. He waited very late to get married.

By 1979, my father was back in his old position. At the time, the government's policy was to encourage older people to step down and make room for their unemployed children. My father could have retired and let me take a position at his factory. But he didn't want to. He was so excited to have his old life back. It was a second chance for him, and he was unable to walk away from it.

I couldn't really condemn him. Anyway, the Bureau of Chemical Industry was good enough to resolve the problem by offering me a job in a small factory that was owned collectively.

This factory had been established under the program of "using state enterprises to support collective factories" (*yi quanmin dai jiti*). Material and human resources from state enterprises were to be used to help small factories in their initial stages of development. Gradually, such support would be withdrawn. These factories were supposed to reduce unemployment levels among those of us who had returned from the countryside. Most of the employees in my factory were like me: "sent-down" – now returned – students.

I worked for a while as a laborer. But, because of my medical training, I was appointed the factory's doctor. Everyone congratulated me. It seemed like a good position. I even went to Shanghai Number Two Medical College for an additional half-year training program. Our factory was doing very well. Everything seemed fine. I got married and had my baby daughter.

I never dreamt I would lose my job.

Whom should I blame for this?

In the late 1980s, a corrupt manager led the factory. He was close to retirement. All he wanted was to line his own pocket before it was too late. He literally sold us out to foreign capitalists by starting a joint venture with a Taiwanese-American businessman. The first thing he and his partner did was to construct a fancy building inside the factory and fence it off as their "joint-venture zone." The manager made a fortune by giving the construction work to those willing to pay the highest bribe. Next, the Taiwanese-American got his cut by dumping outdated poor quality machines on us. Then he disappeared. Our boss got his chance to visit America. So, both partners got what they wanted. They no longer cared whether the joint venture would ever produce anything of value.

Our factory had borrowed foreign currency from the government at the old rate of one US$1 to 5.3 yuan.[1] The debt rose to 10 million yuan at the new exchange rate, which we had no hope of repaying. Our factory had to stop production. The manager said "so long" and retired. What angered us most was that, before he left, he installed a home telephone for "job purposes" and billed the factory. Can you imagine? Even at the last minute he was still trying to grab something for himself.

Six months ago, our factory closed down entirely. We've been given 160 yuan (US$19.25) per month to live on and told to find jobs ourselves. At first, we couldn't believe what was happening. We went to our Bureau to talk to the chief and other officials, hoping they could do something. They recommended we sing three songs: "The Communist Internationale,"

"Unity is Strength" and "The Field of Hope." They claimed these stirring anthems would give us the spirit we needed.

Well, we got some spirit all right. We organized, and began to frequent the Municipal Economic Planning Committee and the General Workers' Union. We pointed out this is supposed to be a socialist country. We're able-bodied and need work to feed our families. We were desperate. Whenever we saw an official in a corridor or in an office we forced him to listen to us. Finally, the authorities decided they'd had enough. They didn't like us visiting them in groups. So they sent a work team to our factory and ordered us to direct our grievances to them. Every day now, the team just sits there, drinks tea and chats freely with anyone who wants to meet with them. It's no real help but it's a good strategy. We had to stop bothering the bureaucrats.

Yesterday, I went to the factory and discovered there were no funds for unemployment compensation, even though we are supposed to be paid in two days. There's no money to reimburse workers for medical expenses. If you get sick you're on your own.

Our newspapers often claim shamelessly that some people got richer after they were laid off because they had the opportunity to pick up better-paid jobs. But not a single person in my factory has a better life now than he or she did before. Since the factory closed down I've tried to get every kind of job. But China doesn't suffer from a labor shortage. Every place I've looked wanted people under 35 years old. I'm a woman in my mid-forties. No one wants to hire me. I've given up all hope.

Rather than bitch about life's unfairness I might as well hang myself. I don't want always to have to compare my situation with people who are better off – especially not with my brothers and sisters. They still have their jobs. Indeed, my second eldest brother is doing very well. He's in real estate and making lots of money. I don't resent the ones who did well. All I want is a job to support my family. I don't expect to be wealthy. My husband's salary is very small. Everything is so expensive today. The average salary used to be 60 yuan a month. Now the lowest basic wage is 600 yuan.

Yesterday I had to pay 375 yuan for my daughter's school fees. I know that if she wants to go to university we'll not be able to pay for it.

My daughter used to have school lunches. In the past, I could afford this. I thought it was a good way to encourage independence and responsibility. I didn't want her grandparents to wait on her every day. But now she has to come home for lunch.

My daughter knows about the changes in our life. She told me: "Mama, I can't compete with my classmates on anything except grades." She is always top in her school. She's my pleasure, hope and everything. She's grown up a lot since I lost my job. When she sees me tired she comes up to me and hammers my back with her fists. "I'll give you a massage," she says.

My daughter knows nothing about the Cultural Revolution. She asks me lots of questions: "Why didn't you go to university?" "Why did people come and take things away from grandpa's home?" "Were they bad people?" It's very difficult for me to share my history with her. It's hard for her to understand. What's the point of bothering her with stories of the past?

When the reforms began I had great hopes. I never expected that things would become worse for ordinary people. I blame our government. Now we're expected to believe that everything about capitalism is good, just as we used to be told that everything about socialism was good. Our government doesn't know how to learn from the West. We copy only the bad things. In the past we were poor, and life wasn't easy. But I never had this feeling of panic all the time, like a heavy rock in my stomach. In the morning, after I've done my chores, I feel lost, not knowing what I should do next.

Let me tell you something. Whenever I cook I put on my doctor's white coat. It's a good use of my profession.

Note

1   In June 1993, the Chinese government devalued the yuan from 5.8 to 8.5 to the US dollar.

10 Li Xiqiang, male: unemployed, and working on a book

Are you OK? Sorry you have to squash yourself in among all these books. I was going to suggest we meet at Xin's home.

I seem to be busy today. This morning, a friend from Japan called and we talked for two hours. Then I hurried to my co-author's home and had a long conversation with him. After this, I went to a hospital to see a friend who'd just been diagnosed with liver cancer. I barely made it home on time. I hope you're not too uncomfortable.

You're right. What you see in this room are all the belongings I accumulated in Japan – more than 7,000 books. When they got to Shanghai the customs officials couldn't figure out what was going on. "Are you a professor?" one inspector asked.

"No."

"A professional writer?"

"No."

The officers dragged thirty cartons of books into their conference room and told me to come back the following week.

When I returned the inspectors hadn't even got started on the books. But they said that, if I would wait, they would open some boxes later. It was the summer of 1994, and very hot. The customs officials were in their air-conditioned conference room, and I was outside covered with anxious perspiration. At the end of the morning, they let me in. They'd opened just a few boxes and had put about thirty books aside. Anything that contained nude pictures or had the word "sex" in the title had been confiscated. I said to myself: "Why did the Japanese use the same character as us for 'sex?' I wish they could've been more original."

None of the inspectors could understand why I had so many books. One middle-aged woman asked knowingly: "Got rich parents, right? Got a two-bedroom apartment already?" She couldn't understand why I hadn't purchased the "four big things" [Refrigerator, washing-machine, big color TV and videocassette recorder that returning Chinese are allowed to import tax free].

I told her: "No. My parents were poor and died six years ago, and I live in an 8 square meter room." She looked at me sharply but appeared to believe me.

The officials never got round to opening all the cartons. But they did confiscate seventy books. When they left for a break I managed to sneak some of them back.

Actually, these books did cost me the price of a two-bedroom apartment: 200,000 yuan. Most of them are about psychology and literature. Psychology's one of the most popular subjects in Japan. The Japanese are introverts. They love psychology.

Books are expensive in Japan. This one cost me 1,000 yuan. But the books helped me survive. I'll explain how later.

I went to Japan in 1987 at the urging of friends. They'd enrolled me in a Japanese language school. Some Japanese businessmen made a fortune operating this kind of business. The year I went was the last the Japanese government allowed young Chinese to enroll in such schools. In 1987, I was 35 years old – an age that would prevent me from getting a student visa today. So, there you are. I got the last flight out.

I didn't go to Japan to make money. At the time, I was at a loss. It probably was the same yawning gap that my friends had experienced. I felt empty, and I wanted to escape a life that had lost all excitement. My mother came to the airport to see me off. She was a short woman. At the last moment I turned around and tried to give her a good-bye wave, but I lost her in the crowd. Three months later she died at the age of 62. My stepfather couldn't take the loss and passed away too a year later.

I was devastated by mother's death.

Mother had remained silent when I told her I planned to go to Japan. She'd showed neither objection nor approval, only resignation.

Twenty years ago things were a lot different.

I was a 1968 graduate: one of the youngest of the Three Old Classes generation. We were all ordered to go to the countryside. But my mother told me to stay with her.

Every day, the neighborhood Up to the Mountains and Down to the Villages mobilization team came to our house beating gongs and shouting: "It's glorious to go to the countryside! It's shameful to be a parasite!" It was the first time we'd had people screaming at our door. Our knees shook and our hearts thumped, but, later, we got used to it. When she heard the sound of gongs approaching Mother would say to me gently: "It's coming; it's coming. Ignore them." Five minutes later, the noise would move on. We would go back to life as usual.

I was my parents', as well as my stepfather's, only child. My parents got divorced when my father was arrested and sentenced to jail in 1954. Mother then married a factory worker who was a very, very kind man. He said to me: "I am your 'papa' now; he (my real father) is your father" (*fuqin*). We were very poor. Mother didn't work and we lived in a tiny attic room that was only 5 feet high. Neither my stepfather nor I could stand upright.

Mother's life focused on me. She took care of me in every particular. She was always there. My lifestyle was certainly different from anyone else I knew. Was it better or worse? I'm sure having a mother with me all the time distracted me. Sometimes I joked about it. I lost a PhD degree under my mother's supervision. A small space of my own might have made all the difference.

My earliest memory of my real father was when I saw him in jail in Nanjing in 1957. I was five years old. I remember walking along a winding path in bitter winter cold. Everything was gray: the prison was gray and my father was gray. He was also a total stranger. I had no feeling towards him whatsoever – only a sense of chill and a terrible fear of that place. It was another five years before I saw him again.

In 1962, my father was released from jail, and he settled in Nanjing. I visited him almost every summer. We spent humid summer nights reading and talking. I discovered why he'd been jailed. He'd had a very rich relative who'd owned half of the old town of Nanjing. In 1948, this man had fled to Hong Kong and told my father to take care of his compound.

One day a woman had knocked on the door and asked if the house could be rented. When father discovered the would-be tenant was a Guomindang army general he was pleased because he thought this would fend off trouble. So, the general moved into the house and became a good friend of my father's. Later, he helped father get a job with the Guomindang government's Department of Public Affairs. Father was well educated in the classics and had been looking for work for quite some time.

After liberation, father had honestly described these events and had never dreamt they could be used against him. But the Department of Public Affairs had been run by a notorious Guomindang figure and my father was accused of being a "cultural spy." The case against him was a travesty. After receiving hundreds of letters of appeal from my father the court in 1962 finally acknowledged it had made a mistake.

In 1966, father was in trouble again. I didn't see him for another six years. He was in a labor camp and twice tried to commit suicide. Once he ran away and was soon caught. When he was asked why he'd tried to escape father raised his arm and the interrogating official flinched. "That's why," Father said. "When you see a blow coming you try to avoid it. You beat me every day, then ask why I run away?"

In school, I was a quiet student. I was asthmatic and a little overweight, so I was never physically active. The thing I liked best – then and now – was reading and talking to friends. The Cultural Revolution gave me opportunities that, otherwise, would never have been available to me. After 1968, I basically shut myself off from the outside world. My universe was my family, a circle of friends and books. It was a satisfying, but somewhat unreal, world. Let me give you an illustration.

One hot, summer night, I was reading Rousseau's *Confessions* under a street light. It was getting late. I was quite absorbed and didn't see a Workers' Patrol team approach. They took the book away from me, scanned the first page suspiciously, and saw the words "Oh Eternal Beauty!" That was it. "You're reading something bad, talking about 'God'." The book was confiscated.

I was very upset because my best friend had lent me this book and there was a long waiting list for it. I felt I had committed an unforgivable error. I ran to my friend's home and told him what had happened. He was silent for a moment, and then he told me not to worry. "The book has a school seal," he pointed out. "We can say you found it in a garbage bin." [1]

That night I couldn't sleep. It was just too painful to lose that book. Suddenly, I remembered that somewhere in Engels' works he praises Rousseau. I jumped up and started to flip through some volumes. Finally, I located what I was looking for. The next day I was back in the police station with Engels. I showed the officers the paragraph I'd found, and, after a heated discussion, they decided they'd better return my book. Clever me. I'd orchestrated the melodrama: "Engels Saves Rousseau."

Still, as you can see, my world could easily be affected by a very small incident.

During the Cultural Revolution I learned English and German in order to pass the time. My texts were Marx's and Engels' original works in German, with a translation in English. I always began with the indices and learned those words first. I used Chinese translations of Marx's and Engels' works as my dictionaries. In 1970, I bought English and German dictionaries for 1.70 yuan. My allowance was 50 cents a month. I made paper jackets for these dictionaries and tried to memorize them page by page.

In 1971, the authorities finally gave me permission to stay in Shanghai on the grounds that I was physically unfit to go to the countryside. I was given a job in the neighborhood public service station. I had to take care of a phone booth, answer the telephone and deliver messages. It suited me well. I usually had a book open.

When Mao died I knew something big was going to happen. Four years later I got the chance to use my foreign language skills.

In 1980, I passed an open examination on the German language and was recruited by the Research Institute of Shanghai Light Industry Bureau. Usually, I translated material about bicycle construction. Two years later I heard that the Shanghai Academy of Social Sciences needed someone to index imported books and magazines for their reference library. I applied for the job and showed the examiners I knew three languages: English, German and Japanese. They gave me the position.

I liked this job very much. For the first time in my life I had access to many foreign books. My task was to skim them all and write summaries of them in Chinese. Whenever I found a book I really liked I kept it as long as possible. I pretended I needed more time to figure it out. For me, it was an ideal position. I felt like "a mouse who had fallen into a rice barrel."

In 1987, clouds started gathering over my head. I had no formal college education and I was threatened with the loss of my job. You ask why didn't I go to university? After the College Entrance Examination was reintroduced in 1977 I made myself sit down to prepare for it. I spent half the day reading Party documents and other political materials but only managed to give myself a headache. I tried again the following day. That evening I accepted I could never bring myself to memorize such nonsense. As a result, I would never pass the required test in political science.

I saw going to Japan as a chance to bring something new into my life. Even today I don't regret my choice, although it had fatal consequences for my marriage.

I got to know my ex-wife through my father.

Father became quite feeble in his later years. This is how my ex-wife came into the picture. She lived next door to him and was very helpful. In fact, she devoted herself to father for many years.

In 1984, father sent me a letter asking if I'd consider marrying this woman. I'd met her on many occasions and had become quite fond of her. The only possible hitch was that mother might object to a daughter-in-law who'd been so close to her ex-husband. But mother agreed to the match. After all, father had needed someone to take care of him.

Father died before the wedding could take place, but I kept my promise and married my fiancée. Less than a year later I was on my way to Japan with the expectation that my wife would soon join me.

The contrast between old, dirty, exhausted Shanghai and bright, pleasant Yokohama was shocking. For the first two months I was consumed with childlike enthusiasm – excited yet uncertain. I entered the language school and found myself a job in a noodle shop. I saw the irony of my situation. I'd always viewed writers of the 1930s, such as Lu Xun, as my heroes.[2] Decades ago, Lu Xun was an exile in Japan, looking for a way to save China. Half a century had passed and nothing much had changed. Like Lu Xun, I'd come to Japan because there was nothing for me in China. I was just another faceless exile.

Like other immigrants, I first went through a period of disorientation and then another one of depression and frustration. I'd hardly settled into my new life when I received news of my mother's death. It was a terrible, terrible blow. My wife joined me two months later. She thought she could help me out of my depression. But it wasn't any good. One day I wrote to a friend that, since mother died, I no longer had a beloved one (*qingren*) in this world. My wife saw my letter and burst into tears. "What am I?" she asked.

Only later I realized that mother and I had depended on one another too much. When I left China I'd sentenced her to death. I was born for her, and she lived for me.

The pain of my loss persisted. If I'd not had these books on psychology I probably would have gone mad. As I read, I played the role of therapist, talking to myself as friend and patient. As soon as I was able to understand my buried emotions I recovered.

Sooner or later we must all learn to deal with the loss of whatever it is we love. Sometimes it's the environment that shaped us or the culture that formed us. Often it's the one on whom we once totally depended.

Finally, I pulled myself together. But it was too late. Six months after she arrived in Tokyo my wife left me without a word.

I quit school immediately. I decided to work full time in order to earn enough money to buy the books I wanted and to support me in China for at least three years after I returned. However, the only way you can stay in Japan legally is to keep your student status. Therefore, I had to become a "black person" [illegal resident]. I kept this status for six years.

I worked night shifts at a coffeehouse and another three hours in the afternoon in the noodle restaurant. Every day I would arrive at the coffeehouse at ten at night with a bundle of books. By two o'clock in the morning the business would slow down and I would have almost three hours to read. Then, at eight o'clock, I would go back home, read the newspapers, watch the news on TV and go to bed. At four o'clock in the afternoon I would go back to the restaurant to cook noodles. I was unable to do jobs that were physically more demanding but paid better. So the only way I could make some money was to extend my working hours.

Every day, my life was the same. By 1994, I'd bought enough books and saved enough money. I started thinking about going back to China. I wouldn't say it was a difficult decision. But I did spend some time discussing it with friends. "To be or not to be?" It was a choice without the possibility of compromise. I'd grown to like Japan. I read so many Japanese works, and I respected Japanese culture. But I missed my own country. I wanted to return, find a girl and start a family.

I haven't found anyone. I miss my ex-wife sometimes. If I hadn't gone to Japan we probably would have stayed together and had a child by now. In a foreign country it's a lot easier for a couple to drift apart and go their own separate ways.

These days I'm working on a book with a friend. Right now, we're doing some revisions. I have a second idea for a book, but I don't know if I'll ever work on it. I'm not a disciplined person. I'm too lazy – too fond of reading and talking, too timid about writing.

I want to write a book about the language code of the Cultural Revolution and describe how the movement manipulated the masses. You ask whether humans are shaped by language? Yes – they live within the limits of their language.

Why was it called the *Cultural* Revolution? Because it was about smashing the old language code and creating a new one. We use language to shape our outlook on the world. Mao told us to "Read a bit of Marx and Lenin," "Learn a bit about Dialectics," and "Read a bit of Lu Xun." But Mao destroyed the chance of any serious intellectual discussion. Marxism became whatever the Party wanted it to be. How many Chinese even remotely understand Marxism? Very few. When someone died people used to say: "He's gone to see Marx." Karl Marx from the Rhineland became one of the family ancestors.

The Cultural Revolution tried to reorganize the whole nation under a new language code. We had Mao's writings, official slogans and eight model operas. They were the only modes of expression that could be used for public communication. Our generation spent its formative years during that period. The language of the Cultural Revolution is still imprinted on our thoughts.

One day, when I was washing dishes in that Japanese restaurant, I found myself humming "Whatever the Party Asks Us to Do We Must Do It" – a song from the Beijing opera "Strategically Capture Weihu Mountain!" Why the hell was I singing that song in a Japanese noodle shop? It was because this kind of language had become an unconscious part of my existence. If you talk to people of my generation you'll find they still use the old patterns of speech. The other day, a friend and I were chatting. Suddenly, he said: "See through the appearance to the essence."[3] Old Mao's thinking is still a part of our daily language.

During the Cultural Revolution very few people managed to locate themselves outside this language system. Qi Baishi was the exception.[4] As Qi was "jet flighted" through screaming crowds during the Anti-Rightist campaign he recited a line from Li Bai's poem: "Monkeys cry to me from both banks but my boat has slid ten thousand mountains away."[5] Qi wasn't listening to the howling mob. He'd put himself beyond their reach.

Toward the end of the Cultural Revolution it was no longer necessary for the Party to work on the masses. It just let us sing: "The Cultural Revolution Must be Good, Must be Good and Must be Good!" Today we are told: "Development is the Core Truth" (*fazhan shi ying daoli*). "Don't question," in other words: "Just accept that everything under the name of 'development' is legitimate and good."

I agree it's more relaxing now. I can write things that wouldn't have been allowed in the past. However, I'm still the outsider. Not like some of the others. So many members of my generation always managed to be the "right guys." The sons and daughters of the Party officials I met in Tokyo, for instance, were Red Guards and "revolutionaries" during the Cultural Revolution. Now, all they talk about is doing business. They're glittering paragons of reform. In spite of everything that's whirled about them they've never stopped being "positive role models."

A couple of weeks ago I was walking down Huaihai Road [now the most expensive and fashionable shopping district in Shanghai]. Lots of people were standing around, gawking at something behind a police line. I couldn't see what was so fascinating. But I wasn't that interested either. I turned away, muttering to myself: "What's going on?"

Suddenly, a teenage boy, dressed up like a Hong Kong hippie, spun around and said to me: "You dimwit. Can't you see they're making a TV show?!"

I was too shocked to respond. Such rudeness aggravated by such a stupid demeanor! I walked away, very upset, feeling anger, the bite of loneliness and the sharp indifference of a society that has never belonged to me.

[At the end of the interview Li produced two pieces he'd written after his wife left him.]

I A pair of red shoes

How my ex-wife and I separated was unusual.

One morning, I awoke to discover she had gone. All of her belongings – the photos on the wall, the passport in the drawer, the Japanese ID – had vanished as I slept. From that moment on I knew nothing about her whereabouts until, one day, she called on the phone to let me know how I could file for a divorce.

My friend in America had a similar experience. His wife, though, took their son with her when she left. Like me, he'd been "sleeping on high pillows with no worry" and had no idea about what was about to hit him. When his child's teacher called and asked why his son wasn't in school my friend learnt he was alone in the world. He hired a detective to look for his family. He spent all his savings.

"I found them!" one day he shouted over the phone. You could hear the happiness.

Ibsen's Nora made an honest statement when she left with a loud slam of the door. But today's "New Female" is less communicative. When she's ready to leave she doesn't bother to say good-bye.

My wife's plans were long in the making. Her actions were deliberate. I was too self-confident. Blindly optimistic, I believed her love was there since I loved her with all my heart. Here I made a fatal mistake. Why should love be reciprocated?

My wife took everything with her. She didn't leave a single photo behind. How many photographs did I take of her? Many, many.

Yet, deliberately or unintentionally, she left behind a pair of red shoes.

Next to the door of our apartment is a shoebox. As soon as my wife and I entered our home we used to remove our shoes and place them in this box. Now, among the black and gray shoes, there is a pair of red shoes. They catch my eye when I return. Sometimes I come in from the night shift, tired and disoriented. It looks as if the shoes have been moved.

"She's back!" My heart begins to thump. I rush upstairs, only to find the same empty room. Where is the specter of my missing wife?

During many years of loneliness I often walked up to the apartment hoping she'd be there. I knew it wouldn't happen but still I dreamt.

Friends recognized I was torturing myself: "The person's gone! What's the point of faithfully keeping her belongings? Throw them away! Please."

They were right. I made myself put the shoes on top of a garbage can. But minutes later I hurried back and retrieved them as if they were lost treasure.

What an unusual pair of shoes! I could never be apart from you. To love someone isn't easy. Nor can we stop loving someone just because they no longer need our love.

II The lighter

My wife used to work in a coffeehouse. One day, she brought home a lighter with the shop's name and telephone number on it. I kept it so I could call her. The shop had a romantic name: It was "Liebe": German for "love."

Whenever we said, "Please give me the 'Liebe'" it was as if we'd said: "Give me some love."

We used the lighter to ignite our gas ring. During the first few months in Japan we were quite alone. I used to joke we used the fire of "Liebe" to prepare a dish that would make us forget the loneliness of a foreign country.

Later, my wife left without a word. I worked two jobs and seldom stayed at home. I hardly cooked anymore. But I needed hot water to brew my tea. Whenever I lit the gas I thought of her.

The "love" lighter lasted a long time. It still had fuel in it when I returned to China. But our marriage didn't last that long.

I could never understand why the love between two people didn't last as long as the relationship between a person and his lighter.

Notes

1 At the beginning of the Cultural Revolution most school libraries were ransacked by Red Guards. Some students took advantage of the situation by bringing books home. Many of the books available during that period were "liberated" school texts.

2 Lu Xun (1881–1936) was a product of the May Fourth New Culture Movement. Two of his short novels – *Diary of a Madman* and *The True Story of Ah Q* – quickly became contemporary classics (English trans. Lu Hsun, *Selected Stories*, San Francisco: China Books and Periodicals, 1994). Lu Xun believed that traditional Chinese habits and customs were partly to blame for China's backwardness.

3   From Mao's essay: "On Contradiction" (in Nick Knight, ed. *Mao Zedong on Dialectical Materialism: Writings on Philosophy*, Armonk, NY: M.E. Sharpe, 1990).
4   Qi Baishi (1863–1957) was a well-known painter who came under attack in the 1950s.
5   *Liang an yuansheng tibuzhu, qingzhou yiguo wanchongshan*. From the poem, "Through the Yangzi Gorges," by Li Bai (701–762).

11 Chen Jianxin, male: college professor

By August 1966, the students in my school had already established two competing Red Guard organizations. I didn't know which to join. Finally, I picked the "Red Shield" organization because it was favored by most of the academically inclined students.

Since the third grade I'd always been a little student "cadre." When the Cultural Revolution started I was in my last year as a high-school student, and I was branch secretary of our Youth League Organization. Of course, it was expected I would get involved in the Cultural Revolution. But most of us were eager to participate. Many people today believe that students in those days were very political, but we were less political than religious. Religion demands commitment, not thought.

We showed lots of initiative though. I remember that I went to the Department Store of Arts and Crafts in the Nanjing Road and ordered Mao badges for the whole school. We sold these badges to every student at 5 cents each. This was before Mao badges became popular, so my friends and I scored big for "Red Shield."

In October 1966, I went to Beijing with several classmates. We waited for several weeks, hoping to see Mao. Finally, Xie Fuzhi came to talk to thousands of us at our Great Exchange transit camp.[1] Xie asked if there were any message that we'd like him to take to Mao and the other members of the Central Committee. Thousands clamored as if with one voice: "We want to see Chairman Mao!"

On the evening of November 24, 1966, the announcement came that "Our dearest, dearest great leader Chairman Mao will receive Red Guards tomorrow." That night, no one slept much. The next morning we arrived at Tiananmen Square just after dawn. Because I'm short I was placed in the first row. I could see the small figures on the balcony over Tiananmen Gate quite clearly. It was easy to identify Mao. Everyone – myself included – was jumping, crying and sobbing: "Long live Chairman Mao!"

Mao waved to us a few times. He was very detached. He seemed alone and untouched. Twelve years later I had the same feeling when I revisited him in his mausoleum. He was dead and really alone then.

My trip to Beijing was the high point of my involvement in the Cultural

Revolution. Soon afterwards, my friends and I were sent to factories as temporary workers, while the government figured out what to do with us. The boys in my school were assigned to Shanghai Number Two Steel and Iron Plant. We were told that permanent positions at the plant would soon be made for us. Then we learned that a Red Guard Conference of all Shanghai middle schools had recommended that students should go to the countryside and to frontier regions. So our original assignments were canceled and replaced with the Four-Facing Policy.

My younger brother and I graduated the same year. He was a 1966 middle-school graduate, while I was a high-school graduate. According to the policy one of us had to go to the countryside. I was the elder, so I said, of course, I would go.

I was assigned to Chongming Island. I still remember the day I went to cancel my city resident registration. I was very sad – much sadder than I'd expected. The officer in the Safety Bureau crossed out the relevant page in my registration book with a black pen. In less than a second I'd ceased to be an urban dweller and become a peasant.

However, after I arrived at the farm I discovered things weren't too bad. The dormitories were clean, and everything was orderly. Our work unit was made up of newly arrived students – 100 boys and 100 girls, divided into ten work teams. I felt as though we were still in school, on a temporary work detail.

The unit was in charge of a fruit farm: the best kind of work one could hope to get on Chongming Island. A fruit farmer does about one third of the work of a rice farmer. We got the fifth and the twenty-first days of every month off. On these days, the roads were full of students coming and going, visiting friends, or just having a stroll.

I enjoyed my three years on the farm enormously. It was an opportunity for me to do lots of reading. Almost every student had brought books with them – more than half of them "liberated" from school libraries. So, with one hand, the Cultural Revolution took away our education. With the other it gave us all those books.

Before the Cultural Revolution many books were considered "unsuitable" for revolutionary aspirants. As a Youth League member, I'd refused to touch anything not approved by the authorities. I never borrowed any western books, and I was suspicious of those who did. It wasn't that I had any good reason to reject western literature. I just wanted to be seen as "progressive."

The Cultural Revolution left quite a hole in my education. But on Chongming Island I could decide for myself what I wanted to study. I read most of the western classics, and spent long evenings discussing them with friends. I would say that my fundamental beliefs and ideas were formed during that period.

In 1972, the government began calling students back to Shanghai. The 1966 high-school graduates were given priority over other students. I was reassigned to a job at Shanghai's Number Three Steel and Iron Plant. The workers in the steel and iron plants were mostly semi-literate. Before liberation they'd been rickshaw pullers, barbers and other low-skilled laborers. They were all quite down to earth.

I remember this was right after the Lin Biao incident. So, my first two months on the new job were spent participating in the "Criticizing Lin and Confucius" movement (*pi Lin pi Kong*).

In the document issued by the Party Central Committee, Lin Biao was accused of calling Mao an "Emperor." This allegation didn't surprise the workers because they too thought of Mao as an Emperor. Most of them believed a missile probably had shot down Lin Biao's plane while he was fleeing to the Soviet Union.

I was put in charge of a study group. Every week, I got half a day off to study Marx's and Lenin's works. It was a nice break for me. I didn't even mind having to write critical articles on Confucianism.

In the factory, I was invited to apply for Party membership. I wasn't that interested, but the factory Party Committee made the decision on my behalf. I was told I could join on May Day 1978. In 1977, however, I took the College Entrance Examination – the first year it was offered. I passed, and was accepted by a university in Shanghai. I quit my job before May Day 1978, so I never actually joined the Party.

When I was a high-school student I submitted several applications for Party membership. Since then, I've lost interest. I still believe in communism: a society without exploitation and oppression. Who would say such a goal isn't worth struggling for? But the Chinese Communist Party no longer believes in its own political program. It's long since stopped pretending to be a communist party.

Going to university was a glorious experience for me. But there was some regret mixed in too because the opportunity came far too late. I was 31 years old – twelve years older than the youngest student in my class. This young student called me "Old Master." He wrote to me: "I look to you to guide my future." It was a nice compliment, but it also revealed how he regarded me.

At the time though, many of the students were around my age. We were all highly motivated. The culture was nothing but study, study and study. Every night, the classrooms were full of people. No one was outside. Everyone was working. Today, every corner of my campus is occupied during the evenings, *except* the classrooms. When I walk across campus at night I see places with lights on where there are no students and places that are dark with many students. I can't imagine what they're all doing.

When I was a university student I published three articles on Chinese contemporary fiction. After I finished my studies, I was given the best job assignment possible – an assistant lectureship in the same Chinese Language and Literature Department from which I'd graduated. At the time, I couldn't have been happier. I never anticipated that a decade later I'd regret my decision to pursue an academic career.

The graduates from my class were given three kinds of assignments: first, government positions; second, jobs in the media and press; and, third, appointments at colleges and universities. Only a few of us were selected for positions at colleges or universities.

Those who became officials now are in positions of authority. Many are managers of companies. Those who got jobs at newspapers, magazines, or TV stations are also doing great. With the onset of commercialization the media are always the first to drop their pants and do whatever is necessary to make money.

My former classmates in government or business now make much more money than I do. As a professor, I've nothing worth selling. All I can do is "moonlight" as an after-hours teacher. My monthly salary is a little over 800 yuan. I'm also eligible for a 200–280 yuan bonus every month, which is determined by how many courses I teach and by how my department's doing.

Universities are now under a great deal of pressure to "create income" (*chuangshou*) for themselves. The only way they can do this is to sell education to whoever can afford it. So they favor students who can pay their own way. Many of these wouldn't normally meet standards for admission. Some universities have been forced to sell off part of their campus to speculators. Universities also offer "workshops." Basically, these sell certificates to bureaucrats.

What I'm describing is pervasive. In my son's middle school, which is a district key school, only one-third of the students were admitted on the basis of their test scores. The rest are sons or daughters of district government officials, rich merchants, army officials and other privileged types. Good students from poor families don't have much of a chance to get into a key school. My son was quite upset when he found out how it works. "It's not fair" was his only comment.

The spread of commercialism does affect a person's spirit. Instead of exchanging ideas, my colleagues now discuss where they can buy things cheaply. Female teachers will rush out to get the same inexpensive outfits. They end up looking identically dowdy. Professors will argue furiously with peddlers over a couple of yuan. It all makes you feel low.

If I could get some satisfaction out of my job I wouldn't complain to you like this. But I don't. More and more, I feel alienated from my work. I teach Chinese contemporary literature. Students show up in the classroom only because they have to. I talk about what interests me, but I'm my only audience. You can guess how I feel. When I was a student, we had so much to talk about. After classes were over, we kept teachers in the classroom so we could continue the discussion. There was a passion for knowledge, and teachers were held in high regard. They certainly gave us their best. Today, the students look at me as if I'm a loser. I know what they're thinking. What do these dead writers have to do with us?

In the past, the government assigned jobs to college graduates. Without a good academic record you could never get a decent job. Nowadays, the graduates find jobs themselves, so knowing the right people is much more important than academic performance. The students call the humanities (*wenke*) the easy-to-pass subjects (*hunke*).[2] For the teachers, "a good grade is the guiding principle" (*yiliang weigang*).[3] We are told to let students pass, no matter how they perform – particularly if they're from minority groups or if they're paying full tuition. Teachers give easy grades and easy tests so that they can please students and get good student teaching evaluations.

One of my students submitted a thesis that was copied entirely from one of my articles. When I questioned him he denied any wrongdoing. I asked: "Do you happen to know a professor called Chen Jianxin?" He just shrugged. He didn't know my name, nor did he care about the author whose ideas he'd stolen. Yet I'd taught him and was his thesis adviser.

The atmosphere outside the universities has become poisonous. So many things attract young people today. They feel they must possess them. Lots of students work part time to make money. They want to dress fashionably, talk fashionably and eat fashionably. People say that the young generation is not like we were – that they can think for themselves. I think it's nonsense. My students belong to whatever's in vogue; they're slaves to their desires.

In the past, there weren't that many things *to* desire. We had time to study and to contemplate. The Cultural Revolution was a disaster but at least people weren't demoralized. Today, capitalism, which is alien to our culture and traditions, has come to China. It's an even bigger disaster. Marx exposed the ugliness of the system more than a hundred years ago. Now we get to relive everything he described.

I think there are two things wrong with us Chinese. First, as Lu Xun noted, we're a forgetful people with a short memory. Second, we tend to be slavish followers of others. Once, we fought for independence. Today, what we won at such high cost we give back to foreign capital. I'm not exaggerating. If you look at all the places with high-rise buildings and many lights – they're all built by foreign investors. If the money were gone the buildings would be empty and the lights shut off. We've handed our country over to others. We've repeated the mistakes of the 1950s. After the Soviets withdrew everything shut down. But Mao had anticipated this and was prepared. In any case, he wanted the Russians out

Hong Kong's return to China is a big event on the 1997 calendar. I don't feel much pride. Don't you see the irony? On the one hand, Hong Kong is returned to us. On the other, we are signing new 50- or 80-year leases with foreign investors as fast as we can, terrified we're not selling fast enough. We're losing our heritage. If we could, we'd dig up our ancestors and sell them too.

You want to know what I think about "New China?" I'll tell you: the government's corrupt, the people are demoralized, the economy's messed-up and the schools and universities are neglected. There's not much future for anyone here – not ordinary people anyway.

Notes

1   Xie Fuzhi was Minister of Public Security at the beginning of the Cultural Revolution. In 1966, he ordered records about "landlords," "rich peasants," "counter-revolutionaries," "bad elements" and "rightists" to be made available to Red Guards.
2   *Wenke* and *hunke* sound almost the same in the Shanghai dialect.
3   *Yiliang weigang* echoes the popular slogan: "Grain is the guiding principle." Both expressions sound similar.

12 Yang Yuan, male: college administrator, and Song Ming, male, his friend: purchasing agent for an industrial plant

YANG: I left Shanghai for Heilongjiang on April 27, 1969. The following day was my seventeenth birthday. I spent it with strangers on a train headed for a faraway place that no one in my family had ever seen or thought much about.

Both my father's and mother's parents left China for Singapore at the beginning of the century. I don't know much about my maternal grandparents since my mother's mother died young and her father remarried. My paternal grandfather worked as a printing worker and managed to save up enough money to open his own shop. My father started working there when he was just a kid.

In 1955, when I was three, my parents decided to move the whole family back to China. Life in Singapore wasn't easy for them. A friend of theirs had recently returned to China, and he had sent back an encouraging report.

My parents settled in Shanghai, and were given jobs in a printing factory. Because they were "Returned Overseas Chinese" (*guiqiao*) they enjoyed some privileges, such as being given an apartment in a good neighborhood. Shortly thereafter, my two siblings were born.

Our new life started brightly, but things soon became dark. My father died from an illness when my younger brother was just a year old. My poor mother became a widow at the age of 31. She never remarried, but not because she lacked suitors. She was very pretty when she was young. Quite a few men proposed to her. But she wanted to raise her children by herself.

I was thinking of my mother on that train on my birthday, knowing she'd also be thinking of me. She'd been in tears since I'd started to pack my luggage.

As the eldest child in the family I'd been given many responsibilities, and I'd tried to do as much as I could for mother. During the summer vacation I cooked and washed for my sister and brother, so when mother got home from work she could have a rest. I got a big allowance: 2 yuan each month. I guess mother tried to make me feel important. I usually spent my allowance on books and candy for my sister and brother. I wanted them to feel they had a big brother.

When I left home my mother almost had a breakdown. However, I knew I should go so that my sister and brother would be given a better chance to stay in Shanghai.

SONG: I had a very special feeling towards my second eldest sister and my youngest sister. Of the six children in our family we were the closest. The three of us all left home to settle in the countryside. This common experience created an even closer bond.

After she failed to pass the College Entrance Examination my second eldest sister went to a farm in Xinjiang in 1963. When she heard I was leaving for Heilongjiang she took a train for three days and nights to come back to see me off. She'd spent all her savings buying things she knew I'd find useful. I noticed she hadn't bought any clothes for herself in the previous six years. But she'd purchased an expensive winter jacket for me.

She also gave me fifty 8 cent domestic stamps. She said: "If you have the stamps, you'll write. I want to hear from you as often as possible." During my five years in the farm I remembered these words and wrote to her every three or four weeks.

Later, my youngest sister was sent to a village in Jiangxi. I couldn't get back to Shanghai at the time, so I sent her the 20 yuan I'd been able to save during my first year in Heilongjiang. I knew that her life in the village would be more difficult than mine. She didn't spend this money on herself. Instead, she bought some yarn and knitted a thick sweater for me. She didn't have enough wool to make the whole sweater, so she undid a scarf my mother had made for her and used this material for half the sleeves.

I'm not so close to the other two brothers and one sister who stayed in Shanghai. They cared about me too, but, somehow, it was different.

YANG: The Up to the Mountains and Down to the Villages movement divided many families. The Four-Facing Policy often created conflict among siblings because the action of one very often had a great impact on the others. Years later, the differences between those who stayed and those who left became apparent. "I let you get your job but I'm not appreciated" is a common complaint from those who went to live with the peasants.

SONG: I wasn't resentful towards the others. I just felt there was greater distance between us. Yang seems more like a brother to me than my real brother. He and I ate and slept in the same place for more than five years. We've shared our most intimate thoughts ever since.

YANG: There were six of us in our residential unit, living like brothers in one family. If anyone received money or food from his home he shared it with all. If Song got some money from his sister or parents he usually bought two cartons of cigarettes for everyone, whereas when I got some extra money I would treat the others to a good meal in the county town. It was the same with all of us on the farm. If you got something you shared it with your closest friends.

The first two or three years in the farm went by fast. I was young, and a question like "What are you going to do in the future?" never occurred to me. The "future" was something far off in the distance. My mind was at peace, and the atmosphere on the farm was harmonious. But things changed quickly when students began to leave for the universities and take advantage of other opportunities. Soon everyone became conspiratorial and restless.

Song was among the first lucky ones to be admitted to a school. He was the purchaser for our unit, which gave him plenty of opportunity to get to know people at farm headquarters. A cadre who was a close friend of the head of the farm helped him. Song made sure he introduced me to this cadre before he left to enroll in a technical college in Changchun.

SONG: Your work unit could recommend that you be sent to school, but the final decision was made at farm headquarters. Yang was a bit slow regarding these matters.

YANG: But I learnt quickly. The following year I made an effort to cultivate a relationship with this cadre. One of the bad things about the Up to the Mountains and Down to the Villages movement was that, at the end, it did tend to corrupt local government. Cadres were given control over something students wanted desperately: the chance to reunite with their families.

Song's cadre friend finally recommended that I be given special consideration because I was a "Returned Overseas Chinese." In 1974, I was admitted by Shanghai Normal University to study mathematics.

SONG: It's not true that, during the Cultural Revolution, the motto "study is useless" was widely accepted. If it had been the opportunity to attend college or university wouldn't have been seen as so golden. Towards the end of the Cultural Revolution study was considered valuable – but it was, admittedly, a different kind of study.

YANG: It's certainly true that, as Worker-Peasant-Soldier students, we didn't have the standard college education. There was too much emphasis on political study and on practical problem-solving. The curriculum wasn't well thought-out. However, we did learn valuable lessons. Education today is too isolated from practical problems. That's not good either.

I graduated in 1977 and was recruited by my own university. I taught freshmen classes and continued to study. I thought I was a good teacher. But, in 1983, all the faculty members from the Workers, Peasants and Soldiers intake were asked to upgrade their qualifications. By that time, the graduates who'd enrolled in 1977 and 1978 [immediately after the end of the Cultural Revolution] had started to fill vacant faculty positions. It was clear we either had to get additional qualifications or leave the universities. It was a depressing time for me.

I enrolled in a so-called "Diploma-to-Degree" program (*dazhuan zhuan benke*). My three years of college education as a Worker-Peasant-Soldier student counted for a diploma only. Now, I had to do another two years' study to qualify for a bachelor's degree. After I got this degree the Dean asked me if I would consider an administrative position. It was obvious I had no option but to comply. That's how I started working in the Office of Graduate Studies.

SONG: In 1976, I finished three years' study in a technical college and was then assigned to Wuhan Steel Plant in Hubei province. I met my future wife in the college. She was given a job in Shanghai's Number Three Iron and Steel Plant. She was happy to be back in her hometown, but sad to be separated from me.

It's different in factories. People don't care what kind of degree you have. As long as you can get things done they respect you. I'm a good organizer, and, before long, management at the factory asked me to become a purchasing agent for the technical department. I was glad to get this position because it let me visit my fiancée in Shanghai. In 1985, four years after we were married, my wife was transferred to the new Baoshan Steel Plant in Shanghai. The plant was willing to offer positions to the spouses of employees as long as they had college diplomas and some relevant work experience.

I was reluctant to return to Shanghai because I had begun to prefer "inlanders" (*waidi ren*) to Shanghainese. Provincial people tend to be friendly, warmhearted and straightforward. People in the north, for instance, don't typically "chop firewood" (*pi yingchai*) [share expenses] with guests after a meal in a restaurant. But they do in Shanghai. Shanghainese have the reputation of being shrewd, honey tongued and cunning, so when I traveled around the country I often concealed where I was from.

Anyway, I wasn't sure I belonged in Shanghai anymore. But I agreed to move back here after the former Party Secretary of Wuhan Steel Plant was transferred to Baoshan. I have a special relationship with him. He was accused of leaking state secrets to foreigners during a visit abroad in 1983 and was arrested. I knew the accusation had to be false. He was far too careful to make such a mistake. I was told about his arrest when I was on a business trip in Shanghai, and I sent a letter to his wife to show my support for him.

After this man was cleared of any wrongdoing he came to my house with his wife. She started crying as soon as they walked in. Among all their friends I'd been the only one to speak out on their behalf. My letter had saved their faith in people. We became very close friends, so I was happy to follow him here in 1986.

I make a little over 2,000 yuan a month. I consider myself a lucky person – one of about 10 percent of my generation. Lots of people aren't so fortunate. Baoshan Steel Plant is a major state enterprise. Our factory is equipped with foreign technology and has adopted Japanese management methods. We're doing well. The government won't let us fail. So, my position is secure as long as I'm careful and do my job.

YANG: To be lucky means to have a job really. Song is one of the few people of our generation earning a good salary. My salary is a bit over 1,000 yuan a month. But I'm fortunate too because I have a reasonably secure position. The environment at universities has changed a lot, but it's still relatively peaceful.

Three of the six close "brothers" from our farm haven't been so lucky. They didn't get the opportunity to go to university. One of them is now out of work and two are working in factories, making very little. We used to visit each other often, but now they don't want to see us. I don't know what to say to them either. It's not their fault. A decent society should be able to provide jobs to all those willing to work. I wouldn't be surprised if they take to the streets in protest.

SONG: The government is terrified people will get desperate. Right now at least, they'll give you enough to eat if you lose your job. I heard that, next year [1997], 600,000 more jobs will be lost in Shanghai. Some people have said the true figure is going be another million out of work.

My job requires me to work closely with top managers. These people are becoming members of a privileged class. The businessmen who took over rural township and village enterprises in the 1980s used to be the ones who had the reputation of being rude and obnoxious. They would run local workshops as if they were personal fiefdoms. Today, managers in state-owned enterprises behave in the same way. Workers call their managers *laoban* (boss, or private owner). The head of my department – a young man in his middle thirties – told me the first day he was on the job "Obey me, and I'll keep you," as if he owned the place.

YANG: Cadres now tend to be recruited from the "over-the-next-century" generation, the members of which are now in their thirties. Maybe it's not so bad. The country needs young people. But the problem is that the members of this generation are often arrogant, ruthless and impetuous. They're better at talk than action. These traits are aggravated by the new entrepreneurial culture. During the Cultural Revolution cadres worshipped Mao's every utterance. Today, cadres worship the capitalist ethos. I don't know whether this is good or not.

SONG: I think these young people are worse than the older generation because, in the past, cadres would at least claim that their mission was to serve the people. Today, cadres make it pretty clear that it's the mission of the people to serve them.

YANG: I visited Guangzhou [Canton, the capital of Guangdong province] last year on a business trip. On the second night, I was treated to an outing at a nightclub. I was shocked to see girls performing strip dances and to observe prostitutes waiting for customers. There were homeless beggar-children everywhere. It wasn't safe to walk alone at night. I was very upset. This isn't what I want China to be like.

I read somewhere that foreigners hope that China will become more like Hong Kong once the colony is returned to us. But Guangzhou is already like Hong Kong! What a frightening vision I was given. Economic development in Guangdong has done little for the country as a whole. A few got rich, but how does this benefit everyone else? Our society is ruined. Look at Guangzhou: it's immoral, ugly and decadent.

Perhaps Shanghai can set a good example for the rest of the country. The city has pursued reform in an orderly way, and has not given in to lawlessness and corruption.

SONG: Well, Shanghai has some of the same problems as Guangzhou, but they're better hidden.

YANG: That's the difference. In Shanghai, bad things, such as prostitution, are not openly acceptable. If you get caught you can be prosecuted.

13 Gao Yunhua, female: unemployed worker

As a little girl I was cheerful and happy – good at school and popular with the teachers. What I enjoyed most was singing in the chorus organized by the Young Pioneers' Palace. Every Tuesday afternoon we had lessons and practice. It was lots of fun.

I was also a member of the Team to Welcome Foreign Guests. When foreign delegations came to the Young Pioneers' Palace we would put on a pretty dress – make-up, too – and wait at the entrance to welcome them. I really looked forward to this.

I've often told my son my childhood was happier than his. Society was a lot safer then, and people behaved better. As children, we played a lot. We weren't given much homework, and what we were given we worked on together. I was a little team leader – given responsibility for the work of a group. Every morning, I would report what our group had accomplished. We supervised ourselves. Nowadays, parents have to sit over their children in order to get them to finish their homework.

I got into a good – but not a key – high school. When the Cultural Revolution started I was close to finishing the end of my first year. We were given one final examination and then everything else was canceled. I remember that, by the end of June [1966], some Big Character posters appeared in our school – most written by teachers about other teachers. Later, some senior students joined in. No more school! Everyone was in a holiday mood. I went to school every day just to read the posters. One afternoon, I got quite dizzy holding my head back to read them all.

I can't think of anyone from my high-school class who was active during the Cultural Revolution. To tell you the truth, we were all bystanders (xiaoyaopai).

In late July, my brother set off to join the Great Exchange. I begged him to take me with him but he refused. I stayed at home, feeling rather bored. Every day, I went out to see some friends and exchange gossip. Once, I heard my best friend's home was being raided. She was monitor of our class: a girl everyone liked. I ran to her home immediately. I knew that her grandfather used to own a jewelry shop.

The house was in a mess. Everything was turned over. My friend looked ashamed. I asked her to have dinner at our house. We maintained a close relationship until she went to America seven years ago.

Most of the kids in our high school came from the area around Huaihai Road. None of us had high-ranking officials as parents, although some of us were from the former bourgeois class. My family was working class.

At the time we never thought about class differences. Only children from cadres' families seemed to care about family background, and I didn't know any such families. My school friends and I stood "heel-to-heel" (*jiao peng jiao*) and the Cultural Revolution wasn't going to change that.

In October [1966], a rumor went around that the government was going to stop the Great Exchange. Afraid I would miss out on this free travel opportunity, I went to my school with a friend to get the papers needed for travel. The following day, she and I went to the railway station to have a look. Tens of thousands of other students were already there, trying to get on a train. We ended up going to Hangzhou. We'd prepared nothing for the trip – no change of clothes, no money, nothing at all. We hadn't even told out parents about our plans. We were far too excited.

We arrived in Hangzhou four hours after we left Shanghai. The next day we managed to get on a train heading north. By midnight we were in Nanjing. The Student Receiving Station arranged accommodation for us at the University of Nanjing. We were also loaned some money and given two military coats. Just as well! The weather was starting to get cold.

There was nothing to do in Nanjing except look at Big Character posters. Later, we spent several days trying to board a train to Beijing, but, finally, we gave up and returned home. When we arrived back in Shanghai we were tired but happy because we had tasted the Great Exchange.

When I appeared at my door my mother cooked me a nice dinner. She hadn't panicked when she discovered I'd disappeared. Can you imagine anything like this today? If my son doesn't get home on time I get very worried. Six months after I'd returned home, however, I did get a scolding when my mother received a letter asking for the 20 yuan I'd been given in Nanjing.

In 1967, I heard we were going to "carry on revolution while resuming classes" (*fuke naogeming*). I ran to my school in anticipation.

"Are we going to have lessons again?" I said to a math teacher I'd recognized outside the school. I was eager to get started because I was planning to become a doctor.

"I really don't know" he replied, looking confused.

My school certainly didn't look as if it was ready to educate us. Old and new Big Character posters were everywhere. The smell of rotten glue paste and ink was pervasive.

Soon, many of my classmates crowded back. I noticed that quite a few of them had put on weight in the past few months. They looked healthy and relaxed. We talked, laughed and gossiped. In fact, that's all we did. Then we were packed off to factories to learn from the working class.

Two years ago, my high-school friends and I had a reunion. I discovered that the few classmates with a "bourgeois" background had all gone to America, Australia or Japan. During the Cultural Revolution "class" was emphasized all the time. As a child I never appreciated what the fuss was about. I wasn't aware of significant social differences among my friends. But, when I think about it now, I realize, of course, that class does matter.

Families with a good class background are more likely to have relatives living abroad. The children can leave and seek their fortunes elsewhere. After the Cultural Revolution "bourgeois" families got most of their property back and were compensated for their losses. But working-class families got nothing. In any case, how could I be compensated for my lost education? People like me are the real victims of the Cultural Revolution.

After several months of working in a factory my school friends and I were told we were going to be settled in the countryside. My parents were prepared for this. They had already contacted my paternal grandmother and other family members in Wuxi [a county about 60 miles from Shanghai] to arrange a settlement for me.

Grandmother was an extremely proud woman. She had three sons; they all worked in the city; and they sent money to her every month, which she saved for them. My parents were happy to send her their daughter because they knew I would be well taken care of. Moreover, I would be raised in the village of their birth.

I was against the idea. I wanted to stay with my classmates. I was not at all enthusiastic about living with grandma. I'd only visited her three times before. But there was no discussion. Father had already transferred my resident's registration.

So in the spring of 1969 I left Shanghai. I wonder what would have happened if I'd stayed with my friends. If I'd taken a different path I might have had quite a different life. Who knows? Perhaps I would have joined the Party and become a cadre. Maybe I would have gone to university. At least, I wouldn't be so alone now.

I didn't have a difficult life in the countryside. I never had to cook for myself. Grandma and my aunt took care of me. However, there were only a couple of dozen educated youths in the whole county. We all lived with our relatives. Nobody paid much attention to us.

During my first two years I received 40 to 60 percent of what the peasants earned. Later, the village leaders were told to apply a policy of "the same pay for the same work" (*tonggong, tongchou*) to the students. After this, I received full credit for a day's work.

I worked five years in the fields. I did get the chance to train as a "barefoot doctor," but grandma said no. She was afraid I'd have to serve as a midwife. "How can an unmarried girl do that kind of job?" she snapped. That was the end of that idea.

I never thought about my future. My time in the countryside was like a prolonged visit: my whole mood was temporary and unsettled. When I reached the age of 20, matchmakers arrived one after the other. I went to see the village leader. "I answered the Party's call to make a contribution to rural development," I told him. "I'm not here to get married." He looked at me and sighed.

"I notice that you've lost a lot of weight since you came here. Really, you don't have the strength to work in the fields. I can't give you any other job because there are no positions open in our township enterprises. Why don't you go back to Shanghai and apply for 'resettlement due to physical condition'? I'll assist you any way I can."

I was speechless. I knew some students had returned home because of poor health. But I never thought I fitted into that category, even though I'd fainted twice in the fields.

I took the train back to Shanghai the very next day. Within a week, my file was on the desk of the District Educated Youth Office. The village Revolutionary Committee had recommended I be returned to Shanghai because of my physical unsuitability.

In order to get approved for resettlement I realized I needed some proof of my "unfitness." For several years I'd sought treatment for an irregular heartbeat and for insomnia. I put together a record of my visits to doctors and presented these to the Educated Youth Office. But the woman in charge just said to me flatly: "I don't think you meet the criteria for resettlement. Don't waste my time."

My file was returned to the village, stamped "rejected." But the village leaders just sent it back to Shanghai. This game of back and forth went on for several weeks.

I soon figured out that the woman who had rejected my application was punishing me for my youngest sister's refusal to accept her assignment. This sister – the seventh in our family – was put in the "soft category" (*ruandang*) after she graduated because three of her elder siblings were already in the countryside and another three were working in factories. She was assigned to study as a chemical technician. We all expected she'd get a job in Shanghai once she finished her studies. However, after she graduated in 1975 she was ordered to go to a factory in Anhui. My mother was furious. She'd had enough. She said: "I'm good enough to be a Party member. I've already sent three of my children to the countryside. My last child is staying here."

The woman in the Educated Youth Office was such a bitch. She had a stone-hard face and used to stare at me with ice-cold eyes. I was so intimidated by her. Every time I went to see her my legs shook, my mouth dried up and my voice cracked. Hoping that she might give up if I made a nuisance of myself, I showed up in her office twice a week. But she never changed her expression, and she refused to budge. I was the one who cracked.

At home, I started crying uncontrollably. The only thing that prevented me from having a complete nervous breakdown was my youngest sister. She was stronger than I. Later, she started going to the office with me.

In 1978, a returned student replaced the woman at the office. He told me he would solve my sister's problem, and mine too. Two months later, my sister got a job in a chemical factory, and I was assigned to a neighborhood factory. The next year my father took early retirement. One of my other sisters returned to Shanghai to take over his job.

Three years at home had changed me entirely. The endless waiting, the repeated humiliation and the defeat afterwards had sapped my strength. In the past, even though I was uncertain about the future, I still had a kind of dream and some hope in my heart. Now all I could do was try to survive.

I got married soon after I was assigned my job. My husband's grandma lived next door to us. He moved in with her after his parents got into trouble at the beginning of the Cultural Revolution. We got to know each other quite well. He went to the country the year before me. He began sending me love letters with lots of brotherly advice, such as: "Eat more." "Don't exhaust yourself." As soon as I was officially resettled in Shanghai I sent a telegraph to his farm: "Get a marriage permit and come to Shanghai." Within two weeks we were married.

Neither his family nor mine had anywhere for us to live. We rented a room from a peasant in the suburbs. Ten months later my son was born. My husband's farm let him work on their boat, which came to Shanghai once a month. So he was able to visit me five days each month.

It was a difficult time for me. No matter the weather, six days a week I had to get up at five o'clock in the morning, wake my baby son, get him ready and leave home before six so I could get to my workplace by seven-thirty. The bus was always crowded. I had to struggle on and off by myself and then ask the other passengers to pass the baby through the window. My child was always so good. As soon as he could, he'd walk to the bus stop with me. It would take us at least 15 minutes.

After three years, my work unit finally managed to get me an 8 square meter room in which to live. There was a critical housing shortage at the time because all the returned students were starting families. Luckily for me, the Chairman of our Workers' Union was a cadre with a golden heart. She spent all her time trying to help workers. Without her I wouldn't even have this tiny room.

For the first ten years of my employment my factory did fine. It expanded in size and developed its own product: the Changfeng hair dryer. During the first three years we were paid 24 yuan a month. Later, piecework was introduced. I worked overtime every week. By 1990 our factory was making good money.

Then, managers decided to purchase some land in Pudong and build a new factory on the site. It turned out to be a fatal error. At the time, we workers welcomed the move because we were assured we would get a better working environment. We were also told we would get subsidized hot lunches and a nursery for our children. Factory managers promised us they would provide transportation so we could get to our new workplace.

Soon after the new factory was completed however, township and village enterprises began to undercut our prices. Some of our technicians left for better-paid jobs. Management gave up quickly. By the middle of 1993 we were told that those who had a big stomach should eat more and those with small stomachs would have to eat less. Let a few get rich first. At a hastily called meeting we were bluntly informed that some of us would "get rice" [keep their jobs] and the rest of us would have to "eat porridge" [lose their jobs].

Everyone was told to write a self-evaluation and beg for a chance to be retained. Management called this: "Strive for and Compete for a Position" (*jingzheng shanggang*). But the purpose of this exercise was to humiliate and degrade us – to make us feel that if we were dismissed it would be our own fault. The decision about whom to keep and whom to fire had already been made.

I woke up one night and couldn't keep back the tears. My son slept by my bedside in a cot I'd bought when he was 6 years old. Now he was 12. I thought to myself: What kind of future is he likely to have? I was pretty sure I was on the "black list" of workers about to be terminated. I'd worked in this factory for more than ten years. It was the only job and life I knew.

I went to see the boss and talked him into letting me work in our factory's retail outlet. I knew he was hesitant because I was too old and plain looking to be a good saleswoman. He needed a young and pretty girl for the job. But I argued that my knowledge of our products should outweigh the problem of age and appearance. He finally accepted my terms. The factory would pay me 140 yuan a month, and I could take a commission on sales

I took this new job very seriously. The first year I managed to earn 400–500 yuan a month. My main customers were state-owned enterprises. They bought hair dryers for workers as rewards or as gifts.

But my job didn't last. By the end of 1995 our factory was forced to shut down completely. Since then I've tried all kinds of work. My latest venture is selling magazines in hospitals. I've a friend who works as a carrier in the postal service. She lets me borrow her uniform. Some hospitals permit people in postal uniforms to sell magazines to their patients. Others don't. Often, I'm chased away. I make very little money, but it's better than nothing.

The only thing I care about in the world is my son. He's studied fine arts since the age of five. He was accepted by a middle school that specializes in music and art. My hope is that he'll be able to get some kind of scholarship for a college education. I know I won't have enough money to pay for him to go to university.

My husband and I have our own separate lives. Since he returned to

Shanghai in 1981 he's not found a steady job. Now he deals in the black market. When he makes money he spends it all. When it's gone he's miserable. We stay together because we've no hope of finding anyone else. Basically, we're finished.

That's my life. You can talk to my husband if you want.

14 Hong Yongsheng, male: historian

I've been to America once – in 1992 when I spent three months at the University of Hawaii. I worked with a professor from the Institute of Far East Studies on *The Book of Changes*. That's my specialty. Last year, I published a book here called *Foreign Studies on The Book of Changes*.

Three months in Hawaii don't qualify me as an expert on the United States. I can only tell you how I felt when I was there. I was constantly reminded how lucky the American people are. Certain places do seem to show God's capacity for kindness. Hawaii has the most pleasant climate I've ever experienced. And, to my great surprise, there are no mosquitoes! I grew up in Shanghai, and the only other place I know is northern China, where nature is very harsh. For me, three months in Hawaii were like a Disneyworld vacation.

My wife wrote to me regularly. There were two main topics of discussion. One had to do with our little girl, and the other was whether I should return to China. I could have stayed in America – either legally or illegally, as do many visiting Chinese scholars. The university was willing to extend my visit. But I had to acknowledge that if I stayed in America illegally I would no longer be on vacation. I asked myself: did I want to sacrifice my career for a menial job in a Chinese restaurant? Besides, I didn't really belong in America. My roots are in this country. So I came back.

I come from a very poor family. Until 1953, when he became jobless, my father owned a tiny liquor store. The "store" was actually just a booth with a counter and several shelves set up in our family room.

I was the first son. Two brothers arrived later. Mother washed clothes for several families in the neighborhood. It was hard work, especially in winter. I always thought her hands were unusually large. In fact, they were permanently swollen because they were in cold water most of the time.

In 1957, the government tried to send some urban dwellers to the countryside. They targeted surplus residents (*xiansan renyuan*) such as my parents who didn't have formal employment. About a dozen families were transferred from our neighborhood to a village in Qingpu, a county outside Shanghai.

We traveled overnight in a small steamboat. I was five years old, and the river seemed very big and dark. Actually, it was only a small canal. Qingpu is water country. In those days you went about by boat. I wasn't a bit excited because I could sense how anxious and unhappy my parents were. Mother had wept and cursed as she'd packed our belongings.

My experiences in the countryside were immediate and vivid. During my first week I learnt about sex and death.

My parents and I shared one big storage room with two other families. Because I was in a strange place I was quite restless during the night. The couple next to my bed woke me up on several occasions. It didn't take me long to figure out what they were doing.

I quickly made friends with boys from the village. They liked to dig up abandoned graves. I followed them around and saw the skulls they'd found. These gave me nightmares. Later, I connected these rotten skulls with the fate of a boy who'd drowned in the river. This kind of incident happened often in the countryside because small kids were left to wander around by themselves. Children would go out to play or to wash in the river and never come back.

On one occasion I nearly drowned too. I'd followed the village boys to an abandoned temple. We had to cross a canal. I couldn't swim, but this didn't stop me from plunging ahead. In a second, I was under water, choking. A kid a year older than I gave me a push back to the shore. He saved my life. I didn't dare tell my parents what had happened.

My family lived in Qingpu County for about eight years. During this period I was in and out of six different schools. It was only in the last couple of years that my parents managed to settle down in Zhujiazhuang, a town near Lake Dingshan. There, I was able to go to school regularly. All the other village schools I attended had one thing in common: a single classroom containing children from the first to the sixth grade. The teachers would circulate from group to group, assigning various lessons. This gave me the opportunity to listen to what the others were doing. When I was in second grade I was already studying with the kids from the fifth grade.

I was particularly fond of one teacher. Every morning, he would take out a book and read stories for an hour. Sometimes it was a short story from *Harvest* literature magazine; at other times it was a long novel. Later, when I became a schoolteacher I did the same thing for my students. Every day, I picked a story from the Hans Christian Andersen collection. The children were so fond of these tales that I could easily control them just by warning them they might be banished from the next story-telling session.

The village schools I attended were primitive and backward. But, in certain respects, they resembled the private tutoring schools of old China. Rural teachers could teach whatever they wanted, and the kids certainly weren't under any academic pressure. I learnt something in those schools I've treasured all my life: a free and independent spirit of learning.

During my family's time in the countryside we often didn't have enough to eat. Father would dry edible plants and herbs, grind them, and mix them with flour. I thought this was quite creative of him. Sometimes, my parents would bring home baskets of carrots. We would wash them, slice them up, and put them out to dry. Then we would have carrots every day for weeks on end. When there was rice for dinner father and I were always served first. Mother made it clear that I was more important than my two younger brothers. It was taken for granted I would be the pride of the family.

In 1965, my father decided that he would appeal to the authorities to let him come back to Shanghai. But the request was denied. Finally, father and mother decided to return anyway, and we rented a small room in which to live. Mother took in laundry again. Father did all sorts of odd jobs. Among other things, he worked as a day laborer and as a stevedore. My brothers and I couldn't go to school because we weren't registered as city residents. Near our home was a key elementary school. I used to watch the kids through the fence and feel very despondent.

By that time, I'd already developed an interest in history and in classical literature. My uncle used to take me to Fuzhou Road, and we would spend the afternoon in the Bookstore of Chinese Classics and in the Cultural Relics Store. I would find a quiet corner and sit and read for the whole afternoon.

So when the Cultural Revolution began, I wasn't in school. At first, I really didn't understand what was happening. However, my parents were delighted by the sudden turn of events and joined others in the street to shout "Down with the Capitalist Roaders!" In the evenings they went to political meetings where they accused Party cadres of oppressing the masses.

At one such event mother broke down completely. She told everyone that officials in Shanghai had accused our family of taking rations away from city folk. She said that when we'd been ordered out of the city I'd burst into tears and told the authorities I could get by on tap water.

Actually, my parents weren't in the slightest bit political, but they hated the bureaucrats who'd sent them to Qingpu. The Cultural Revolution gave them a chance to voice their grievances. I don't see anything wrong with this. Before the Cultural Revolution Party officials often treated people such as my parents with indifference and contempt.

Looking back, I would say that the Cultural Revolution didn't significantly alter my family's situation. We did get our city registration status back in 1967. But, apart from that, our lives were unchanged. Before the Cultural Revolution we were poor and powerless. Afterwards, it was the same. If Mao wanted to bring democracy to the masses he failed.

I should have been in the class of 1968. However, as I hadn't formally graduated from an elementary school, the authorities decided I should be classified as a sixth grader. You might wonder why they bothered to make such a ruling, considering no schools were open at the time.

But the decision did have a major impact on my life. Instead of going to the countryside like the rest of the 1968 class, I was assigned in 1971 to a factory in Henan province. The factory was built by the Shanghai Steam Engine Plant to help develop heavy industry inland. It was staffed exclusively by Shanghainese.

I enrolled for a year's training in the Shanghai Steam Engine Plant, and, in 1972, I took the train heading north to Henan. I was singing and smiling all the way. I'd always wanted to go to northern China – the birthplace of our nation. Henan was rich in history. Could any other place have offered me so much?

For the first time ever I was given a desk of my own in a 14 square meter dormitory room I shared with a co-worker. How happy I was!

In Henan I made four good friends – all a bit older than I. One studied Chinese water painting, one learned English and the other two, like myself, were fond of classics and history. Later, three of us were appointed teachers in the factory's elementary school. We spent weekends and school holidays walking in the countryside and climbing mountains.

During my eight years in Henan province I visited nearly all the important historical sites. My friends and I also composed classical poems. I thought about seventy-five of mine were good enough to keep. I still have them. After I left Henan I stopped composing poetry, but now I've started again. Classical poetry best expresses my current mood.

I loved the time I spent in Henan. This vast land generously opened up to me its fullness of history, its space of imagination and its humanity. I love the people of northern China. They've inherited more of what is truly Chinese than the people of southern provinces, which were long influenced by alien cultures.

By 1978, I felt it was time for me to leave Henan. I chose Shandong province as my next destination: another important wellspring of Chinese culture. I took the College Entrance Examination and applied to the History Department in Shandong University. Unfortunately, I failed the political study and foreign language exams. I wasn't too upset because I was so sure of myself. However, it made me lose interest in studying as an undergraduate. I decided that if I ever wanted to go to university I would apply directly to graduate programs. I never took the College Entrance Examination again.

I started publishing some articles on Chinese history. Because of these, I was invited to lecture at history and sociology seminars organized by the Shanghai Academy of Social Sciences. I left the factory in Henan and moved back to Shanghai in 1980.

During this period I applied to several universities, but I was consistently rejected because I had no baccalaureate degree. Finally, in 1986, I was admitted as a graduate student in the Chinese Philosophy Institute at the Shanghai Academy of Social Sciences. In my entrance exams, I got the highest scores on all subjects, except political study. During my interview I was asked a couple of questions about Marxism. I talked non-stop for half an hour, trying to make a good impression. The examiners let me pass. Later, I was told that the chief examiner knew next to nothing about Marxism. Just as well!

I graduated in the summer of 1989. I was still a student when the student demonstrations broke out in the spring of that year.

The previous year I'd been a visiting student at Beijing University so I was quite involved in the events leading up to the occupation of Tiananmen Square. I had quite a few reservations about some of the student leaders.

In 1988, Beijing University was very lively. Students got together nearly every evening. The main topic of discussion was gossip about high-ranking officials. These top leaders were ridiculed for their ignorance and stupidity. The students believed the future was theirs. They were frustrated and felt they were not being taken seriously. They talked grandiosely and rather stupidly, making comments such as: "Today I study, tomorrow I save China." The following year this kind of attitude surfaced in the students' utter contempt for the government and in their aloof and elitist attitude towards the masses.

At the beginning of the 1989 student movement I was just an observer. However, on April 26, 1989, a *People's Daily* editorial declared that the students were "counter-revolutionaries," and, three weeks later, the government imposed martial law in the capital. This made me see things in a different light. I joined the demonstrations in Shanghai, and I signed my name and my wife's and child's names on petitions that opposed the official pronouncements about the students.

What really scared the government in 1989 was the emergence of independent workers' and students' political organizations that began to cooperate. This was unprecedented. It reminded the government of what was happening in Eastern Europe. It had to take a hard line.

We don't really know all that happened in Beijing on June 4, 1989. We got the news through the *Voice of America* and, of course, through the official media. On June 6 and 7, thousands of students and civilians in Shanghai held a memorial service in People's Square for those who'd died in Beijing. All traffic stopped for two days. Busses were left on intersections to block all roads leading to People's Square.

People were very anxious about the students' safety. Rumors spread that soldiers were moving towards Shanghai. People set up barricades and stopped trucks loaded with members of the Workers' Militia.[1]

Zhu Rongji [then Mayor of Shanghai, who became Chinese Premier in 1998] behaved very intelligently. He did what was necessary to defuse the situation. Basically, he gave everyone a chance to let off steam. But he insisted on mustering the Workers' Militia. These soldiers were armed with nothing but a helmet on their head. Nonetheless, the helmet was a symbol of authority and power. At first, people identified Militia members with the government and pelted them with objects. The Militia were caught in a bad situation. They'd been ordered not to let workers assemble in the streets.

By June 10 the street demonstrations in Shanghai came to an end.

Now you probably feel no trace of the excitement we experienced in 1989. There's nothing left. Nobody's interested in anything except making money. Wang Dan's sentencing didn't even cause a ripple among the students in Shanghai.[2] The market economy has dissolved people's unity and ended their commitment to social causes.

However, the market economy unexpectedly and positively impacted social science. Articles that are creative and independent are much more likely to be published now. No one's interested in official propaganda. This creates a good climate for us. We can say very critical things as long as it's phrased in academic terms. Read some of our articles for yourself. They're quite bold.

What matters to me are my own personal beliefs and standards. I think there's something deeper and wider than our limited life experiences. I've named this room "The Room of the Three Happinesses": Spiritual Happiness (my intellectual life); Physical Happiness (my family's life, our immediate environment); and Future Happiness (my child's life). I'm quite content, let me say.

Notes

1   Somewhat equivalent to the National Guard in the United States.
2   Wang Dan, a student leader during the protests in 1989, was given an eleven-year sentence on October 30, 1996. He was convicted of conspiring to subvert the government.
    On April 19, 1998, Wang Dan was put on an airplane to the United States for "medical treatment."

15 Zhang Aixiang, female: small business owner

My husband's putting me on the spot. I guess he's right to say he can't tell you about his life without talking about me. We've been together a long time.

My father was a peasant from Shandong province. He joined the Liberation Army in the early 1940s. In 1958, he answered the Party's call to transform the "Great Northern Wilderness" (*beidahuang*) and, together with thousands of others, he moved his family to Heilongjiang. Father could've got a job in the county town but he got into an argument with his superiors over his job assignment. In a rage, he decided that he would settle in a remote village at the far northern edge of the province and become a simple peasant.

The village had about twenty families who lived in a mountainous area at the edge of a forest. The trees were so dense you couldn't even see your neighbor's house. At the time, I was 6, and I had an 8-year-old sister and a 3-year-old brother.

I wasn't able to go to school until I was nine. Because my mother had to work as a laborer I had to take my small brother and a new baby sister with me. My brother wasn't too bad, but my baby sister was a lot of trouble. She cried one minute and wet herself the next. It disrupted the class. When I complained to my mother she decided it would be best if I quit school. I wept, but I had to obey.

After I'd stopped going to school about a month, the teacher came to our home. He wanted me to return. "Come back," he said. "You can bring as many brothers and sisters as you want. We're all very poor in this village so it is all the more important that you learn."

The school was a one-room cabin. The teacher let me have a table to myself, so my little brother and sister could sit on either side of me. Altogether, I had six years of schooling.

When the first students from Shanghai arrived in our village in 1968 I was already a full-time laborer. By this time my mother had given birth to two more sisters. Now, we were a large family with six children.

Like everyone else, I was very excited about the new settlers. We used to cluster around the doors of the students' homes, peeking and chatting.

Later, the students chose some villagers to be their friends. I became a frequent visitor to their collective households.

My husband came to the village with his sister. I was his sister's friend first. In 1970, I was appointed the first woman team leader in the village, and my future husband became the accountant for our work team.

The villagers chose me to be their leader because I had a reputation as an "iron girl" (*tieguniang*). I worked as hard as the men. After I became team leader I worked even harder. In autumn, we cut grass to prepare the winter food for our animals. If a male laborer cut 100 bundles of grass I'd cut 110 – no matter how long it took. My parents said most people tried to get away from work but they had to try to get *me* away from work.

I remember one incident in particular. I was harvesting beans in the field, and it was getting late. My father came to check on me. He tried to pick up a bundle of beanstalks I'd cut, but he couldn't lift it. He took off his shoe and started beating me. "You work as if you don't want to live anymore," he cried. "You stupid little fool! Don't you know how to take care of yourself. If you're injured what are we going to do?" He felt he had to hit me to get my attention.

But I was born like that. I didn't change. People liked me, and thought of me as a hardworking and trustworthy person. I joined the Party when I was 19 years old. The following year I became Party Secretary of our brigade.

My husband and I liked each other the first time we met. We were both 16 at the time. I was a peasant and he was the city boy. But it wasn't until six years later that Chui and I opened our hearts to each other. That year his sister left the village to attend a college in the provincial city. I asked Chui if he was going to leave too. "No," he replied, "I want to stay here with you."

In 1977, before Chui and I could plan our wedding, the students in the village began to return to their families in Shanghai. A couple of them abandoned their peasant girlfriends and boyfriends. My husband was his family's only son. His parents put a lot of pressure on him to go back home. Chui's mother was planning to take early retirement so her son could replace her.

My parents were in panic. They warned me that I should not allow Chui to return to Shanghai. "If you let him go," they warned, "it will be the end of you. You'll be abandoned and humiliated and our family will never be able to hold up its head again. No other man will want a rejected woman."

I knew that Chui wanted to go back to Shanghai, and I also realized that, if I asked him to stay at the village, he probably would. I cried and cried. I never doubted that it was my duty to put him first. Finally, Chui did leave, but he also promised he'd come back to marry me.

My parents thought it was all over. They threw my belongings out of their home and ordered me to leave. They weren't going to shelter a disgraced daughter.

I picked up my stuff and moved into the brigade office. I recognized my parents probably were right and that, sooner or later, I'd get a goodbye letter from Chui. But I also realized it was pointless for me to try to force myself on him.

A month passed. One day I walked into the office and found that all my belongings had gone. My mother had sent my sisters to move me back home. I went to see my parents. They just said: "Now, please, do forget him."

Chui would send me letters often twice a month. In every one, he would repeat his promise that he was going to return to marry me. In 1980, almost two years after he had left the village, Chui asked me to come to Shanghai before the New Year. He wanted us to get married the day after the New Year's Celebrations. Again, my parents were infuriated. "It's not possible," my father raged. "How can my daughter go to her husband's family without a proper greeting? It's embarrassing." I felt the same way. How could I go to Chui's home all by myself?

But Chui begged me not to worry. He didn't have the time or the money to travel to our village. If I could just forget about the ritual and the costume, he told me, we soon would be husband and wife. So I said goodbye to my parents and arrived in Shanghai on my twenty-eighth birthday. Two weeks later, Chui and I were married.

It was obvious no one in Chiu's family approved of the match. I was greeted coldly by his family. We rented a place in a poor neighborhood and ate with Chui's parents. Two months later I was pregnant.

Shanghai's winter is very damp as well as cold – something I'd never experienced before. During winters in Shanghai it's the same temperature inside and outside the house. We were spared this in Heilongjiang because, there, all the houses are heated in winter. I couldn't speak the Shanghai dialect and was ignored by my in-laws. It was hard to sit with them at the dinner table as a total stranger. I wanted to cook meals for Chui and myself, even though it would have cost more. I also wanted to work – no matter what kind of job it was.

I didn't have Shanghai resident registration, so I couldn't be formally employed. The only jobs I could find were temporary. I had to beg for them. I did all kinds of work. But no matter what I did I was always given the worst job and paid the least. I was the scapegoat whenever things went wrong. "Crows are black wherever they go."

One boss gave me extra work during the lunch break. Other people were resting, while I was cleaning, sweeping and stacking things. I said to the boss: "You take advantage of me because I'm a temporary worker."

"That's right," he patiently explained. "That's how it works."

At home, I was often in tears. After my daughter was born the situation only got worse. My job paid less than 20 yuan a month. Our income couldn't support us. My mother-in-law's face got grimmer and grimmer.

One day, I said that I would like to go back to my village. This drew an immediate reaction. "Why don't you get a divorce?" my mother-in-law said. "You've created a lot of difficulties. Go back to Heilongjiang and find someone suitable for you. Chui can find a wife with Shanghai resident registration. You'd both be happier." I felt as if I was stabbed in the heart.

I ran back home and told Chui what his mother had said. He was very angry: "If she says this again," he said, "you can tell her that, wherever you go, I'll go with you." Later, he told his mother the same thing: "Don't turn me into a disobedient son. I'll never leave her." The topic of divorce was dropped.

I missed my family and the village very much. Sometimes in the street I heard people speaking the northeastern dialect (*dongbei hua*), and I would follow them to listen to the familiar and sweet sounds of my own tongue. In 1984, I did go back to the village with my husband and daughter. My child and I stayed for eight months. Then, something unexpected happened.

I became pregnant again. But I didn't realize it until four months later. I'd always had irregular periods. When my parents found out they were delighted. They wanted me to have the baby. I wrote to my husband – who'd gone back to Shanghai by this time – to give him the news. He and his parents were shocked. A letter arrived urging me to have an abortion.

I wanted to keep the baby, and my family supported me. "Give birth here," they told me. "No one in Shanghai will know. We'll raise the child if you can't." In Shanghai, a second pregnancy would have caused problems. But not in the village.

For several days, I debated with myself whether to have the baby. Sometimes I felt I wanted it and other days I worried about how I would cope. Time passed. The pregnancy entered its eighth month, and, by then, of course, it was almost impossible to abort the child.

Finally, my father-in-law sent me his verdict. He said that I was very foolish to keep the baby since my husband and I couldn't provide for our first child. My parents saw his letter and changed their minds. If I was still going to be his daughter-in-law, they said, I'd better obey him. Otherwise life would be very difficult for me.

I wrote to Chui and asked him to tell me face-to-face what to do. When Chui arrived in the village he was silent for a while. Then he exploded: "Why did you ask me to come?" he cried. "Now, I have to order you to have an abortion. Otherwise, how could I face my parents? If I'm not here I don't see and I don't know. You could have had the baby." He broke into tears.

The county family planning office said that it would be dangerous for me to have an abortion. They told me they would inform Shanghai that the local office had given me permission to have my child. They said that, since Chui and I were both Party members, we wouldn't be punished.

However, the pressure from Chui's family was unrelenting. He was reminded, once again, what a mistake he'd made to marry a peasant girl. I couldn't stand his sad and miserable face anymore, so I gave in. If I had to die I would. I felt I just didn't care any more.

The county hospital performed the abortion. I don't want to recall that day. I was in a coma for two days. Later, the nurse told me that my husband had passed out when he saw that the baby had thick, shining black hair. Chui didn't eat, sleep or talk until I came to. No one will ever understand how we felt. [She breaks down for a while].

Two months later I went back to Shanghai. I was still weak. But I had to look for work again. I heard that schools were trying to find people who could type their text materials. I thought I could get a typewriter and work at home. It was a good idea, but I didn't have the 700 yuan I needed for the typewriter.

My sister-in-law heard about my dilemma. She talked to her mother. One evening she came to our home with a typewriter. My mother-in-law had bought it for us. I was a bit moved.

The first month I only made 16 yuan and 80 cents (US$5.25). I typed very slowly, spending most of my time looking for characters. The second month I made more than 80 yuan. Gradually, I got some steady customers. However, half a year later, I figured out what I was doing wrong.

I was paid a maximum 1.20 yuan per page of typing – more often, 80 cents a page. I had to work almost non-stop to type 100 pages a month. But the people who did the printing were paid 3 cents per page. They were able to earn half my monthly income in one day. I decided I should do the printing as well as the typing. This meant I had to buy a cylinder press.

My husband said: "You're standing on top of one mountain and now you want to climb another. Why don't you just continue with what you are doing." But I insisted. I rented an old press to give it a try. As soon as I got this machine Chui became very supportive. He fixed and oiled it for me.

My first big job was to make 220 copies of a fifty-page lecture I first had to type. I worked half a month to finish the typing, and then printed and bound the copies in a week. When I delivered these copies I was paid 800 yuan. Can you imagine how I felt? I'd never seen so much money in my entire life.

I said to my husband: "800 yuan has made me crazy. I wonder if we could ever make 10,000?" I spent half my earnings on a new printing machine, and, over the next two months, I paid my mother-in-law back for the typewriter.

Six months later business started slowing down. People had begun to switch to power-driven printing presses. Several of my customers told me that they would give their business to someone else unless I could get one of these machines.

Either I had to find 12,000 yuan to buy a new printing press or I would have to acknowledge that my business had failed. I didn't have the money. All I had was 2,000 yuan. It was 1987. I thought at the time that no one could possibly have that much money.

It was summer. In the evening, everybody went outside to get some cool air. Some neighbors noticed my unhappy face. "What's wrong?" they asked. "You're so quiet." I told them my problem. "How much are you short?" they replied. "Maybe we can help."

I didn't really expect any assistance, but, to my surprise, two of these neighbors – one a truck driver, the other a retired worker – offered to lend me 3,000 and 4,000 yuan respectively. With almost 10,000 yuan in hand, I went to my in-laws for help. They came up with the rest of the money.

I turned half of our room into a workshop and moved the new machine in. I set out immediately to get orders. For the next three years my husband and I worked day and night. The printing press was never shut off. I worked from seven-thirty in the morning until one-thirty a.m. the following day. My husband had his regular job from eight to five. After dinner he went to bed and slept until one. Then he worked from half past one until seven-thirty.

Three years later we got three more presses and my two sisters came to work for me. I also hired two additional workers. The business moved to a four-room house. In my best year I made nearly 100,000 yuan. I bought a three-bedroom apartment.

My in-laws treat me quite differently. Now they smile a lot. Although I'll never be close to them I try to be fair. When air conditioners came on the market I put one in our new apartment. I cannot stand the summer heat in Shanghai. As I enjoyed the cool air I thought of my husband's parents. I told Chui we should buy one for them too. He couldn't believe his ears. "Are you serious?" he kept asking. He knows how much humiliation and pain I suffered because of them. Finally, he was convinced I was sincere. He was very excited. The next day he got up very early and stood in line for hours to buy a Japanese air conditioner.

People tell me I'm too kind to be a good businesswoman. I've helped seven other people open their own printing shops. "I've never seen anything so stupid," I was told. I did, of course, lose some business to those I helped. However, if there's enough rice everyone should get a bite. Maybe it's not how you should think if you want to run a business.

I've had a lot to worry about recently. We've been notified that we'll have to move our workshop. The new superhighway is going to run right through it. I've lived in uncertainty for two years. We were never sure what was going to happen. I prayed that the road would go a bit left so our print shop would be spared.

Now, I have to shut down – temporarily at least. Even if I find a new place my business will be cut in half. I get very little compensation from the government. It's difficult for people like me to get any assistance or consideration from the authorities. When you're in the way they move you out, regardless of the losses you suffer.

Is there any way you could help?

16 Lin Yuling, male: publishing editor

I could talk three days and three nights about the Cultural Revolution. It was the most memorable period of my life.

I was born in 1944. Because I was asthmatic I was in and out of hospital as a child. I lost a lot of schooling as a result. Formally, I was a member of the 1966 graduation class, but, actually, I was a lot older than the others.

My father had owned a tiny factory that had gone bankrupt just before liberation. Nonetheless, he was a former capitalist and that's what was officially recorded about our family.

The Cultural Revolution didn't take me by surprise because, for me, many of its traits were foreshadowed. For instance, by 1963 few students from "bad" family backgrounds were allowed to go to top universities. Beijing University accepted one of my classmates, whose scores were poor, because she'd claimed her family was "lower peasant." I'd always been keen on Chinese history, but I realized it was unlikely any good university would offer me a place.

I was acutely aware of the unfairness of these political categorizations because my family was very poor. Father worked in a factory. We'd had to pawn some of our possessions because his salary couldn't support four children. That's how ridiculous the whole thing was.

Still, the Party's policy was subtle because the door to advancement was not completely slammed in our faces. Instead, we were told that, while family background did matter, individual performance also could make a difference (*jiang chengfen, zhong zhai biaoxian*). We were the same as the whites and the blacks in America. Like us, blacks were told they could become honorary whites so long as their behavior was flawless.

Everyone tried to conform. We all became Young Pioneers, then members of the Youth League. Basically, we were all cut from the same cloth.

In November 1965, Yao Wenyuan's article "On the Play 'The Dismissal of Hai Rui from Office'" was published in the *Wenhui Daily*. Yao [later, one of the "Gang of Four"] was a notorious leftist and well known for trying to politicize everything. Even so, I was shocked at the severity of his attack. I said to myself: "Yao's trying to get Wu Han [author of the play] executed."[1]

Yao's article lit a fire under the intellectuals, and many of them wrote articles both for and against the play. What no one understood at the time was that Yao's article was "bait" that was intended to entice the "snakes" out of their holes.

One middle-school student, called Ma Jie, sent a letter to the *Wenhui Daily*, arguing that an uncorrupted feudal landlord and official such as Hai Rui was still better than a corrupt communist official. I mulled over Ma's letter, found I agreed with it wholeheartedly, and began to draft my own essay entitled: "In Response to Yao's 'On the Play "The Dismissal of Hai Rui from Office"'." When I'd finished a week later it was 9,000 words long. Two of my classmates – both from working-class families – read the essay and agreed with it 100 percent. In fact, they were so enthusiastic about it they took it in person to the *Wenhui Daily* and insisted it be printed.

The newspaper rejected my scribblings. Before long, though, everyone had heard about my efforts to get published. At school, one teacher said to me sadly: "Young people don't understand how high the sky is nor how deep is the earth" (*tiangao dihou*). Needless to say I was lucky my writings were not widely distributed. Among other things I'd called Yao "an expert in fabrication and distortion." That, in itself, would have been more than enough to get me into a whole heap of trouble.

I would say that when the Cultural Revolution began about 98 percent of students in Shanghai were followers, not instigators. By contrast, Beijing contained a high number of families headed by high-ranking Party members. Students there were politically well informed and willing to take the initiative. Shanghai students had to follow a movement that had begun elsewhere. They couldn't initiate political struggle because they didn't really understand what was going on. I was one of the few who was able to put things in historical context. I'd read many books on the history of the Chinese Communist Party, so I could recognize that the current upheavals were but the latest of several "left-mongering" phases.

In August [1966], people from my father's work unit raided our home. They raked through my parents' belongings but saw nothing there worth confiscating. All they found in my mother's money-box were receipts from pawnshops. Finally, they had to satisfy themselves by carting off about 500 books I'd bought over the years.

Those books were my life. I'd spent hours in bookstores deciding what I should purchase with the small allowance my parents gave me. I was left with just three volumes – a collection of Sándor Petöfi's poetry and two of Nikolay Gogol's novels. That was about the only time in my life I cried.

I was so upset I fell ill the next day and had to be hospitalized again. I spent two months in bed, paralyzed with severe asthma. My little sister looked after me. We both missed the Great Exchange. But I didn't care.

From the moment they took my books away I was finished with the lot of them forever.

Because of my hostile attitude I soon became estranged from most of my friends. Let me give you an example. I really liked one girl in my class. One day, she came to my house attired in green army fatigues. When she began to lecture me on the importance of revolutionary action I ridiculed a verse students were singing at the time: "Beat wolves with sticks! Kill tigers with guns! To be a revolutionary you need Mao Zedong Thought!" "There's no logic," I objected. "How are these things related?"

When my young friend noticed what I was reading she became even more agitated. "We're living through a period of class struggle," she pointed out. "Why are you sitting at home reading Shakespeare?"

"What's wrong with Shakespeare?" I retorted. "He was good enough for Marx and Engels."

The girl left in a huff. The special feelings I had for her started to dissipate.

I noticed at the time that the most active and radical Red Guards tended to be those Youth League members who previously had been the most ardent conformists. At this earlier stage they were psychologically repressed because they'd forced themselves to obey all the rules. For them at least, the Cultural Revolution was a real liberation. Kids who'd been "pets" in the past were now the most enthusiastic about trashing authority.

In 1968, I was living at home as an unemployed youth. I had plenty of free time. I was lonely and depressed. Also, I was desperate for companionship. At the time, the bookstores had few books. Nonetheless, they were a good place to meet people who had some volumes to trade. I met some remarkable people in these shops. One was a Qinghua University student named Wang. After Wang had joined Kuai Dafu's Beijing organization "Jing Gang Mountain" he'd became suspicious about the real forces behind the Cultural Revolution. He'd returned to his hometown, Shanghai, to avoid the coming "bloodshed" as he put it. It was the first time I'd ever heard anyone use terms like "conspiracy" or "coup" to describe what was happening in the nation's capital.

Because of my association with Wang I came to know perhaps the most unforgettable person I ever met.

This was a very gentle looking man. I never asked him his age but it was obvious he was in his forties. I heard that he joined the Party when he was an English student at Beijing University just before liberation. He was ordered to spread revolutionary ideas by enrolling in the science department at another university. He didn't want to abandon his English studies but lacked the courage to explain this to the Party. So he returned to Shanghai and disappeared. Effectively, he voided his party membership. In 1957, he was declared a "rightist." I don't know why. My guess is that his disobedient past came back to haunt him. He was sent to a farm in

Xinjiang. After he contracted tuberculosis he was allowed to come back to Shanghai.

Wang and I often met this man in tearooms and took strolls with him. He never invited us to his home, nor did he visit ours. For a long time I knew him only by his family name – Zhu. It was clear he didn't want us to know about his past or his private life. Wang and I used to spend a lot of time just listening to him talk.

Zhu knew a lot about the Soviet Union and Eastern Europe. He could read the few foreign periodicals that were available at the time. Although these were mostly the newspapers or magazines of socialist or communist parties in Western Europe they did provide a window on the rest of the world. Zhu told us about Stalin's purges in Russia, "deStalinization," and the "Czech Spring." He said that 2,000 Rehabilitation Committees had been set up in Czechoslovakia. That really seemed to impress him. I think he was hoping the same thing would happen here.

About six months after I'd met Zhu a couple of Red Guards from my school appeared at my door. This was during the summer of 1968. "There's something we want to talk to you about," they said. I knew at once why they had come. A week earlier my neighbor, Chen, had been detained by the Red Guard organization at his school. Chen and I weren't close, but I'd trusted him enough to let him join Wang, Zhu and I a few times. Obviously, Chen had informed on us.

I was taken to an empty classroom at my school. As soon as I walked into the room someone stepped up and punched me in the face. The blow was so violent I blacked out for a moment. My nose was broken, and the blood poured out. They wanted me to confess all the counter-revolutionary crimes I'd committed. I was scared, but I wasn't going to give in that easily. I didn't know how much they knew already.

After a couple of hours they told me that Chen had already confessed and had agreed to help them arrest Wang. I was told we would go to Wang's home, where we would meet up with Chen. I think the Guards made up this story in order to get me to lead them to Wang. This would also trick Wang into believing I'd collaborated.

The evening was very humid. People were sitting in the street in order to get some air. I imagined Wang at home with his elderly parents, with no conception of what was about to happen. Wang was an only child. I wanted to cry. I took wrong turns, again and again, trying to postpone the ordeal.

When finally we arrived Wang was chatting with some neighbors. He pointed to his bare torso and calmly said: "Let me get dressed." He acted as if he was just going out with a few friends. He told his parents he would return in a couple of hours. That night Zhu was brought in also. I still don't know how they managed to get hold of him.

Wang and I were locked in a room for the night and guarded by a student. We were forbidden to talk to one another. Zhu was locked up elsewhere. When we saw him the next day he had two black eyes and bruises all over his body. He sat at a desk, hunched over a blank piece of paper in front of him. Every now and then, Guards shouted at him and struck him over the head. He didn't say a word, nor did he look at us. The whole time he was smoking cigarettes one after the other, just staring at the piece of paper. I kept looking at him, hoping he would make eye contact. But he never did.

I started writing my confession. I was prepared to go to jail and even die. I realized there was no longer any point denying what I'd said. I'd compared Mao to the First Qin Emperor, and Jiang Qing [Mao's wife] to Empress Wu. I'd rejected the Cultural Revolution. I was a black heart.

At last I finished and was allowed to go to bed. In the middle of the night shouting awakened me: "Someone has jumped from the building! Help us!"

Wang and I were rushed into the corridor and made to face the wall. I was shaking uncontrollably. I knew it was Zhu.

Zhu had jumped out of a third floor bathroom window. The window was quite high. He'd died instantly. Two of the students were visibly shaken. One seemed deeply disturbed. He kept saying to me: "I hit him once. Why did I do it? I wish I hadn't done it. I really wish I hadn't. Please don't do anything to yourself." I felt sorry for him. He was only 13 or 14 years old.

The following morning Wang's friends arrived in force to rescue him. They pretended to be from another Red Guard organization, and they showed the Guards who were holding us captive a piece of paper with a red seal on it. They said Wang had to be taken to his own school to be investigated. The ruse worked. I was imprisoned for another week.

The head of the Red Guard organization at my school was a real bastard. He wanted to establish the existence of a counter-revolutionary conspiracy so he could take credit for crushing it. Our file was sent to the Security Bureau, which refused to accept it. The police were unimpressed: "What's this about? Counter-revolutionary students? They're too young. Go away and get some education." Later, I learned that the Security Bureau was in chaos. No one was in charge. So I was released.

A Worker Propaganda Team was sent to our school to try to get hold of the situation. I was called in. The team leader, a middle-aged man, talked to me. He said: "If other people repeated what we said about Chairman Mao and the Party they would go to jail for at least five years. Shouldn't you be a bit more careful?"

I was startled he'd used the expression "we said," not "you said." I sensed he was sympathetic. My interrogator then suggested it was all the fault of Liu Shaoqi, the revisionist.[2] Apparently I was one of his victims.

I knew how to take a hint. So I wrote a long self-criticism and blamed everything on Liu Shaoqi.

After Zhu died I had nightmares. Night after night I would wake up in a cold sweat. It was too painful to get in touch with Wang. I didn't see him again for months.

Wang is now working at a university in America. Two years ago he wrote a long essay to commemorate Zhu. He called it "A Swan by the Stream that Runs Forever."

Zhu loved western poetry. Once, he showed us about thirty poems he'd translated. One of them was Charles Baudelaire's "The Swan." That's why Wang chose that title.

When I learned about Mao's death I hoped change would come but I never expected it would arrive so quickly.

One of my friends at the time was a schoolteacher. His school was located in a former church building. He lived in a tiny tool room in the church tower, where he'd listen to the BBC and to the Voice of America. One day, he told me and some others to come to his room. He said excitedly: "Something important has happened." Without waiting to find out what it was, we began to celebrate. We punched the air shouting "Good! Good!"

Our friend told us that the foreign broadcasting stations had announced that Jiang Qing, Zhang Chunqiao, Yao Wenyuan and Wang Hongwen [the "Gang of Four"] had just been arrested. This was a week before anyone else heard about it.

I don't think there'll ever be another Cultural Revolution. The more materialistic the Chinese become the less likely it is they'll ever follow a single man or party into such religious craziness.

Through millennia of Chinese imperial history we've had several dark periods. The Ming dynasty was one such epoch. But the black periods always produced a few extraordinary officials such as Hai Rui. When the Emperor went too far someone would stand up and tell him that the sages' teachings were so and so and that the ancestors' rule was such and such and that, in short, you don't measure up. There were always a few mandarins willing to throw off their "black gauze caps" and resign. In imperial times, "Heaven," other sages and the ancestors were all above the Emperor. The Confucian bureaucrats would call on these Powers whenever they were needed.

Above Mao there was nothing. Mao created the Party, the army and New China. There wasn't a single high official who could stand up to him. Mao was extraordinary. He exploited the weakness, the selfishness and the mediocrity of the rest of them. He turned himself into an unchallengeable Emperor.

Very few of us could have done it.

Recent developments in China give me some hope, but not a lot. We're now enjoying a kind of freedom that never existed before. As long as you don't organize secret societies or terrorist groups to overthrow the government you can swear at the leaders and do pretty much as you like. I suppose this is the maximum amount of freedom allowed by any state.

In 1989, the government had a reason to be scared. For the first time ever, Chinese workers tried to organize themselves outside the Party. The CCP found itself on one side of the conflict. The working class was on the other.

Workers have fewer rights today than before. Managers act as capitalists, with the full force of the state behind them. There's no higher power to stop them abusing their office.

There are many social issues that should be addressed today. Since the May Fourth movement Chinese literature has shown it's capable of looking at modernity critically from without. Lu Xun was the best of them. But look at the self-interested, egotistical, elitist and vulgar intellectuals who dominate China's literature today. They talk about "Degree Zero" writing – meaning no emotion, no critical insight and no thought. No one wants to follow in the steps of Leo Tolstoy or Romain Rolland, both of whom recognized that a writer must *first* develop a heart and a sense of right and wrong.

Writers today tend to fall into one of two groups. The first are interested only in money. They resemble the pornographers of the Ming and Qing dynasties, and they copy from Hong Kong and Taiwanese pop culture. I call their work "dropping-pants" literature. Basically, they're whores.

Jia Pingwa's *The Abandoned Capital* (*Feidu*) typifies the genre. With a mind full of dirty things, Jia belittles women in a manner worse than any of his predecessors. He depicts them as mannequins without "hearts or livers" (*xingan*) [incapable of thought or feeling]. He says all you need to know about women is that they crave sex.

I think the government is encouraging this kind of trash. It wants the masses to graze on the garbage of stupid stories, mindless violence and endless sex. This type of literature is called "non-lofty" (*fei chonggao hua*). It's valuable to the authorities because it's completely indifferent to political reality, social issues or human suffering.

Those in the second group of writers are interested only in themselves. They don't have the time for any other topic. Yesterday, we had "expressionists" and "modernists." Today, we have "postmodernists." Tomorrow, we'll endure whatever new fad western intellectuals inflict on us.

Among the narcissists are the so-called "feminists" – at least that's what they call themselves. Intellectuals such as Lin Bai and Hai Nan write about their disappointment with men, and they celebrate their lesbianism as if such feelings are worthy. But where's their awareness of the real issues facing Chinese women? Have these "feminists" ever laid eyes on the mothers who've lost their jobs? Do they care about the young girls who are sold and sexually exploited? Of course not. Such low types are not worth their attention.

If you study our literati you'll see how important heredity is in the power structure. At the top is the elite: the established big-name people and the writers from families well connected to political power. The sons or daughters of high officials chair almost all the regional Writers' Associations. So, different regions come under the domain of different fiefdoms. It's all quite feudal. People such as me, who come from a common background, can't compete.

My generation's era is now drawing to a close. Last year, I went to a reunion at my old high school, where once I was imprisoned. I noticed that the members of our class hadn't achieved that much. All that we possess are our faded recollections – often quite bitter.

Few of us had many opportunities for careers, education or lasting personal relations. Like those of many others of my generation, my marriage was one of convenience. My wife is a thoroughly decent woman. But we don't have anything in common except the dining table and the bed.

It's sad, but I can't pretend otherwise.

Notes

1 Wu Han, a historian, writer and the Vice-Mayor of Beijing published the play "The Dismissal of Hai Rui from Office" in 1961. Wu praised Hai Rui, a celebrated Ming dynasty official, for courageously opposing the Emperor's misrule. At the time, most intellectuals recognized that Wu's play was an allegorical treatment of Peng Dehuai's criticism of Mao during the Great Leap Forward (1958–1961).
2 Liu Shaoqi (1898–1969) was President of the People's Republic before the Cultural Revolution. In the early 1960s, he was widely regarded as Mao's successor, but he was later condemned as the "Number One Capitalist Roader" and dismissed from office. He died in prison of pneumonia.

17 Dai Buqing, male: unemployed worker

People often say that those with an easy childhood end up with a tough life. That's certainly true in my case.

I was the youngest of four sons. When I was a baby my 8- and 9-year-old brothers used to compete for the privilege of pushing me around in my pram. I was seen as special.

At school, my eagerness to follow all the rules made me very popular with my teachers. In the fourth grade I became leader of the Young Pioneers. My world was rosy. It was taken for granted I'd go to a good middle school and then to university. "Xiaodi (little brother) is academic material," my brothers used to say. They were convinced I'd become an engineer or a professor – someone important anyway

Only when you get to my age can you look back and see all the forks in your life. That's because, by then, everything has become history.

In 1969, I went to a farm in Jiangxi province. It was a good assignment. Jiangxi is a rice region, and, as a worker in a state-owned farm, I was paid monthly. My eldest and second-eldest brothers – both factory workers – had told me to stay at home, and had offered to support me. In order to take some of the pressure off me, my other brother had already left for a farm in Heilongjiang. But I wanted to go to the countryside. I didn't want people to believe I was a coward.

My first year at the farm was very tough. At the time, my ambition was to become a "commander of ducks" (*yasiling*). When I saw the duck herders driving their flocks with a long, dangling bamboo stick I decided this had to be the best and most romantic job a countryman could have. Actually, it's not that easy. In early spring, the water in the rice paddies is always freezing cold. Duck herders are in and out of the water all day and get chilblains and bleeding cracks all over their feet. Nonetheless, compared to the backbreaking work in the rice fields, the occupation of herder looked like paradise to me. Unfortunately, I never quite managed to get the position I wanted.

Instead, I worked as a laborer for two years. In the third winter, the whole unit was sent to dig irrigation ditches for the local commune. I was given the task of writing "battlefield" reports about enthusiastic and hardworking people. I submitted my first report in just three days. The Party Secretary of our commune was very impressed. He couldn't believe I'd come up with so many good stories so quickly. He decided I was too good to work as a ditch digger. So he borrowed me from the farm and put me to work as his propaganda secretary. I could hardly believe my luck.

I knew I would do very well in my new job because it fitted my personality. I could never be an official, but I'm a good assistant. I worked in the commune for over a year. Often, I had to accompany the commune cadres to remote settlements. One thing I can tell you is that cadres in those days were mostly good people – not like rural cadres today. They traveled by foot, by bicycle or, occasionally, by tractor. They ate "assigned meals" (*pafan*) provided by peasant families. The peasants were very poor. We usually were given rice and pickled vegetables.

I remember one incident in particular. I'd accompanied the head of the People's Militia, who was delivering goods to a village. The village leader took us to a peasant's home. This man gave rice to us and porridge to his children. The peasants were very traditional. You always gave the best you had to your guests. The head of the People's Militia felt very guilty about the children and left them half a bag of cookies he'd bought for his own daughter. In those days cookies were a rare and special treat.

After a year in the commune I went to farm headquarters to work for our Department of Public Affairs. During my seven years on the farm I spent just two years working in the fields. If things had remained as they were I'd probably have stayed on that farm, quite content. At the time, I never dreamt that, one day, the government would let all 20 million students return home.

But by 1977 everyone on my farm was trying to leave. Farm headquarters were filled with people making all kinds of demands and threats. Rumors were widespread: "Number Three Unit is out on strike." "Someone got hold of a gun, and demanded an official seal on his paper." Girls allowed to leave often were suspected of sleeping with someone in authority. At the time, there was a song called "Sacrifice your Youth (*qingchun*) [implying 'virginity'] to Your Superior (*shouzhang*)!"

One by one, most of the students left the farm. Dormitories were turned into pigpens. Like the others, I didn't want to be left behind, so I returned to Shanghai in 1979. I was eager to start a new life. I'd joined the Party in the countryside, and district officials in Shanghai arranged an office job for me. I worked once more for a Department of Public Affairs.

For a time I was happy. In 1984, I married another resettled student. Although our combined salaries were less than 80 yuan a month we looked forward to the future. I enrolled at an evening college to get a diploma in secretarial science. The district government paid my tuition.

Sometimes I think that in a country such as China personal efforts don't mean that much – particularly during periods of social upheaval. I believed

I was on the right track when I got my diploma. I thought it would give me better opportunities for promotion, not to mention job security.

By the middle of 1988, however, things didn't look so good. My wife's factory was in trouble and had started to lose orders to township and village enterprises. The district government began to cut its staff. I lost my public affairs job and was transferred to the District Government's Collective Enterprises Bureau. I was assigned to a bankrupt workshop and ordered to help save it.

None of us had a clue what to do. Finally, we decided to start a new business manufacturing stuffed toys. For a time everyone worked with blind enthusiasm. The female workers did the cutting and sewing, and the male workers ran around Shanghai trying to find buyers. But our efforts were fruitless. No one wanted the toys. The workshop was turned into a storage room.

A relative had gone to Japan two years earlier, and she agreed to help my wife enroll in a language school in Tokyo. Most Chinese use these schools to get a visa to enter Japan. As soon as they're settled in Tokyo they all look for work. My wife and I bought a signed document of financial sponsorship through a dealer so she could get a student's visa. It cost us 15,000 yuan on the black market.

My wife left China in the summer of 1989, just after the Tiananmen Square incident. Our daughter was only 3 years old. Obviously, the separation was hard on my wife. She's never talked much about it. She's tougher than I.

In 1993, I managed to get a temporary visa to visit my wife. I wanted to work too.

The day after I arrived in Tokyo my wife took me to some restaurants to look for a job. I got a job as a dishwasher in the first week. So my wife and I began a routine of working, eating and sleeping. Without our daughter, we had little else to do.

During the half year I stayed in Japan I never overcame the terrible, terrible loneliness. I missed my daughter so much that I was unable to go to sleep without talking to her in silence for a few minutes. I worked in the restaurant for about four months. When the expiry date on my visa arrived I told my wife I wanted to go home. She cried and wanted to come back also. But she couldn't. She'd decided to earn enough money so that, in the future, we'll have some security and be able to provide for our daughter. I really don't know how much money we'll need.

Sometimes, I hope my wife will write and say that enough is enough and that she's returning. I have no job now, and my daughter and I depend on the money she sends every month.

By now, I think, my daughter is used to life without a mother. She knows mummy's living overseas to make money.

I saw many sad people in Japan. The dependents of university students there are called *jiazu zhiza* (staying dependents). "Zhi" can mean "immovable" or "trapped" deer. Many of these dependents had a good education and a promising career in China. They'd sacrificed all this for a chance to work abroad. Many of them were between 25 to 40 – at a stage in their lives when they should have been developing their careers. I met quite a few Chinese in Tokyo with MA or PhD degrees who worked as dish-washers.

When I got back to Shanghai I found the workshop I'd tried to help had been turned into office rental property. All the workers had been sent home. There was no money left for pensions or medical expenses. My parents asked: "Why did you bother to come back? We were taking good care of Jinjin [their granddaughter]. There's no future here for you."

I'm still paying my monthly Party membership dues: half of 1 percent of the 275 yuan I receive every month for living expenses. As long as I make the payments I remain a member of the Communist Party. It's a joke. They still count me as a supporter of this "proletarian" party whose policies have impoverished and destroyed me.

18 Xu Xinhua, male: high-school principal

To me and to the rest of my generation the Cultural Revolution meant more than ten years of turmoil and personal hardship. Our lives are all quite different today, but one thing we have in common is that we're all marked by our early involvement in a great political movement.

Mao called on us to go to the countryside (*xia xiang*); Deng asked us to jump into the sea (*xia hai*) [become entrepreneurial]; and Jiang told us to get off our posts (*xia gang*) [let go of our state jobs]. It was a logical development. If there'd been no Cultural Revolution there wouldn't have been the need for capitalist economic reform.

In the 1960s and 1970s, society created and rewarded idealistic, romantic and energetic young people. Even though there was lots of suffering, hardship – and plain stupidity too – we got through that time all right. Now, we're middle-aged. I find today's social environment hostile. I don't think things are going too well for us.

I went to Heilongjiang in 1968. I wasn't given much choice. My two elder brothers had jobs in Shanghai, so that meant I would have to be a peasant. I willingly agreed to settle in a village near the Sino-Russian border. No one else wanted to go there. It was too far away, and too cold.

I traveled to the Great Northern Wilderness believing that hardship is the best way to build character. The village was tiny. Most of the peasants had never seen anyone from a big city before, and everyone showed up to greet the first group of students. Their lives were primitive. People had never even seen toothpaste or toothbrushes. I drew lots of stares when I showed up in the fields wearing shorts. The critical glances made me ashamed of my bare legs.

Five years after my arrival there were thirty students living in the village. One of the students took a couple of men back with him to Shanghai so they could learn how to make cakes and cookies. Soon afterwards, the village opened its first bakery. It was the first in the county.

We students did bring some change to the countryside. You can't say we didn't contribute to local development. The county I went to received 30,000 students, which increased its population by more than 10 percent. Within five or six years the student-settlers occupied more than half of

Party and government positions at all levels. In my village alone, students served as team leader, Party Secretary and female cadre.

I went all out in my work so I could become a "Model Educated Youth." On many occasions I knew I was pushing myself beyond the limits of my physical endurance, but I didn't know how to hold back. I truly wanted to try my utmost. I actually managed to work harder than the peasants. In the end I split my shinbone.

Three years later, when I came home for a visit, I looked very much the northern peasant.

My friend and I took a ship from Dalian to Shanghai. We arrived in the late afternoon. Our immediate reaction was that we no longer belonged in this city. Our clothes were old and dirty, our hands were rough, with horny, cracked nails and we looked as if we were used to hard labor. Because we felt so embarrassed we decided to stay by the Huangpu River until it got dark.

On the way to the bus station I accidentally bumped my bag into a passing bicyclist. The man jumped off his bike and shouted at me: "You stupid peasant! Don't you know how to walk in the city?" I grabbed the bicycle away from him and raised my arm as if to strike him. Suddenly, he saw my face and seemed to realize I was a student-settler. He bowed to me immediately: "Very sorry brother, forgive me my blindness."

My home visit didn't cheer me up. Instead, I felt rather depressed. I returned to the village as soon as the vacation was over.

I come from a working-class family. In school I was an average student. I never gave much thought to political matters. Like most of the students at the time, I suppose I believed in Mao and the Party. When the Cultural Revolution changed my life for the worse I didn't complain. Only after the Lin Biao incident in 1971 did my faith begin to weaken. My father once told me that he stopped worshipping idols after he saw a craftsman urinating over the clay used to make a Buddha. I know how he felt. By the early 1970s I'd lost my political innocence and my simple beliefs.

The year after my return to the village, universities and colleges started recruiting Worker-Peasant-Soldier students. Local factories also began to recruit some of us, and people with good social connections began to take advantage of the new policies. When the first student left the village the whole atmosphere changed. From that point on everyone was restless. I thought that my best bet was to work hard so I could get a recommendation for university.

In 1974, I was nominated to study at China East Normal University in Shanghai. This time around I came home with pride. My parents were very happy, not just because I was back but also because I was the first from our family to go to college. I'd earned this place for myself.

I studied physics at university. Education then didn't stress academic excellence. But our training wasn't completely worthless. We were expected to solve many practical problems. One third of our study time was spent in factories, working with production teams. I thought it was a good way to learn. I only wish I'd had five or six years of study, instead of three.

I was eager to perform well in the classroom. My life certainly wasn't any easier than it had been in the countryside. I went through three years without having one Sunday off. We studied every evening until it was time to go to bed.

When the Cultural Revolution came to an end I was happy. I thought now there'd be no more fighting among the people at the top. The bad guys were gone. I never anticipated how quickly the political culture would turn against us, making us victims twice.

I'd entered university with pride in my heart. But when I graduated in 1977 as one of the last of the Worker-Peasant-Soldier student cohort China was in the midst of another transformation. The College Entrance Examination had just been given for the first time since 1966, and those who'd passed were already on campus. "Worker-Peasant-Soldier student" soon began to mean "worth nothing very much" (*bu zhiqian*). Before we knew it, we'd become worthless rejects of the Cultural Revolution.

In the 1980s, when educational credentials became the main criteria for hiring and promoting teachers, things got a lot worse. I was a physics teacher in middle school and was still stigmatized by the label "Worker-Peasant-Soldier graduate." I decided I didn't want to be categorized this way for the rest of my life. So, with support from the school district, I enrolled in another college program, and, in my spare time, I got another degree. These were three very stressful years.

Sometimes I said to myself that I was born at the wrong time. My brother is four years older than I, yet his life was quite different. He got a job before the Cultural Revolution began, and started his family when he was in his mid-twenties. His two children enjoyed free university education and now are earning good salaries. My child, who's in middle school, won't get a free college education. We'll have to pay for his tuition. In addition, my brother has over thirty years in his job. We've been told that changes in state employees' pensions won't affect those with more than thirty years service. So, my brother has a secure retirement, whereas I don't know what will happen to me when I get old. I became principal of this high school five years ago. My job's getting increasingly difficult. The students are difficult to manage, and the parents are less and less involved in their children's education. Around 20 percent of the students come from broken homes – either the parents are divorced or they're unfit. We've parents who neglect their children – something that was unknown in the past. Many of these parents have no jobs, or are self-employed.

My wife teaches first-year students in middle school. She has more problems with the parents than with the students. The parents are in their late thirties – quite different from the members of my generation. They make many demands but show little willingness to help the teachers.

The other day my wife visited a student's home. The parents were playing mahjong with some friends. They didn't bother to stand up to greet the guest but continued with their game. My wife got very upset and told them that if they wanted to know why she'd come they'd better see her in school the following day. They never bothered to show up.

The students in my school – which isn't a key school – aren't terribly interested in studying. Most of them will end up in a vocational training anyway, not college or university. They all know that it's more important to have the right parents than it is to perform well. Families with power and connections get their children into a good school by paying higher fees. They can also arrange suitable employment. To study hard guarantees nothing today. It's not difficult to understand why students aren't motivated.

My parents never had any problem talking to their children in the old style. I always took what they said seriously, and tried to follow all their rules. This kind of attitude is increasingly rare now. The real change in people's outlook and behavior has come in the last twenty years. In the 1950s and 1960s people still respected and honored traditional Chinese morality.

Our government has one moral education campaign after another. They know the problem's bad. But government campaigns aren't the solution. They just create more bureaucracy, more paper work and more reports for me to file. Meanwhile, someone such as my wife who's on the front line has a real battle on her hands. She's not just dealing with the kids but confronting society as a whole. After all, it's society that created these young people.

My biggest problem is finding reliable staff. Young graduates come and go like sightseers on horseback. As soon as they've a better offer from another employer they're off. I'm very reluctant to accept new college graduates unless the Education Bureau forces me to. Over the last couple of years I've started hiring teachers from other provinces. Even though they're better qualified they can only be hired on a temporary basis. Still, they always work very hard.

I can't pretend the administrators know what they're doing. There's no consistency. If, today, some of them visit Germany they'll return with the German model of education fresh in their minds, so we'll be told to learn from Germany. If, tomorrow, they go to Japan we'll be asked to imitate the Japanese. It's a typical "dragonfly-dipping-into-the-water" syndrome. The administrators stop briefly and move on as soon as they've attained a minimal level of satisfaction and a superficial understanding. For someone like me, who's near the bottom, it's next to impossible to keep up with the ever-changing and often quite meaningless directions.

As the bureaucracy increasingly relies on quantitative measures the time I spend on paper work gets longer and longer. Nowadays, everything is measured by numbers. It's like trying to make live things dead. Frankly, I believe that 80 per cent of the reports I submit are never read by anyone. Now I understand why Mao hated the bureaucracy so much.

I suppose I'm giving you the impression that my job makes me suffer. In fact, I love my job, but it's frustrating. I can't make independent decisions. I wish I could run the school with more autonomy – then I'd be a real schoolmaster, not just a caretaker.

19 Cao Zhenshan, male: foreign trade coordinator

My father owned a tailor's shop before liberation, so our family was classified as "petit bourgeois" (*xiaoyezhu*). I was never asked to join a Red Guard organization, but this didn't bother me too much since I wasn't interested in politics. But I did worry about my future job assignment. I wasn't eager to go somewhere particularly unpleasant just because someone with influence decided I came from a "bad" family background.

I thought I'd better meet with the Assignment Work Team at my school before they did anything I might regret, so I went to their office and showed them a paragraph from Mao's "Analysis of Social Classes in China." This document classified someone who worked for himself as "half proletarian." I pointed out to the Team that, if Mao's thinking was correct, I shouldn't be put in the same category as children from the bourgeois class.

The Team members appreciated my input into the discussion. Instead of sending me to the countryside they assigned me to a machine tool factory.

About the only activity I enjoyed during the Cultural Revolution was reading Big Character posters. After I traveled to Beijing on the Great Exchange I went to several university campuses and copied hundreds of posters. Later, I'd compare my notes with others, hoping I'd recorded a particularly interesting nugget of gossip.

I remember the day I saw Mao. The cars approached swiftly, and, then, suddenly, the whole of Tiananmen Square went crazy. As Mao swept by, my eyes were riveted on him. I didn't notice any of the other leaders. It was like a dream. Recently, I told my son about this experience. He didn't understand why it had meant so much to me. I don't think you can make young people today feel about leaders as we once did.

That was about the extent of my involvement in the Cultural Revolution.

In the factories, the Cultural Revolution was about power and about organization, not about ideology. What mattered was what political faction you belonged to. As a young apprentice, I wasn't much involved in all the political infighting. But, through ignorance, the innocent can still suffer. I took up with some people who happened to be the enemies of our

Party Secretary. For quite some time I could never understand why this man was so cold towards me. By the time I'd finally figured it out I'd learned a valuable lesson. From that point on I was never in too much of a hurry to make new friends in an unfamiliar environment.

After I got my first job I soon discovered that, although the workers were supposed to be the masters, in reality we were exploited. So I decided I'd better become a cadre. Cadres only had to move their lips while the workers toiled. But I never made it. I guess I just wasn't ambitious enough. But, then, thanks to President Nixon, my luck changed.

When Nixon visited Shanghai in 1972 I was among ten workers selected from my factory to be part of the municipal government's "Welcome-Nixon" Work Team. Thousands of us from work units all over Shanghai began to prepare for an American President's first visit to China.

I attended a week-long workshop. The government had a "sixteen-word" policy for us to follow: "Not humble, not arrogant; not hot, not cold" (*bukang bubei, buleng bure*) – I can't remember now how the rest of it went. Anyway, we were instructed to patrol the streets the day Nixon was in town. We had to take the places of all those who normally would have been out and about. We were ordered to keep everyone else inside. If a housewife wanted to buy some soy sauce or salt we were supposed to get it for her. All Shanghai residents had been instructed to get their shopping done the previous day. Still, someone might forget and wander outside.

We were cautioned we'd probably come across foreign journalists poking around, trying to interview people. If this happened we had to be "not humble, not arrogant; not hot, not cold," etcetera. It was all complete nonsense. We never came across one damn foreigner! Nonetheless, we did our best to impersonate ordinary people. It was a very cold day and my feet were freezing. I wanted to jog a bit to keep myself warm, but I worried that if I did the Americans might spot me and suspect I wasn't an ordinary pedestrian.

The good thing for me that came out of all this was that, after Nixon went back to America, the official who had organized the workshop I mentioned earlier appointed me to work for our Bureau's Department of Public Affairs. This Department was planning a touring exhibition to demonstrate model examples of blackboard propaganda. I have excellent handwriting. So I worked in the Bureau for about three months. Afterwards, I was treated rather differently in the factory. Sometimes I'd be released from work to help with propaganda.

In those days everyone got the same salary when they finished their apprenticeship: 36 yuan per month. Why 36 yuan? It was because this was equivalent to the average pension. In 1970, retirees had enough money to live on. Now they don't. My father has a pension of just over 300 yuan a month. It's not enough to feed him.

The 36 yuan salary rate lasted for six years. The first raise came after the end of the Cultural Revolution. There were 3 yuan, 5 yuan and 7 yuan raises. Most of us got a 5 yuan raise. As long as everyone was guaranteed the same income life was worry-free. People became indifferent to the big picture – I mean the larger economic situation. Now, I pay much more attention to the economy. If anything bad happens it will affect us immediately.

If the Party lessens its grip on power China will be in chaos – particularly now that the market economy is beginning to engulf state-owned enterprises. About 1 million workers were laid off this year [1996] in Shanghai – at least that's what we were told at meetings. The government is trying to keep unemployment within certain limits in order to avoid social unrest. Two years ago my wife lost her job in a textile factory. The textile industry was the first to get hit, then the metallurgical industry, then, this year, the electronics industry.

Layoffs devastate the families concerned. A million people might lose their jobs, but the overall number affected is much higher. Recently, a family of three died in Shanghai because the father decided there was no point in them living any more. He and his wife had both been laid off. One day he went to the market to buy meat for his family. He had 10 yuan. When the butcher cut a piece that cost a little bit more he asked for some to be trimmed off. The butcher got very impatient and became quite insulting: "It's only another 80 cents," he pointed out. "If you really can't afford it I'll let you have it for nothing."

The man went home, mixed rat poison with his food and gave it to himself, his wife and their child.

This incident made the government nervous. It ordered that couples should not be laid off at the same time. Right now, half the state-owned enterprises are suffering losses, which means that next year even more people are going be out of work. The government does try to reassign some of the unemployed. My wife was one of the lucky ones. Now she works in the railway station.

I'm lucky too. In 1980, I heard that the Light Industry Bureau was forming its own foreign trade corporation as an intermediary agent between foreign companies and the Bureau's own factories. That year, government let production enterprises trade directly with foreign companies. I knew the person who was put in charge of organizing the foreign trade corporation so I went to see him. "I can only offer you a job in the storage room," he told me. "Are you sure you want to take it?" I can tell you I didn't hesitate. I knew I would have a much better future in his corporation than in my factory. I also realized I needed an education, so I spent three years in evening class studying for a business degree. In 1984, I was promoted to trade coordinator.

Now, I make about 4,000 yuan a month – a very high salary. I've nothing to complain about. Of course, I realize most people my age are not so fortunate.

My corporation makes a good profit – particularly since the movement to a market economy accelerated after 1992. To be quite honest, it's not so much the boom in trade as the loopholes in regulations. Everyone knows this place is a gold mine. Not surprisingly, all of the new college graduates hired by our company come from the families of high officials. Who's our Vice-Manager? [He names the son of one of the most powerful officials in Shanghai]. Sometimes I feel this place is run like a family business. Upper management spends much of its time traveling abroad, soliciting business for sons and daughters – all in the name of "reform" and the public good, of course! I assume the same kind of thing happens in America and in other countries. However, it's so prevalent here that the government should take some care. People such as me who get just a small share feel it's unfair. But how about the people who get nothing and hear almost daily about the rapacious antics of the "coterie of princes" (*taizidang*)?

You may have heard about Zhou Beifang, the son of the President of Capital Steel Company. I was told he's going to be executed. Last year, Zhou was charged with embezzling millions in state funds. He and Deng Zhifang, Deng Xiaoping's second "prince" son, were very close friends, and, together, they founded the infamous *shouzhang sifang* company. [The title of the company includes a character from both "prince's" names: viz. *fang*. It also suggests "Chief in all Four Directions".] These people are unbelievably avaricious, and they show incredible arrogance.

I heard that Jiang Zemin has warned leading political figures to check up on their children's activities. He knows the Party can't afford many more scandals. In his communication Jiang cited an old saying: "Sons will sell their inheritance without a hint of feeling." Personally, I believe the young princelings are *baijiazi* [wasteful and irresponsible heirs] who are ruining what they've been given. A good family can be destroyed in this manner. So can a country.

Have you heard this joke? Last year, Jiang Zemin went to see Zhao Ziyang and asked him what he thought of his anti-corruption campaign.

Zhao probed Jiang about his sincerity: "Do you really want to clean up corruption," he asked, "or do you just want to put on a show?" Jiang admitted he was torn.

"Well," said Zhao, not helping much: "if you end corruption you'll destroy the Party (*wangdang*); if you don't you'll destroy the country (*wangguo*)."

This about sums up how people feel.

The anti-corruption campaign has put some pressure on cadres – on a few "small chickens" (*xiaoji*) anyway. One of the department heads in my company was sentenced to seven years in prison. He took about 400,000 yuan in bribes. He helped some enterprises in Shanghai "export" raw materials and semi-finished products to companies in Shenzhen that turned around and resold their "imported merchandise" at inflated prices to third parties. The enterprises in Shanghai got exporter tax rebates from the state and the companies in Shenzhen got Hong Kong dollars for their sales. The third-party companies that purchased the "imported merchandise" got state subsidies as well. Everyone did great – except for the state.

I think that the problem with our country is not the lack of good plans but the lack of good people to carry out the plans. If you were to ask me why Mao was a great leader I would say that, regardless of his faults, he inspired many people to believe in him and fight his battles. In his day people didn't care as much about material things. Today, we don't have leaders capable of providing spiritual leadership. Therefore, everything comes down to economic success. If reform goes well the Party's okay. If it fails we're finished.

Recently, we've been treated to quite a few TV specials on the "Long March." There's also been an upsurge in the number of public lectures about the need for "spiritual civilization." This kind of thing makes me nervous because it's a sign the leadership's getting jittery.

I've told my friends they'd better save some money for their retirement. I'm quite sure we can't rely on the government. Look at my father's generation. They worked all their life for the state and now they don't have enough to get through their final years.

20 Cai Jinzhi, male: general manager of a state farm factory

One step after another my life's journey reaches this point. It's not been easy.

I was born into a revolutionary family. Against my wealthy grandparents' wishes, my father joined the Liberation Army in 1946. At the time he was a university student, but he gave up his studies to join the Southern Expeditionary Forces so he could help liberate people from the Guomindang. After the war my father returned to his home village, 20 miles outside Shanghai. He immediately got involved in local government and ultimately became Party Secretary of Fengxian County.

As a child I wasn't particularly diligent. In 1966, I was about to graduate from high school and had little confidence that I would pass the College Entrance Examination. However, as the "first son" of the county I was expected to sit the exam. I spent lots of time preparing for it. When it was canceled because of the Cultural Revolution I was very happy.

At the beginning of the Cultural Revolution students in the countryside were slow to grasp what was happening. I wasn't particularly interested in the movement. I think this had something to do with my relationship with my father. I never got to know him very well. While my mother and other brothers lived in our home village, my father stayed in the county town several miles away. We seldom saw him.

My father soon was in trouble. Since he'd occupied the Number One position in the county he quickly became the Number One Capitalist Roader. So, you see, I'm made up partly of red and partly of black bones.

People didn't trouble mother or my brothers. They knew we'd not stayed one night in the county government compound nor eaten one meal in the government dining room. We'd had nothing to do with father's "capitalist crimes."

During the Cultural Revolution I observed many political ups and downs. But I wasn't interested. I'm a very pragmatic person with no interest in political ideology.

After father was criticized I became increasingly reclusive. To compensate for the emptiness in my life I arranged an apprenticeship for myself. I'd always loved working with my hands so I thought I'd make a good carpenter. It was embarrassing for a high-school graduate to become a carpenter, but I didn't care. My master was a carpenter in Jiangnan Shipyard. He was illiterate and didn't know how to draw or read blueprints. After I showed him I could do both he accepted the carton of cigarettes I'd bought for him. In this manner I attained my first job.

My father died of pneumonia in his early fifties. It wasn't a serious illness. I think he just gave up. His death changed me. I felt from then on that I'd take care of my brothers and myself on his behalf. I decided I didn't want to stay home and be a peasant. I thought that with my new skills as a carpenter I could find a job in Shanghai.

One of my father's old friends had been rehabilitated as the head of a District Handicraft Industrial Bureau. I went to see him my first day in Shanghai. I knew he could help me find a temporary job as a carpenter. A month later I started working in a construction team organized by his Bureau.

I was hired as a temporary worker. First, though, I had to persuade the government of my commune to let me work in Shanghai. I was told to hand over 40 percent of my salary to the commune. I could keep the remaining 60 percent. This was how surplus agricultural labor was organized in those days. We were called "Four-and-Six-Workers" (*siliugong*) because we had to share our earnings with local rural government.

I was the only high-school graduate in my work team. So it was a case of "when there's no tiger in the mountain the monkey can call himself king." Before long, I was asked to teach the others how to read and draw blueprints – this gave me pride and some authority. Although I was only a temporary worker no one looked down on me.

Both my superiors and my team workers thought I was a very capable person, and, in 1972, they gave me a chance to attend an eighteen-month program for workers at Tongji University. Students were expected to complete this program in their spare time. I continued to work during the daytime and studied at night. Finally, I was awarded a certificate that's completely useless today.

Afterwards, I was made leader of my production team. But I told my superior that, if I were going to lead the team, I would insist on one thing. Workers could take as much time as they wanted for political meetings. However, I reminded my boss that the Party's slogan had recently become "Grasp the Revolution to Promote Production" (*zhua geming cu shengchan*) so when it was time for production I wanted to see everyone working hard. The boss gave me his full support.

Soon, I started a "production quota" management. Everyone knew what he or she was supposed to do. If you had to go to a four-hour meeting – no problem, but the rest of the day you had to make up for lost time. Naturally, I was careful not to give anyone a chance to claim I'd used production to suppress revolution!

After two years I successfully turned a production team that was in debt to the tune of 28,000 yuan into a work unit that made a profit of 46,000 yuan. Everyone was happy. The team was a so-called "small collective unit" (*xiaojiti*) made up mostly of temporary workers. We could keep some of the profit ourselves. I was given a salary of 90 yuan per month. At the time it was high.

As a temporary worker I was not eligible for housing when I got married. I had to build a house for myself. I spent all my savings – 1,200 yuan. It took me a whole year to build a two-room house in my home village.

This made me angry. I thought that if I were formally employed I could get help from the government. The money I had to spend on my house could have helped my younger brothers. I had a duty to build houses for them too. It took me another six years to save up enough money to construct houses for my brothers. The house for the youngest brother was the best. By then we'd had lots of experience.

Anyway, I went to see my superior. He promised me I'd get a formal position when the opportunity arrived. I decided to give him another year. There were other construction teams willing to hire me. With my certificate from Tongji I could easily have found another job. I waited. A year passed and nothing happened.

That was in 1975. I became increasingly restless about my situation. Then I heard that a newly established state farm in Fengxian was looking for skilled workers to strengthen its labor force. The farm was near my home. Although I'd have to relinquish a larger salary, and also give up living in Shanghai, both my wife and I would get "iron bowls." I went to the farm headquarters and signed myself up. I moved to the farm at the beginning of 1976 and was given the responsibility of building a furniture factory.

That's how I started working in this state farm.

Twenty years have passed. I'm proud of what we've achieved. When we started there was nothing. Today, the farm headquarters is like a small city – we have everything a city has. The farm owns over thirty factories. Seven of them belong to the Handicraft Industry Company, which is under my supervision. These all make furniture. Two factories are engaged in foreign trade. Around 90 percent of state farm employees work in factories. The remaining 10 percent lease our land and hire peasants from Jiangsu province to do the actual farming.

I joined the Party in 1978. I am the Vice-President of this state farm. I report to the Department of Industry and Trade. A journalist for one Shanghai newspaper came to visit us and wrote that we "built up a fortune from toilet seats." That's quite true. I'll explain what she meant in a moment.

In 1983, I went on a tour of America and Canada funded by the Municipal Farm Bureau. We visited furniture-manufacturing companies. I recognized that our factory would not be able to make high quality furniture, but I also thought we could make a few simple things. At that time, our furniture factory was primitive: we had just 80,000 yuan of assets. I was aware of the tremendous business opportunities. But I didn't stand a chance of competing with the big state enterprises. Still, there was a fire burning inside me.

My opportunity came unexpectedly. One day I was in the Municipal Foreign Trade Bureau in Shanghai. I heard someone several offices down shouting – obviously a foreigner, and very upset. I learned it was an American, who'd contracted with the biggest furniture manufacturing factory in Shanghai to make moldings. He'd just discovered that this factory hadn't done what it had promised. Now, the American was refusing to deal with the factory and was threatening to cancel the contract.

The officials in the Foreign Trade Bureau were in panic. They didn't want to lose the business, and, more importantly, they didn't want to lose face. I told the officials they should give me two months to see what I could do. If I could produce moldings meeting all the requirements they should give me the contract.

This was in 1984. After two months I'd demonstrated I could produce what was needed, so I got the deal. The municipal government gave me a loan in foreign currency to buy machines from Canada. The machines were a bit out-of-date, but good enough in comparison to what we'd had before. However, I soon discovered those machines basically were useless because what they made no longer was in demand. Many enterprises suffer from this kind of problem. You import specific machines in order to manufacture a certain product. But when the demand for this product dries up, or when you lose out to other enterprises, the expensive machines become just useless iron.

I didn't go bankrupt because I switched to producing toilet seats for the same American businessman. We established a relationship based on trust. Later, the American company made a joint investment with us. The factory you visited this morning is now a joint venture, with 40 percent of investment coming from the American partners and 60 percent coming from the state farm. The Americans got their money back in two years. They're more than happy.

Our main products for foreign trade are kitchen and bathroom appliances such as cabinets, dowels, towel-holders and solid wood doors. They are standardized products that are relatively easy to make and are always in demand. We can't compete with Japan and Holland in making bedroom furniture. But our solid wood doors sell for about US$135–140 per piece at export price.

We get our materials from two sources. Hardwood timber comes from northeastern China. It's all white ash. Plywood comes mainly from Thailand, Malaysia and Indonesia. Unfortunately, these countries recently have increased the export price for plywood from US$70–80 per cubic meter to US$140–150 per cubic meter. So I've got problems here. I've got to develop new products or find other suppliers.

You ask why America with its vast resources wants to use the disappearing Chinese forests to make its bathroom fittings. Well, I guess that timber is still cheaper in China than in America. Also, labor costs are much cheaper here. The highest annual income of a worker in my factory is about 10,000 yuan, and the average worker's annual income is between 5,000–6,000 yuan [US$580–700]. No comparison, right?

Our workers have lots of benefits though. Our farm has about 3,000 formal employees and about the same number of contract workers. Including dependents, we have about 10,000 people. The formal employees get a full package – including medical care, children's education, pensions and housing. Every family gets a two-bedroom apartment of 45 square meters. The farm pays 30,000 yuan, and the family 20,000 yuan, towards the cost of this apartment. But the family owns it. The profits we make largely go on this kind of thing. Our farm is like a small society. Everything has to be taken care of.

I've visited the United States more than a dozen times. If you do business with Americans you ought to get to know them better. Some Americans work for us as salesmen. Once, some students came to me and told me I should hire them because they're Chinese. "No," I said to them, "I won't." I'm selling things in America. Chinese salesmen cannot be as effective as Americans.

I like to do business with foreigners. They are calm and reasonable. Not like many Chinese. One day, a Hong Kong businessman called me up late in the evening, claiming I'd delayed shipments. I said I'd shipped the goods from my factory on time, and I wasn't responsible for other people's incompetence. He became quite abusive. Finally, he calmed down and said that he'd forgiven me. I replied: "Don't be so Chinese. I never took any blame."

I want to make it clear that you [a Chinese journalist who was also present at the interview] are not going to write any articles about me. "People fear being famous like pigs fear being fat" (*ren pa chuming, zhu pa zhuang*). I want to keep my life as quiet as possible, all right?

I don't care about personal material rewards very much. Of course, everyone wants a good life. But the factories are more important than my personal interests. If my factories don't operate profitably I'm nothing. If I just think about enriching myself – say I get a million dollars – the money won't last forever. People shouldn't just concern themselves with personal gain. Even in capitalist countries not everything is about material rewards, right?

My salary is more than 1,000 yuan a month. My wife and I save half of our joint income. We save up partly for our son who's 22 years old. He's dating now. I can't believe my son is old enough to date girls. I care about him very much. No matter how busy I am, I never spend a Sunday away from my family as long as I'm here. I don't go home every day. I often have to spend nights in Shanghai because of business.

Yes, I was honored as a "Model Party Member" recently. But I'm not a political person. Too many meetings – I just can't take it. But I still have to show up on numerous occasions because I can't afford to offend people. Frankly, I hate these complicated relationships. If I quit this job I'll never become a Party or government administrator.

I'm confident about our factories' future. Right now I'm shifting my attention to the domestic market. People in the large cities – particularly in Shanghai – have started to demand better. interior materials for their houses. As private ownership increases, people look for better quality furniture. They want wooden cabinets, hardwood furniture, and hardwood floors. I see a big market developing. I'm not that stupid to sell things to Americans thousands of miles away only to miss the opportunity right under my very nose. I've already decided to shift our focus to the domestic market.

I want to say this again [to the Chinese journalist]: please don't write anything about me! I have a fear of people making publicity out of me. It's pointless. You can help advertise our products. Now that would be helpful.

21 Lin Juan, female: editor of a woman's magazine

Both my parents came from very wealthy families. At home, *Waipo* (maternal grandmother) was in charge of everything. She put me under her wing from the day I was born. She really spoiled me. We had a live-in servant for the chores. I didn't have to do anything except my homework.

When the Cultural Revolution began I was in my first year of middle school. I wasn't directly involved in the movement but I did try to emulate the role models. That's why I ended up in Heilongjiang.

My class was "Completely Red." Everyone had to go to the country-side. I saw this as an opportunity to create some distance between my family and myself. I figured my parents would try to stop me leaving Shanghai because they knew I wasn't like the others. I planned to over-come my family's resistance, confound everyone's expectations and emerge as a model student. But things didn't turn out like that.

Because I was the best writer in my class I was asked to edit our school's Red Guard newsletter. One week, I had to attend a workshop that took me away from home for a couple of days. When I returned one of my teachers greeted me with a big smile on his face. "Congratulations!" he said. "Your father's such a good man. You can be proud of him." I had no idea what he was talking about.

It turned out that, while I was safely out of the way, my father had attended a mobilization session at my school. At this meeting he'd signed me up to answer the Party's call. He told everyone that his daughter might seem "progressive" in school but that she was a spoiled brat at home. He claimed I was lazy and had never laundered as much as a handkerchief in my life. He ended by telling everyone it wouldn't hurt a privileged kid like me to taste some "bitterness" in the country.

You can imagine how I felt. I was livid. My father had made me look so stupid. Actually he's a pathetic figure. Because of his "bad" family back-ground all he could think about at the time was how to be politically correct. He wanted to demonstrate he was more revolutionary than the real revolutionaries. He put his own interests before those of his wife and children. I know he didn't care about me. What made me feel worse was that my mother didn't raise her voice against him.

Now, I had to decide where I should go. My father put on his democratic face and pretended to have a family council. He told me he wanted me to make the decision so I wouldn't be able to blame him if anything went wrong.

I chose Heilongjiang because I knew it was where the true revolutionaries went. I'd been strongly influenced by speeches given by some older Red Guard leaders. One of these had told us he planned to set up a *kangda* university in this faraway province.[1] His words were inspiring. In my mind's eye I could picture the vast land, the sweeping forests, the simple peasantry and the long border facing a hostile Soviet Union.

Grandma congratulated me on making a good choice. She pointed out that, if I joined a state farm, I wouldn't have to cook my own meals. She couldn't accept I might ever be capable of doing something for myself!

Five days later I boarded a train with other student-settlers, and I was on my way to help develop the Great Northern Wilderness.

First, it was a big train, which headed north for four days. Then we sat on a shabby, local train for another day. Next, we had a long journey on a broken-down old bus. Finally, we disembarked. The prospect wasn't encouraging. Everything was bleak and windswept. A tractor turned up for our baggage, and we were ordered to walk 7 miles to farm headquarters. By the time we arrived it was dark and cold. Most of the girls were in tears. I was beginning to suspect I could have made a mistake, but, unlike most of the others, I refused to cry.

On the tenth day, things got a lot worse.

We'd arrived in April, but the weather was still very cold. During the night it fell to minus 20° centigrade. Our dormitories were freezing. Someone suggested we keep the stove lit all night and redirect the vents so we could get more heat. While we were asleep some sparks escaped and set fire to a straw mattress. Before we knew what was happening our room was in flames. I had to rush outside in my underwear. Everyone else was screaming hysterically.

This was my opportunity. "Comrades," I shouted. "Stop crying! Let's sing a song." I led the group in verses from Mao's Quotations. Slowly, raggedly, everyone else joined in. When workers from other units rushed to the scene they were greeted with cheerful singing, not hopeless wailing. They saw me as I wanted to be seen. My spirits were uplifted. I'd transcended personal weakness.

Seven of the students were badly burned and were taken to the county hospital. Some cadres from Shanghai happened to be visiting the town and sent back news of the fire. By the time this news got home the story was that there'd been a major disaster and that only seven students had survived.

My father went to the Municipal Educated Youth Office with other parents. He'd appointed himself their leader. The parents were very upset and demanded to know what had happened to their children. My father told the authorities that he would pay everyone's train fare to Heilongjiang out of his own pocket. He made such a nuisance of himself that he was reprimanded for trying to stir up trouble and got another notation put in his record.

After a couple of months at the farm I no longer felt inferior. I told myself that I'd not only do everything well but also that I'd outperform everyone else. Before long, I'd become a "Five Goodnesses Soldier" (*wuhao zhanshi*) ["ideologically correct," "morally clean," "hard-working," "healthy in attitude" and "physically fit"]. But, because I was so driven, I wasn't particularly popular. My annual evaluations had comments in them such as "arrogant, and does not have a good relation-ship with the masses." I sincerely accepted these criticisms but didn't really know how to correct them. I couldn't help wanting to be the best.

What I missed most were my books. I was always a keen reader. In the third grade I'd read the "big books" (*dashu*) of Chinese classical literature written in the old style. Then, I discovered that one of the girls on the farm had a whole set of classical novels. Her sister had packed them for her. However, this girl wasn't able to read the difficult text. I told her that, if she lent me the books, I'd tell her the stories, chapter by chapter. She agreed. I ended up reading the stories so often I can still recall every detail.

Some of the officials in the farm were cadres from Shanghai. They'd been demoted and sent to this faraway land to become "king of the kids." Their families had accompanied them. Most of these cadres were college educated and had joined the Party before liberation. At first, I was attracted to them and felt I couldn't match their revolutionary zeal. I suppose I was looking for father figures that could give me some guidance.

Looking back, I realize these cadres were losers. They weren't committed to us, they didn't trust us, and they were always looking for an opportunity to get out – or, at least, get their children out. As soon as they could, these cadres assigned their own children elsewhere.

The first such chance to leave came when some of us were selected to be Worker-Peasant-Soldier students. Up to that point I'd been content, even though the life was tough. However, when I saw other people leaving I became resentful.

I asked for a three-month leave to go back to Shanghai. What surprised me was that as soon as I got home I was my old self again. I slept until midday, ate a lot, argued with my father and fought with my brother. I forgot about the farm. When it was time to go back I'd gained nearly 30 pounds and had a very fair complexion.

I should pause and tell you about my family. My father's father gradu-ated from the Japanese Imperial University in Tokyo. He taught at Sichuan University in Chengdu. His two eldest brothers inherited the family's estates and were executed during land reform in 1952.

Land reform in Sichuan was unnecessarily harsh. Do you know why? It was because Deng Xiaoping came from a big landlord family in the province. In order to show he'd distanced himself from his "bad" family background Deng encouraged the movement to go way beyond what was constructive.

According to my father his uncles were enlightened landlords. After liberation they didn't dare oppose land reform. They handed their estates over immediately but it didn't do them any good. They were both killed anyway.

In 1958, my grandfather was sentenced to ten years in prison for his "criminal activities." He'd criticized land reform and organized a demonstration in front of the provincial government's building in Chengdu.

I didn't know about any of this when I was a child. After 1958, my father had cut off all relations with his family. It's difficult now to understand how people could behave like that. Father later told me he'd done it to help his family. But it didn't help me at all!

In 1973, when I was back in Heilongjiang, I applied to join the Youth League. I didn't mention my grandfather in the application because I knew nothing about him. I did list my father's "political problem." I'd had plenty of opportunities over the years to be reminded about that.

My father got a degree in economics before liberation. He joined an organization called the "Economic Development Strategy Advisory Committee" that was sponsored by the Guomindang. It was more political than academic. Father thought he was going to save China. Instead, he created a long-standing "problem" that was continuously being dredged up by people who didn't like him. Actually, most people didn't like him.

I never expected that father's background would affect my admission to the Youth League, and I was devastated when I was denied admission. I was reprimanded and told I'd concealed "serious family problems."

I sent a letter to my father demanding an explanation. As he'd been backed into a corner he had to admit that his own father was a convict. The farm in Heilongjiang sent two people to Chengdu to investigate my background. They discovered that the old man had died in jail in 1967. I don't know how father took the news. He never said anything to me.

In the late 1980s, I traveled to Chengdu to look up the house where my grandfather used to live. It's a big house. Strangers have taken it over. Grandma died shortly after her husband passed away.

In 1974, I began work as a teacher in a brigade elementary school in Heilongjiang. I wanted the job because I loved the idea of being a teacher. The previous teacher was a friend of mine. At the beginning of the Cultural Revolution both her parents had been sent to May Seventh cadre schools for two years. She was the oldest in her family, so she'd taken over the responsibilities of looking after her younger siblings. She was 14 years old when her parents left.

My friend had been a teacher for two years. Everyone had fallen in love with her. She'd cut the kids' hair and even made clothes for them. Of course, she'd had plenty of opportunity to work on these skills. Whenever it was raining or snowing she used to carry the small children to the school on her back. She'd spent her own money on pencils and books. When I assumed her position I realized I had an obligation to carry on the good deeds she'd started.

However, I knew I was a better teacher than she was because I'd read a lot and I wrote very well. I said to myself: maybe I can't make clothes for the children but I can certainly show them how to write letters for their parents. That's the most practical thing country kids can learn. I didn't want my students growing up like their mothers and fathers, who were mostly illiterate.

I was a good teacher. I'm not going to be modest about it. I loved being a teacher. During my time in that school I sent all the best kids to the county high school. I was well known as a model teacher in the county town, and I was often asked to give teaching demonstrations. The county government asked me to teach at the high school. I had to decline. The universities had just reopened and I wanted to enroll.

As soon as they heard that the College Entrance Examination had been reinstated, many people at the farm quit what they were doing. Many of them just packed up and went back to Shanghai to prepare for the exam. The farm was half deserted. I stayed in my school. I didn't have the guts to leave my job right away. Because of my sacrifice I unexpectedly failed the College Entrance Examination.

The following year, I spent more time preparing for the exam, and I passed. Northeast Normal University accepted me. I studied Chinese literature and language.

After graduation, I was assigned to work for the Women's Federation in Shanghai, and, in 1986, I was appointed Chief Editor of one of the Federation's magazines. That's how I got involved in women's issues.

Over the last five years my life has changed dramatically. I've shown I can adjust to a rapidly changing environment. I'm the kind of person who can't stand to be left behind. I look for opportunities and I grab them. Compared to many others I'm shrewd and business-minded. I'm catching up with the world. But the real masters are the members of the young generation. They have clear, material goals and they'll use whatever means are necessary to achieve them.

As the editor of a leading women's magazine I've established myself as an expert on women's issues. I'm often asked to give lots of speeches on the image of women, on their relations with men, on career choices, family, education, culture, shopping and so on. I've been on TV many times. Right now, I'm presenting a TV show that introduces people to new products. To tell you the truth, though, I'm not really interested in women's issues. Neither is the public.

At the age of 44 I'm still not married, so I can't claim to be an expert on motherhood. I didn't consciously choose to be single. Sometimes I think it has something to do with my father. I always saw him as a very weak figure. As far as our family's concerned, frankly he's useless. My disappointment with him probably affected my relations with other men.

I'm not saying I'll never get married. However, I don't think my life would be as good if I had a husband. As an acknowledged expert on women's issues I earn about 3,000 yuan a month, from speaking, consulting and TV fees. With no family to worry about, I can live comfortably and save up some money. I've worked hard. But I'm never going to make a killing.

As editor of a magazine I get a lot of under-the-table kickbacks. For instance, I can ask for a 10 percent commission fee from every advertiser who wants to do business with me. Many companies are eager to pay me to get the exposure they need. I admit I was a bit slow at first because I was still thinking "wrong versus right."

I make good money even though I don't make big money. But in my line of work you get a lot of extras, and you certainly get to attend a lot of dinner parties. That's income too, right? I'm still a salaried member of the Women's Federation, but I only have to come here once a week. Most of the time I'm running around the city going to meetings, giving speeches and attending dinner parties. I'm planning to start my own consulting business. There's lots of money to be made doing that kind of thing.

To answer all your questions, I'm neither satisfied nor dissatisfied with China. People should try to make the best out of a situation. There's no point bitching. If you want to know what I think might be missing from my life I'd say it's probably the lack of one friend on whom I can depend. Everyone today wants something from you. So, naturally, the same principle governs my relations with others.

I went back to Heilongjiang last year. Every student but one had left the farm. I went to visit her. She'd married a local farmer and was completely integrated into the community. Before I went to her house I warned myself to be tactful. I was expecting her to be unhappy. Much to my surprise, she seemed quite content. I'm much more successful than she is, but she'd prepared presents for me. I was quite touched.

She has a wonderful husband and a daughter who's getting ready to go to university. She laughs a lot. When I left her home I felt a little bit jealous.

And, suddenly, I didn't feel quite so sure of myself.

Note

1 The original *kangda* (anti-Japanese universities) trained military officers and political cadres in the Chinese soviet bases during the Sino-Japanese War (1937–1945).

22 Chai Beihua, male: manager of a printing shop

My friends feel sorry for me. They think this job has forced me to sacrifice my passion for literature. My wife complains I spend all my time here: "It's a position the size of a sesame seed," she says, "but you act as if it were a watermelon." Like many of my friends, she thinks I'm a bit foolish. But there's a secret I've haven't shared with any of them: I'm happier now than ever before.

In 1984, I finished my manuscript on the history of Chinese contemporary literature. I'd worked on this project since 1972. During the Cultural Revolution I read many writers from the 1920s and 1930s. They're not well known because they're ignored in all the official histories. I discovered these writers were diverse in outlook. Some were anarchists, others were more left than the Communists; some were urbane, others traditional.

In the 1920s and 1930s, Chinese intellectuals experienced the kind of freedom our ancestors enjoyed during the time of "One Hundred Schools" in the period of Spring and Autumn [707–476 BC]. During the 1920s and 1930s China was in constant turmoil, and was often governed by warlords. There was no centralized authority and no overall control of ideology. If intellectuals ran into trouble in one place they could pack up and leave for another. In Shanghai, writers would avoid Guomindang repression by moving from one foreign concession to another.

After I discovered these writers I became very excited. It was a surprise to learn that intellectuals had an independent voice so recently in our history. I began to collect all the materials I could find. See those twelve boxes up there? They contain thousands of data cards.

I wanted to write a biographical history of these writers that didn't have a political agenda. I tried to make it as accurate and as objective as possible. After I finished my manuscript I sent it to the People's Publishing House. Months later, they told me that they were interested but that the manuscript needed more work.

I started revising the manuscript, but, then, something happened that made me put my project on one side. I went to see an old professor in China East Normal University to ask about some data. We chatted for hours. During my visit, one of his old students showed up. This man was a member of a Research Institute [he names it]. He was asked to organize a business venture that could generate some money for his Institute.[1] He'd founded an organization in pursuit of this goal and had named it the "Educational, Scientific and Humanistic Organization" (ESHO).

After he learned that I'd worked in the printing trade for more than fifteen years, this man asked me if I would help him start a printing shop. Members of the Institute had translated several foreign works, and they were eager to print and sell them. But, in order to do this, they had to use a state publishing house's presses and share the profits. If the Institute could build its own printing shop it could control the business from beginning to end. The plan intrigued me. Less than a month later I quit my job.

The capital for the printing shop was going to be raised by workshops ESHO would offer on philosophy, history, economics and literature. However, these seminars didn't make much money. Next, ESHO founded the Shanghai Entrepreneurs Friendship Club. This was designed to promote horizontal social exchanges among the managers of state enterprises.[2] The Club was popular, and generated a lot of money from membership fees. In 1985, ESHO purchased a building site in the Shanghai suburbs.

Investors were found who were willing to help fund the construction of an apartment complex on the newly purchased site. The printing shop would occupy the first floor of the building. Once construction was finished the investors would be repaid in apartment units.

For a while, everything seemed to be going well. The complex was nearly complete. However, some of the people running ESHO got out of control. They used Organization funds to invest in a township factory in Ningpo which, I believe, was run by their relatives. Before long, ESHO was bankrupt. Someone at the Institute wrote to the municipal government requesting an investigation. Because the complainant alleged that 1 million yuan of public money had been embezzled it didn't take long for an investigative team to show up.

This team reported that the Institute was illegally involved in the real estate business and had engaged in various kinds of mismanagement resulting in the waste of state property. It fined the Institute 700,000 yuan.

The members of the Institute couldn't pay this sum, so they made a deal with a joint-stock limited liability company. In 1988, the company was given this plot of land and the half-finished building complex. In return, it paid the fine. I said at the time that it was a big mistake. I was right. Four years later, that plot of land was worth 5 million yuan – not including this building.

ESHO already had purchased two printing presses. The company that now owned the building told me that, if I employed ten of their workers, I could use these machines and start the printing business as previously planned. I was paid a small salary, and I had to turn over all profits to the company. Company managers didn't think I would make much money but they were wrong. I managed to generate quite a good income for my employers. But, before I agreed to be manager, I insisted on three things. First, I wasn't going to join the Communist Party; second, I wouldn't do personal favors for anyone; third, I didn't want any political meetings on the shop floor.

In 1992, the company made a formal agreement with me. I could lease the printing presses and the first floor of this complex for 80,000 yuan per annum. Profits over and above this would be mine.

I have a good working relationship with company managers, who mostly leave me alone. As long as I hand over 80,000 yuan a year I can run this factory as my own little fiefdom. However, I am supposed to attend management meetings.

Recently, at one of these meetings I got into an argument with the Chief Manager. He'd called the meeting to discuss a plan he'd put together to remodel the upper floors of this building as a hotel. He told us the project would require a 20 million-yuan loan.

It didn't need a person of superior intellect to see that the plan was doomed to fail. Right now, there are more than enough big hotels in Shanghai. Also, it would take the company fifteen years to pay back 20 million – assuming, of course, that the hotel made enough money to keep up with the payments.

I pointed out that no one in the room had any experience in the hotel business. "Where are the guests going to come from?" I asked. "This building is in an outlying suburb. Who's going to stay here, and why?" No one else asked any questions. They were all too busy arguing about what to call their new hotel.

My speech made the boss very uncomfortable. He warned everyone that he was in charge of this building, not anyone else. Hearing this, I got to my feet and walked out. I'm not a Party member, nor am I an employee of the company, so there's little they can do to me. A few days later, however, the boss called to tell me he'd appreciated what I'd said. He told me he now recognized I was the only one who'd made any sense.

Since I took over this business I've built it up. I've bought six new presses, and I now have significant reserves of paper and printing ink. I'm careful to avoid getting into "triangle debts" (*sanjiaozhai*). I only deal with businesses that can pay cash. Triangle debts are a very serious problem. They occur when one business isn't paid and, so, has to give IOUs to its suppliers. Immediately, the business is both a creditor and a debtor. It can't pay its debts because it's owed so much money. Before long, everything freezes up. Many state enterprises are ruined this way.

Why does this happen so often? I think the problem is the lack of overall supervision. Many projects are launched for no good reason and with little capital investment. Inflation is a big problem too. For instance, a company has 10 million to invest in a new factory. The actual cost is 15 million. The company borrows 5 million from a bank. A year later, the project is half finished but the cost has risen to 20 million. Now, the company can't pay the construction company. In order to keep the project afloat, the construction company stops paying its suppliers. When the factory finally is finished there's no money left to begin production. So, the company goes back to the bank. This time around, the bank raises its interest rates and shortens the loan period. This means bigger payments. Everyone is desperately trying to survive at the margins. If the new factory makes a good product, maybe everything's fine. But if the scheme was shaky from the start the company collapses very quickly.

The state-owned printing factories in Shanghai have gone bankrupt one after another. Now, there are only two left. Many factors contributed to this state of affairs. Competition from township enterprises is one such factor. Printing is not that complicated. A peasant can buy a printing machine and operate it at home.

Some cadres in Shanghai help township enterprises set up business. They act like sponsors, selling equipment to these rural businesses and making sure everything works smoothly. Cadres close to their retirement age [60] regularly do this kind of thing. Surely you've heard the expression "the 59 phenomenon." Often, the small businesses that cadres help start are really for family or friends. Nothing appears to be illegal. But the state-owned industries are hurt. They can't survive when cadres deliberately set out to undercut them.

State-owned enterprises are at a disadvantage in a competitive environment. The odds are stacked against them. The problem worsened after the state further decentralized economic management [in 1993]. The government hasn't just relinquished authority, it's also laid off many of its responsibilities.

About 75 million people work for state enterprises in the cities, and the numbers are falling. Nearly 30 million people work in private enterprises. Many of these private businesses are joint ventures or wholly foreign-owned enterprises. The state enterprises have to pay pensions and medical costs for millions of retirees. Since the recent reforms state enterprises are supposed to contribute to a fund that supposedly will pay 70 percent of medical expenses for public employees in the future. Patients and their immediate work units will pay the other 30 percent. I don't oppose such taxes in principle. But the reality is that state enterprises are burdened by increasingly punitive social security taxes.

The township enterprises and small factories in the countryside don't make any contribution to their employees' health or pension costs. In the private sector, employers can write whatever contracts they want with their labor force. Furthermore, small private companies often avoid paying any business tax at all, and joint or foreign-owned businesses in the Special Economic Zones pay much lower taxes than the state enterprises.

The only way to reform state-owned enterprises is to privatize them. Many state businesses are in a hopeless situation, and the majority are in debt. It's pointless expecting such industries to compete when they have much heavier costs to pay and when they're clustered in sectors of the economy that offer little opportunity for growth. The government should auction off bankrupt enterprises in order to try to revive them. The process has already begun. I think it's a step in the right direction.

Our government has made too many concessions to foreign capitalists. Some of the subsidies they give to foreign or joint enterprise businesses have damaged domestic industry and made robber barons of the foreigners. We're not a country starting from nothing. Before reform, we had an industrial base, and this shouldn't have been dismantled in the service of foreign capital. What happened was a disgrace. Many good Chinese products with a long history were pushed aside by foreign products.

I've had several dealings with foreigners. Once I was offered a salary of 5,000 yuan a month and a car. I refused all the offers because I won't work with compradors and opportunists. The people who approached me were Japanese and Taiwanese. The Japanese recruit Chinese students who are studying in Japan.

Both the Japanese and the Taiwanese had the same idea. They wanted to start a joint venture, and they planned to devalue the assets in this factory, so, by investing a given sum of money, they would have a bigger share of the business and a larger share of profits. When I refused to help one student told me I was making a big mistake: "You're not a Party member," he pointed out, "so why should you care?" I was outraged. I'm always criticizing the Party. But this isn't Party property. It was started with public funds, and so the assets belong to everyone. I told this Chinese middleman he should be ashamed of himself.

Despite everything, I'm very optimistic about the future. I think our country has completed the stage of primitive capital accumulation. It's a period of greed, cruelty and destruction that can't be avoided by any nation that wants to modernize. Now, I find that the frantic pursuit of money is slowing somewhat. People have begun to realize that not everyone can get rich quickly and that certain rules have to be followed. Let me give you an example.

Wenzhou [a coastal county in Zhejiang province] used to be known as the capital of pirated goods and counterfeit products. Many people were involved in various kinds of trickery, making money any way they could. The merchants in Wenzhou grew fat at the expense of their victims. But now we have entered a new phase. Capital is being put into legitimate, long-term business enterprises. The family businesses that used to specialize in shoddy, counterfeit goods have all disappeared. If you go to Wenzhou today you will find modern factories and good schools.

Fifteen years ago, the first entrepreneurs to take advantage of reform were the "bandits." Their only ambition was to grab money. Many of them actually *were* bandits – people with criminal records. They were without a sense of social responsibility. Their businesses tended to be exotic restaurants, massage parlors, private clubs and karaoke bars. They were people of poor quality, and a corrupting influence.

Today, a new group of entrepreneurs is coming to the fore. They have long-term business interests and a sense of decorum and responsibility. I'm not alone in thinking this way. Wait for another ten or twenty years. The business class in China will be quite different. Believe me!

My great-grandfather was a peasant turned businessman. During the Guangxu era [1898–1906] he owned two famous ham stores in Shanghai and Hong Kong. He also ran a pig farm and a ham factory in the countryside, so he controlled the whole operation from beginning to end. He was a thrifty person who lived simply. He knew how to build up a business.

After my father came of age he was sent to study business management at university. Both great-grandfather and grandfather recognized the value of a modern education. My ancestors were people with vision. Sometimes, I wonder what China would have been like if we'd not had a revolution. Before long, I think, we would have had many Chinese Rockefellers.

Father graduated with a business management degree, which was useless at the time. He taught political economy at a Party school for many years. Now, father's retired. But he shows a lot of interest in this printing shop. In fact, he visits so often he's become quite a nuisance. He behaves as if we own the place. He told me once that he felt our ancestors' spirit was being carried on by me – a member of the fourth generation.

I have a big dream. One day, I want to run this printing shop, a publishing house and a bookstore. Then, I will control the product from beginning to end – just like my ancestor. My biggest fear is I'll never get the opportunity. I've only another fifteen or twenty years to make it happen. It'll probably take that long before privately owned publishing houses are permitted.

In 1989, I felt my dream was almost within reach. At the beginning of the year I was introduced to a Taiwanese professor. He wanted to invest in my factory and organize a publishing house here on the mainland. We had a long talk, and got on very well. He told me that, in Taiwan, ideological control was very strict. Presidents of Taiwanese universities all have to be members of the Guomindang. He was surprised to find there was more openness and freedom here than in Taiwan. He was going to use my presses to publish works that were outlawed in Taiwan. I was very excited because I thought I'd found a partner who shared my aspirations. This professor asked me to draw up a contract, while he traveled to Beijing to work on another business project. But after the crackdown in June he never came back. He sent me a message. It said: "I hope we'll get another chance one day."

In 1989, I didn't sympathize with the students. I saw enough turmoil during the Cultural Revolution. Mao was the greatest advocate of *geming* (revolution). I hate these two characters. China doesn't need any more revolution. What we want is *gailiang* (reform).

What happened in Tiananmen Square was turmoil. The students were activists (*huodongjia*), not leaders able to articulate solutions. Ordinary people were drawn to the demonstrations because of their opposition to corruption, inflation and the lack of democracy. After the students abandoned these concrete issues and began to play to foreign audiences their movement became fragmented and isolated.

The students were more interested in displaying their emotions than in addressing real issues. They were like the founders of Solidarity in Poland: activists with no ability to govern. When Solidarity took power it was a disaster. It would have been the same with the students. If we'd let them rule China they'd have become dictators too.

Economic development will bring political reform to China. It's just a matter of time. But I don't think we'll have a multi-party system. I believe reform will occur by strengthening the power and autonomy of the People's Congress. In the past, I've voted three times for representatives to Congress. On the first occasion, the government let us choose two out of three candidates. I didn't know any of them, so I crossed out all three names. The second and third times I handed in a blank ballot. Since then I haven't bothered to vote. One day, when the people can choose political representatives, I'll participate.

I've never been afraid to speak out. One day, two people from the State Security Bureau came to see me. They wanted to visit me on a regular base. They didn't want me to inform on others. They just asked me to speak frankly about certain policy issues. They questioned me about Taiwan. I said China would get Taiwan back when our economy overshadows theirs, and this will happen before too long.

I also told these officials that I'd heard that some female workers of my age had lost their jobs and could no longer support their families. They'd had to sell their bodies. I pointed out that if a mother and a middle-aged woman becomes a prostitute it can only be out of desperation. If the government can't, or won't, do anything for these poor women – well, that's the end of the Party. These visits lasted about six months. Later, I heard that my comments were sent to headquarters in Shanghai.

I spend most of my time in the factory. My apartment is next door. People can call on me whenever they want. I don't mind at all. On weekends, my wife and I take our daughter into the city center. We don't go shopping – it's too expensive. We just look around and then we go to a fast-food restaurant to have lunch. Our monthly income is about 2,000 yuan. We spend most of it on our child. She's in boarding school during the week.

That's my story. I enjoyed talking to you.

Notes

1 Not an uncommon practice. Many Chinese universities, research institutes, etc., are expected to start their own business ventures so they can generate funds for themselves.
2 Under centralized state planning, the managers of state enterprises usually communicate vertically with their Bureaus (upwards) and with suppliers (downwards).

23 Xu Yaoming, male: manager of a herbal medicine trading company

Many books were written about our generation's time in the countryside. My story's probably quite ordinary – just one of millions that was never told.

I spent several years in an army reclamation farm in Heilongjiang province. The farm was close to the Soviet Union, so it was heavily militarized. Just two months before I arrived in Heilongjiang armed clashes had broken out between China and the Soviet Union. Both sides wanted control of an island on the river between the two nations. Many people feared war was likely.

I was a 17-year-old kid from a working-class family, and I thought it was an honor to be sent to serve in the "frontier land against Soviet revisionism." The idea of a military lifestyle greatly appealed to me. I saw myself as a soldier, resolutely patrolling gun in hand.

In May 1969, my fellow students and I left Shanghai and traveled by train to Mudan, a mining town in the far north. From there, we were bussed to farm headquarters. It took us three hours to hike to our residential unit. The snows were melting and the ground was muddy and slippery. When we arrived we looked liked dirty monkeys.

As soon as we got to our unit we were told we wouldn't be given home leave for at least two years. Several of the girls from Shanghai began to weep. I could understand why, and felt very sorry for them. Everything was cold, damp, miserable and very primitive.

On our first night in our new home, we were given a good dinner of pork dumplings. But the next day – and most of the following days – all we got was the typical northern dish of steamed sorghum buns and dried vegetables.

Military training was a big part of our life. We drilled regularly, and we were shown how to bivouac, hike long distances, patrol and shoot. We posted sentries every night. Now I realize how stupid most of this was. We dug miles of defensive ditches that quickly collapsed. If the Soviets had come across the Heilongjiang [Amur] River we'd never have stopped them. The only weapons we had were surplus army rifles, left over from the anti-Japanese war. The Russians had modern, fast patrol boats, but we just went up and down the river in wooden pontoons. After a while we stopped taking the military side of things quite so seriously.

The labor was very hard, but I think what bothered us most were a vicious species of mosquitoes the local people called *xiaoyao* (little biter). These were most active during the harvest season. At twilight, they would rise from the nearby marshes and attack us in a swarm. Our bodies would swell with welts, and we'd often get feverish and sick. We'd wrap ourselves up from top to toe, trying to leave no skin uncovered. Even so, every summer we'd be covered with new bites and old scratches.

Our diet was very poor. Invariably we were given the four "same old things": potato, turnip, cabbage and pickles. The frost-free season in Heilongjiang is very short. There are only three months when you can grow fresh vegetables.

Many students couldn't take the hardship, and a few even tried to escape to Russia. During moonlit nights in winter it was easy to walk across the river. But the Soviets returned defectors at the point of a gun. Those sent back would then be charged as "traitors" and "Soviet spies." Obviously, the Russians didn't think we were worth keeping. Before long, everyone realized there was no point running to them.

Other than work and military duties there wasn't a whole lot to do. The most popular pastimes were drinking, smoking and card playing. Gang fights also were quite common. The gangs were based on the students' home regions. In our farm, we had the "Beijing," "Zhejiang" and "Sichuan" gangs. The authorities always worried that gang-related activity would get out of control. We had guns, so maybe they had a reason to worry.

The farm administrators were all ex-army personnel. They were mostly good-hearted Party members, but they were also single-minded and puritanical. They tried to prevent us forming romantic attachments because they believed "talking love" would interfere with our duties. Of course, it was impossible to stop us taking an interest in each other, and there were quite a few sexual incidents. Sometimes, the authorities played tricks on us that were quite indecent. Once we were woken up in the middle of the night and sent to investigate "suspicious activities from the hostile country" [the Soviet Union] under Number Two bridge. When we arrived we discovered a boy and a girl busily engaged in sex. The authorities relied on public exposure to solve the problem. Once a girl was identified and humiliated she usually was too embarrassed to keep on with the relationship.

During my fourth year at in the farm I came down with appendicitis and had to undergo emergency surgery. Normally, this kind of operation took half an hour and required an incision of from 2–3 inches. But my operation took four hours and left an 8 inch scar on my abdomen.

Two surgeons operated on me. One was an older army doctor and the other was a much younger man. These two men were involved in a long-standing political dispute, and it didn't take long before they started arguing again. I knew what was going on. They'd given me some anesthetic but it hadn't completely knocked me out.[1]

As soon as they'd opened me up the doctors began to quarrel about how to proceed. The shouting soon turned to personal abuse. Meanwhile, I lay on the operating table, bleeding, and sweating in pain with my side cut open. Finally, I shouted in desperation: "Please! In order to succeed you must unite!" [a popular political slogan during the Cultural Revolution]. When this didn't have the desired effect I quoted Mao: "Be determined and strive for success. Sacrifice in order to overcome your difficulties!"

When people learnt what I'd yelled from the operating table, they thought, at first, the episode was comical. Of course, at the time, I didn't see anything remotely humorous about my situation.

Because of the botched operation I was no longer classified as physically fit. As a result I was excused labor in the fields and transferred to our unit's kitchens.

Here, I met one of the most important figures in my life. Without his influence I would be a different person today. His name was Meng. He was a handyman but well respected by everyone. After we'd become close friends I discovered that, in 1938, he'd been a member of the Eighth Route Army and had participated in many battles against the Japanese. I tried to persuade him to ask for the recognition he deserved, but he wasn't interested in notoriety. He'd made a conscious decision to live quietly on the farm.

There was something very deep and unusual about Meng. I never heard him say anything petty or stupid. He was always willing to share with people, and he never asked for anything in return. He was a very private, moral person with a great deal of inner strength. In those days, most people wanted a political identity – just as, today, most people are interested largely in material things. But Meng wasn't motivated by personal considerations.

Because I came from Shanghai I was accustomed to a variety of food. As soon as I was put in charge of organizing our kitchens I tried to improve people's diet. Meng and I decided to raise chickens and pigs, and cultivate more vegetable plots. Before too long our kitchen was providing the best food on the farm.

In 1974, I went to a Commercial College as a Worker-Peasant-Soldier student. At college, I studied traditional Chinese medicine. We were trained to identify and to evaluate the various herbs and remedies. That's how I got involved in this business.

After I graduated in 1976 I was assigned to the Commercial and Trade Department of a northern province. I learnt about Mao's death on the first day of my new job, while I was standing in the street waiting for a bus. I don't remember now how I felt. I can't say I was conscious of the birth of a "new era." For many years thereafter my life went on as usual. The real changes came in the 1990s when the market economy became all-important. There's little ambiguity in society today. Money is everything.

Is this good or bad? I think the question's irrelevant. If you want to keep your job you must swim with the others. Just about every transaction in my business involves some form of bribery or favoritism. People no longer think in terms of whether something's right or wrong.

Our government constantly lectures us on "clean and upright modes of business." But if you insist on being "clean and upright" today you won't get anywhere. The disease is epidemic. In the past, business arrangements were sealed with small gifts of pens or teacups. Today, it's a matter of how much *fens* (cash) you're willing to hand out.

The production and sale of Chinese medicine has two traditional centers. One is in Shanghai, which controls the market in the northern half of China. This market is still relatively well controlled and supervised. The state-owned herbal medicine factories here are still honest.

The other center is in the south and west: in Guangdong and Sichuan. These provinces control the market in the southern half of the country. In the early 1980s, the government relaxed regulations and allowed entrepreneurs in the south to trade medical herbs as agricultural products. This created many new opportunities. But as soon as local entrepreneurs took over the production and distribution of traditional medicines most state-owned enterprises went out of business. Local entrepreneurs developed their own trading networks and built their own facilities. The state factories couldn't compete. Too many employees and dependents burdened them.

In the past, government control of all kinds of medicine was quite strict. Several years back I worked in a province's Department of Quality Inspection. Every deal between producers and sellers had to be checked and approved by us before the products could be released. The people in my Department knew we were responsible for quality and purity. But, today, there's no supervisory agency. Most of the written regulations are ignored. Fraud is widespread.

Many herbal remedies are faked. For instance, cooked rice can be rubbed into tiny balls, dried, dyed yellow and sold as bezoar (*niuhuang*).[2] It's easy to be fooled. Recently, in Hunan, I tasted one herbal cold remedy and discovered it was just sugar and rice powder. The producers offered me a very high commission to help them sell their product. I refused, but they had no problems finding other retailers. My boss once purchased fake medicine that ultimately had to be destroyed, costing us 42,000 yuan. The makers had bribed him. He was fined 30 yuan for making a "mistake."

Fake herbal remedies don't usually kill people, but the same can't be said of fake western drugs. Frankly, Chinese-manufactured drugs are no longer reliable. A couple of years ago, two people in Shanghai died after they were injected with an "antibiotic" medicine that was completely inactive. For a time, pressure was put on the government to do something about the situation.

I don't want to go into the darkness with you. I know too many of the people involved. I was told you could be trusted. But you don't live here. If these stories are revealed people will ask you about your source. I have to make a living here. I can't afford to tell you everything I know.

Most Chinese work hard and have a good heart. Do I love my country? Very much. I want to play my part in helping China become strong and wealthy. But, sometimes, you see so many upsetting things you feel you're being dragged down. I tell myself I shouldn't do anything that would harm the country or the people working for me. If you're in a position of responsibility you must look after the people you work with – no matter whether they're above or below you.

I've been given several important administrative positions because I'm known as a "clean" person. On several occasions I was honored as a "Model Worker" by the municipal government. Actually, I'm not extraordinary – I'm not like some of the cadres in the past. A close friend of mine, who died of cancer a couple of years ago, once did something truly extraordinary. In the early 1960s, he voluntarily asked for demotion and cut his own salary because he thought the nation was going through difficult times. Can you imagine anyone even thinking like this today?

Over the years I've had many contacts with various Party and government cadres. I do think there's a difference between the generations. The cadres who joined the revolution before liberation are mostly good people. Those promoted in the last thirty years are likely to be bureaucrats who're only concerned with their own station and its associated privileges.

I didn't support the June Fourth [1989] demonstrators. They acted as if they wanted another Cultural Revolution. They were anarchists, not democrats. Mao said that the destruction of the old was a way of creating something better. But what can the students offer that's going to be better than the Communist Party? If this country falls apart ordinary working people will be the first to suffer.

Did I sound too leftist when I talked to you? I'm sorry. I'm still an idealist. I always have been. I haven't lost hope.

Notes

1   During the Cultural Revolution it was not uncommon for surgeons to operate without anesthesia. Sometimes, acupuncture would be used to dull the pain.
2   A concretion found in the alimentary organs of many ruminants.

24 Song Xu, male: lawyer

Six years ago, one of my old university classmates came back from America with the story of how he was making a salary of US$28,000. At the time it seemed an astronomically high sum. I couldn't imagine anyone having this kind of income. I was envious and a bit resentful. At university, this man had been the dumbest among our circle of friends. We'd called him "Old Slow." Now, everyone was a lot more respectful. But, in those days, just going to America was enough to make you a star.

This year [1996] our friend returned for another visit. We had another reunion, but nobody was particularly interested in the visitor from abroad. I now make close to US$20,000 a year, and I'm developing my career exactly as I wish.

I no longer envied "Old Slow." Instead, I felt sorry for him. He looked aged and tired. Later, I heard his son had got into trouble in America and was involved in some kind of gang activity.

Don't take this personally but people in Shanghai have started to make fun of students coming back from abroad. Do you know what they say about them? They dress like country bumpkins (*tuli tuqi*); they keep tight hold of their money (*xiaoli xiao qi*); they don't talk like westerners but they don't sound Chinese either (*busan busi*).

The cultural climate in Shanghai has changed a lot. When Ronald Reagan came to Fudan University in 1984 lots of students hid tape recorders under their coats so they could record what he had to say. They thought the American President was a Pope revealing divine truth. In the 1980s, young people had almost religious feelings about the United States. America was seen as a mythical land of freedom, wealth and democracy. No one thinks like this anymore.

The United States has been very arrogant and hostile towards China. Americans are too stupid to realize that, just because we often criticize our government, we're happy when the American governing class gives the world a lecture on what's wrong with China. We criticize our government because we're affected by its policies. The United States opposes our government not because it's concerned about us but because it wants to preserve its own cultural and political hegemony.

By the next century the US government is going to be a source of great trouble to China and other developing countries. The United States has initiated several aggressive military campaigns against many such societies. It thinks it has the right to police the world and force other countries to bow to its will. The United States will do anything to preserve its hegemonic position. Inevitably, China will become America's main rival.

Have you read "*China Can Say 'No'?*"[1]

I don't agree 100 percent with the authors. China should sometimes say no to the United States but we still have to do business with the Americans. We're now getting nearly $US1 billion a month from trade with the United States. Of course, what's far more important than maintaining a good relationship with foreigners is for our government to maintain a stable domestic environment. The best way to resist outside powers is to make sure your own people are happy.

I became a lawyer in 1983. Back then, the Chinese legal system was virtually non-existent. "Law" was whatever the Party's and government's policies happened to stipulate. But, in 1979, the People's Congress approved a new criminal code, and the courts began to assign lawyers to defendants. Actually, only a few people got legal assistance at the beginning since, after 1949, the profession had basically ceased to exist.

My first client was a former Roman Catholic priest. He was an old man who first was sent to jail in the 1950s. This time around his crime was to have interfered with the government's family planning policy. He'd told young women that abortion was a sin.

The government's policy towards religion was based on the "Three Selfs": [religious groups should preach to themselves, not proselytize; educate themselves; and govern themselves]. The priest wanted to work for the Vatican in Rome, so he'd violated the law. When I visited him in jail he tried to convert me to Christianity. It was obvious he was senile and had lost all touch with reality.

In those days we were more like social workers than lawyers. All I could do was get my client more privileges and a little more freedom in prison.

Over the last five years, working as a lawyer has become very profitable. The job is no longer socially insignificant. The reason for this change is more economic than political.

The market economy and the spread of privatization have helped foster a war of all against all. In a predatory market environment people soon turn to law to protect their interests. I can tell you that all the legal cases in China have economic roots – it makes no difference whether they're criminal or civil. All the cases I've handled deal with economic matters. Either you're trying to resolve economic disputes or you're dealing with criminal matters stemming from people's often quite desperate attempts to survive.

My firm is state-owned, but its day-to-day operations are market oriented. We keep 28 percent of legal fees paid by our clients. We can accept or reject cases, and we negotiate payment with clients ourselves. I'm earning good money now – more than I ever dreamt I'd make.

In western societies many lawyers ultimately become politicians. I know why this is. After working so closely with people entangled in economic issues I have a good grasp of how society actually works. I know where the power lies, and I know how to get things done. Unlike many other members of my generation, who can't seem to cope with change, I've adjusted quite well. I pay close attention to what's going on, and I adapt.

Many people now like to claim that, during the Cultural Revolution, we were victims of indoctrination. Well if we were "victims" it was our choice. The Red Guards behaved as they did not because they had been "tricked" into being idealists but because they'd figured out how best to respond to their environment. What's so unusual about that?

I became a Red Guard out of self-interest. I wanted to belong, and I was personally ambitious. What I did then is not that different from what I'm doing now. Money's the sign of prestige and success today, so money's the new idol of our society. During the Cultural Revolution politics was the measure of success, so Mao was the idol.

In 1968, I was assigned to a textile factory. Two years later, everything was in complete chaos because of the One-Attack-and-Three-Against Campaign. Each morning we would find Big Character posters stuck all over the factory. At the end of the day these would be covered by new pronouncements and declarations. It was all quite silly.

Textile workers were more involved in the Cultural Revolution than other workers. Most of the leaders of the Workers' Rebellion Organization came from textile factories. Every time the wind from Beijing shifted new disputes would break out. People got political credit by acting crazy.

Let me tell you about the head of a Workers' Rebellion Organization in one of the textile factories. This man was ambitious but also very stupid. He desperately wanted to locate a "counter-revolutionary" so he could demonstrate political accomplishment. He wanted to move up in the world. Finally, he came up with a plan.

Shortly thereafter, the workers in his factory got a shocking piece of news: a counter-revolutionary slogan had been found on a piece of paper in the men's latrines. It wasn't particularly imaginative. It read: "Down with Chairman Mao."

This called for an immediate response. A factory-wide meeting was called, and the head of the Workers' Rebellion Organization announced that a "counter-revolutionary clique" was on the loose. Before long, suspicion fell on an old engineer who'd happened to visit the latrines just before the note was discovered. He was detained and pressured to confess. But, after three days of interrogation, he'd admitted nothing.

The head of the Workers' Rebellion Organization had appointed himself chief interrogator. He got so wrapped up in his duties he didn't go home. His wife needed to contact him, so she came to the factory and left him a note.

The head was called Xi Ermao. Unluckily for him, his name had the same two characters in it, as did the offending slogan: "Xi" and "Mao." The similarities were too obvious to ignore, and, after some encouragement, Xi's wife admitted that her husband had made her write the derogatory note. Within an hour, the factory was full of posters demanding that workers unite to "Smash the Dog's Head of the Counter-revolutionary Xi Ermao!"

The next time the little commissar was spotted he was back in the latrines. Only this time he was cleaning them.

Today, he'd be quick to tell you he was once a "victim" too.

You want to make a comparison between my generation and the generation that followed? The members of my generation do still have an interest in larger political issues and do still care about society as a whole. I find it difficult to have a serious conversation with young people. If I tell them that coal miners in Heilongjiang are out on strike, asking to "Protect Eight and Strive for Nine" (*baoba zhengjiu*) [guarantee eight months income; strive for nine] they react with complete indifference. Their minds are on whatever happens to be in front of their eyes. But what's happening to the coal miners is of relevance to everyone in China. It reflects the two great disaster zones in the Chinese economy: the state-owned enterprises and the regional differences in the pace of development.

Deng Xiaoping said that we should maintain and improve middle and large-size state-owned enterprises. But the policy today is to let these enterprises expire. In my opinion, no serious effort has been made to save them. The state-owned enterprises are like ulcers in our economic system. The government knows what it must do to clean the ulcers – it should cut them cleanly away. Let them die, and then renewal will be possible.

The main problem with public industry is the separation of management and ownership. The people who manage state enterprises have one boss and one big pocket. The boss is the government and the big pocket is public money. The government is a political not an economic actor. So it doesn't care if businesses are managed profitably.

Every manager uses his post to get a bigger apartment, a larger salary and, maybe, a couple of trips abroad. People can see that managers are getting worse and worse. Meanwhile, state-owned factories are getting poorer and poorer – even though the people who run them are getting richer and richer. It's no surprise people say that state managers work for the Communist Party during the day but dream of their own personal fortune at night.

Because it's big-pocket money, state managers don't care if they lose some cash – as long as they still get their share. I have one client who's a retired cadre from an industrial bureau in Shanghai. Just before he left his post he got involved in financial disputes with another state-owned company. In the middle of legal proceedings he said "'bye" to me and took off to visit his daughter in America. He'd helped her start her own business with a Chinese company.

This old man was given a nice apartment in Shanghai and a generous retirement package. The factories he once managed are now bankrupt. He'd got his company involved in a disastrous joint venture that had lost millions of yuan of public money. But he's living the good life. He couldn't care less about the lawsuit.

There are many ways that public money can be diverted into individual pockets – including those of foreign investors. In joint ventures, for instance, the assets on the Chinese side are typically undervalued or even used for free. Recently, the municipal authorities in Shanghai appraised the value of public assets in joint ventures and discovered that they were undervalued by 40 to 60 percent.

In 1994, the government Commercial Inspection Bureau checked one tenth of the equipment supplied by foreign investors. The claimed value was $US22 billion. The real value was US$18 billion. Frankly, it's corruption and ignorance on the Chinese side that makes this kind of thing possible. Do you think it would happen if the enterprises were privately owned?

Do I worry about the social consequences of so many people losing their jobs? I do, but what choice do we have? It's the unfortunate fate of my generation. We'll live to see a strong and wealthy China, but it's the next generation that will reap most of the benefits.

The regional imbalance in development is potentially very dangerous. We're one political entity, but we have two economic systems: one coastal, the other inland. If the inland provinces can't benefit from the economic boom then China has no hope of becoming an economic powerhouse. I think that the government understands this, and will confront the issue – the sooner the better. Right now, it's encouraging capital to purchase bankrupt state enterprises in the hinterland.

In 1989, I supported the students in Beijing. Rebellion shows one's spirit. Like Mao, Deng had become an ancestor. However, looking back, I recognize that another revolution wouldn't have done China any good. We must be careful not to equate the idea of democracy with a wholesale rejection of the idea of government.

Like I say, I sympathized with the 1989 protesters. But I thought it was humiliating when the government let the United States fly Fang Lizhi out of the country.[2] Obviously, the act was in defiance of Chinese jurisdictional authority. Fang was a wanted person. But the government just said: "Oh, let's forget about it. It's easier this way." What kind of message does this send about our legal system? It's not as if we don't have one.

I have to take my daughter to her piano lesson now. It's usually my wife's job, but she's away on a business trip.

It was no trouble talking to you. You seem to care about China. I'm optimistic. We'll make it, as long as we keep cool and have a good plan.

Thank you.

Notes

1   Song Qiang, Zhang Zhangzhang and Jiao Bian (eds), *Zhongguo keyi shuobu* (*China Can Say "No"* Beijing, The United Industrial and Commercial Publishing House, 1996).

   When this book was published it quickly became a bestseller. It expresses nationalistic and anti-American sentiments, which have become more prevalent in the Chinese media over the last few years.

2   Fang Lizhi, a prominent intellectual, was accused by the Chinese government of helping to instigate the 1989 protests. After the Tiananmen Square demonstrations were suppressed Fang hid in the US Embassy in Beijing. He was flown to the United States on May 25, 1990.

25 Wang Xiaoying,[1] female: member of the Shanghai Writers' Association

A newspaper article recently described me as "a writer from the 'Three Old Classes' who writes about the 'Three Old Classes'." It's true. All my stories and novels are about people from my own generation. But after I read the article I said to myself: why *am* I so concerned with the past? It's an obsession shared by so many members of our generation. The world today is so lively and colorful, so full of promise and opportunity. Yet we turn our backs on it. We look inwards and backwards, not outwards.

As time's gone by we've become even more fixated on a past era. But why? Recently I figured it out. It's not that we don't understand the past. We can't come to terms with the present.

We're lost in the present. That's why we try to locate ourselves in things past. Let's face it. Our generation no longer has much of a role to play. We're actors and actresses in outmoded costumes, standing around, looking out of place and slightly ridiculous. We all see ourselves in this metaphor but we still can't believe what's happened.

After the Cultural Revolution came to its end we were described as a "lost generation." People thought that once Mao left the scene his "children" would become "lost sheep." But, by the mid-1970s, most of us were tired of the endless strife. We knew a crisis was brewing. When Mao died we didn't feel lost. We welcomed the prospect of change.

At first we were treated generously. People recognized the losses we'd suffered. In 1977–1978, I was among those who wrote "scar literature" (*shanghen wenxue*). But I wasn't just grieving about what had happened to me and to millions of others. I wanted to work through my experiences.

Our sense of loss came not in the 1970s but in the 1990s. Twenty years after the Cultural Revolution came to its end our society has completed its process of rebirth. Now it's a completely different environment. New China is about self-interest and the personal struggle to survive. As our society gets colder and crueler we'll just get older and less sure of ourselves. Now we're approaching our fifties. We've got parents to take care of as well as children. Many of us have lost our jobs. We're not in great shape. Our biggest problem is we've lost our bearings. To use one of our favorite expressions: *kanbudong* (it's all quite incomprehensible).

I do think history can single out a generation and play a cruel joke on it. It happened to us. We were raised as idealists, we saw the death of idealism and now we're spared to live in this materialistic world.

My parents' generation didn't experience anything like this. They became revolutionaries during a period of national crisis, and they were key players most of their lives.

My mother is a former high-ranking cadre. She has no regrets. She doesn't like contemporary China and doesn't pretend to understand it. But she's serene. She knows that the great challenges and crises of her life are all behind her.

The young generation's custom-built for the present, so they're not out of place either. We're phantoms caught between two worlds. The shards of idealism are lodged in our hearts. But the world's not for idealists anymore.

You probably think I'm becoming self-indulgent and sentimental. But let me tell you a story. This happened in the summer of 1969, nine months after I became a worker at Huangshan State Tea Farm.

We'd had several days of pouring rain. Early one morning, before it was light, we were awakened by shouts and whistles. Someone was screaming: "Get up! The water's rising!" We rushed outside. We could hear that the nearby mountain stream was running much faster than usual.

One team of twelve boys and girls was ordered to save rice bags and fertilizer from storage shed on the other side of the stream. The rest of us worked feverishly to create dikes to protect dormitories and offices.

In the middle of the morning, the loudspeaker crackled into life. An urgent voice ordered our team leader to come at once to farm headquarters. We knew something bad had happened.

Hours later, we learned that eleven people were missing. The rickety old bridge over the stream had collapsed as soon as the team set foot on it. By the time the students arrived its surface was already under water. Obviously, it was dangerous to attempt a crossing. But the team members didn't hesitate. Hand in hand together they plunged ahead.

When we heard what had happened we fell silent. Then, a few of us began to sob. The authorities sent out a rescue team. Only one boy had survived. He'd managed to cling to the branches of a tree. The others were washed downstream. It took nearly a week to find all the bodies. One of the dead was my closest friend: Lu Hua.

Lu should never have been at the farm. She was assigned to a factory in Shanghai. But she was the leader of our school's Red Guard Organization. She gave up her city registration and volunteered for the farm so she could stay with her friends. On the day we'd left Shanghai Lu had said: "Let's not cry. Our loved ones want to see us smile. We'll sing a song together." She cheered everyone up. She was such a brave person. She died when she was 22.

Today, people would say how stupid she was to risk her precious life for a few sacks of rice and some fertilizer. But, to her, the bags across the stream and the order to save them were more important than personal considerations.

I've just published a novel called *Once We Had Love*. The title refers to the idealism we all once shared. I spent six months interviewing people of my generation, and took another year to finish the book.

After it was finished I was invited to a book-signing ceremony. To my surprise, many, many people showed up. I had to go home and get my own 100 author's copies in order to satisfy all the demand. I was deeply moved. Nearly everyone there was from the Three Old Classes.

We're now told that the Cultural Revolution was a national disaster that victimized everyone except Mao, the "Gang of Four" and the Red Guards. But, during the Cultural Revolution, nearly all the nation's youth willingly joined Red Guard Organizations. We wanted to serve. The future we hoped to build never came, but this doesn't mean that all our sacrifices were meaningless and now are best forgotten.

Our generation represents the tragic spirit of an era. Overwhelmingly powerful and conflicting forces shaped us. Some were good, others evil.

A few weeks ago I was talking to my mother about the past. I asked her whether she believed she was a victim of the Cultural Revolution. She thought for a moment. "In one way or another," she replied, "everyone was a victim."

She was right. When a whole nation goes through a dark period no one is spared.

Thirty years ago I was a young activist. My father was a well-known poet who had joined the communists long before liberation. My mother was the Party Secretary of one of Shanghai's district governments. What mattered to us were loyalty to Mao and the Party. We had intense political discussions every weekend.

I had no doubt we were contributing to world revolution. The Party had told us that the two-thirds of the world's population that were oppressed would be liberated by us one day. Many years later, a friend in Huangshan – obviously more sophisticated than I – told me that working-class people in the west lived better than we did. She said *we*, not workers elsewhere, were part of the two-thirds of the world's population that were oppressed. At the time I was shocked.

During the Great Exchange, while I was still in high school, I went to Beijing to be received by Mao. When I returned to Shanghai the first thing I saw was a Big Character poster on the station wall. It proclaimed: "The Municipal Government is Rotten to its Core."

I knew at once that my mother was in trouble. If the Municipal Government was rotten to its core then, in all probability, so, too, were the ten district governments.

I rushed home and found no one there except our old nanny. She told me that my mother had been taken away in a truck to be exhibited as the Number One Capitalist Roader. They'd put a stone board around her neck. The string cut her quite badly. Members of the Workers' Rebellion Organization had taken Father prisoner in his work place.

I was devastated. I'd thought I was a revolutionary and that my parents were old revolutionaries. Suddenly I found out I was a whelp of counter-revolutionaries. But, even at that time, I didn't doubt Mao or the Cultural Revolution. I thought either my parents had done something wrong or the rebellious organizations had made a terrible mistake.

That's why I volunteered to go to Huangshan. My two sisters went to Heilongjiang. We just wanted to get out of Shanghai.

I would have to say that my life was sheltered before I left home. I really didn't know how ordinary people in China lived. I arrived at the farm with lofty and romantic notions. It didn't take long for the illusions to be dispelled. The work was demanding and the food was terrible. We had meat once a month.

Life in the countryside was monotonous. Often, both boys and girls turned to sex. We were about 20 years old and full of energy. What else were we supposed to do? We wanted companions as well as sexual partners. The companionship could be open. But the sex was forbidden. Only a few refused to cross that line. I was one of them.

However, I did form a partnership with a boy called Yijie. He was close to Lu before she'd drowned in that terrible flood. All three of us were from the same school in Shanghai.

Lu's body was recovered nearly a week after she died. I helped wash her, and I dressed her in her best clothes: a blue cotton jacket and green trousers. Yijie pinned a Mao badge on Lu's chest. In those days you honored someone by showing how loyal he or she was to Mao. Then we buried our friend on the mountainside.

The next day Yijie was charged with committing a counter-revolutionary crime. He was told he had revealed his hatred of Mao by burying his picture. The authorities ordered Lu's grave dug up and the badge returned.

Yijie was always the black sheep on the farm. In Shanghai he'd been involved in the Zhongshan Alliance. There were numerous investigations into his involvement with the anti-Zhang Chunqiao faction. Each had ended with an "inconclusive" evaluation. Basically, Yijie was on continuous probation. This time, too, he was let go with a warning.

Gradually, Yijie and I lost faith in Mao and the Party. I think, for us, the pivotal event was the Lin Biao incident. After that we became increasingly cynical about politics.

In 1972, some of the older students were given a chance to leave the farm. Two years later, most of my class had returned to Shanghai. I was on the list for transfer too, and I went to farm headquarters to tell them I wanted to give up my place to Yijie. The officials saw me as a stubborn young woman who'd fallen in love with an unworthy man. But, to our surprise, both Yijie and I were given jobs in Shanghai.

We left Huangshan Mountain in the summer of 1974, and were married two years later. In 1977, we enrolled in university. Yijie studied history at Fudan University, and I majored in literature.

In 1981, Yijie went to the University of Virginia as a graduate student in their History Department. I never went to visit him. I was too busy with my own work. I didn't want Yijie to stay in America, and I made it very clear to him that I would never leave China. I'm a Chinese writer, so what would I do in America? Yijie finished his Master's degree in 1983 and came home. We wanted to start a family.

Sometimes I feel I shouldn't have dragged Yijie back to China. I should at least have let him stay long enough to finish his PhD. Whenever I see him unhappy about his job I feel so sorry for him.

Last year, Yijie got financial backing from a Hong Kong real estate developer to establish a research institute on urban environmental planning. Since 1990 his main interest has been urban management. Chinese cities are developing rapidly, but no one knows how to tame these "monsters." Yijie wants to be a pioneer in the field.

Now we are experiencing a lot of difficulties with Yijie's university. I told Yijie that he should compromise with the bureaucracy. The most important thing is his project. He's nearly 50 years old now – there's not much time left if he wants to achieve something.

We're not Party members. Yijie applied, and was turned down, eight times – most recently in 1988. His persistence was the source of quite a few jokes among our friends. Now Yijie recognizes there's no reason for him to join the Party. He loves his country and that's enough. Once we were told socialism would save China. Today we're expected to believe that the market economy will solve all our problems. The trouble is that the propaganda is no longer persuasive. Probably the only thing that will hold us together is nationalism.

I was drawn to Buddhism six years ago. I was 41 at the time and badly wanted a child. I'd had one abortion when I was in the university because I didn't think I'd finish my studies if I had a baby. It was a difficult decision, and also the wrong one. Later, I miscarried three times. I was very upset and started to go to the temple to offer prayers.

Marx was right. Religion is for the vulnerable. Buddhism gave me the strength to keep going. I had my baby girl when I was 42. She's the gift of my faith.

Most of our income is spent on our daughter. She's in private school, which costs 300 yuan a month in tuition, plus other expenses. Yijie and I don't have many needs. Maybe it's because we grew up poor and never had much money to spend. Yijie won't even enter a restaurant.

The last two years I've worked on a long novel. A publishing house gave me 10,000 yuan to write it. Long novels aren't lucrative, but we're all right.

Mother lives with us. Father died some years ago. We pool our money so we can have a good meal together every day. I think of myself as a lucky person.

Note

1   Not a pseudonym.

Index